Modal Counterpoint, Renaissance Style

Modal Counterpoint, Renaissance Style

SECOND EDITION

Peter Schubert
Schulich School of Music
McGill University

New York   Oxford
Oxford University Press
2008

Oxford University Press, Inc., publishes works that further Oxford University's
objective of excellence in research, scholarship, and education.

Oxford   New York
Auckland   Cape Town   Dar es Salaam   Hong Kong   Karachi
Kuala Lumpur   Madrid   Melbourne   Mexico City   Nairobi
New Delhi   Shanghai   Taipei   Toronto

With offices in
Argentina   Austria   Brazil   Chile   Czech Republic   France   Greece
Guatemala   Hungary   Italy   Japan   Poland   Portugal   Singapore
South Korea   Switzerland   Thailand   Turkey   Ukraine   Vietnam

Published by Oxford University Press, Inc.
198 Madison Avenue, New York, New York 10016
http://www.oup.com

Oxford is a registered trademark of Oxford University Press

Library of Congress Cataloging-in-Publication Data

Schubert, Peter, 1946–
   Modal counterpoint, Renaissance style/Peter Schubert.
      p. cm.
   Includes bibliographical references (p.) and index.
   ISBN 978–0–19–533194–3 (spiral (comb))   1. Counterpoint.   I. Title.
   MT55.S29 2008
   781.2′8609031—dc22

                                                    2007032910

Printing number: 9 8 7 6 5

Printed in the United States of America
on acid-free paper

Contents

Contents

Preface

This sixteenth-century counterpoint textbook contains some familiar elements, such as exercises in the five species and numerous examples of relevant repertoire. However, it also introduces counterpoint teaching materials from the sixteenth century that offer insight into the musical thought and style of the Renaissance. These have been drawn from over a dozen treatises and adapted for today's classroom.

Highlights include placing repeated motives against a cantus firmus, making new settings of familiar French chanson melodies, and embellishing a first-species canon. Another feature, setting Lutheran chorale melodies in simple four-part texture, ties in well to studies of harmony. In a general way, counterpoint is a good prelude to harmony because voice leading and linear embellishments are studied in a simple two-part context apart from harmonic progressions. The book contains appendixes on text setting and writing a canon against a CF as options for study. Because this book provides examples of music in many genres and styles, it can easily be integrated with music history courses.

Teachers using this book have praised two pedagogical innovations in particular. The first is a wealth of graded exercises: each chapter contains exercises at four levels of length and difficulty, from short ones with simple right and wrong answers to long ones requiring more musical judgment. These provide teachers with a wide range of possible assignments and in-class activities, including improvisation. The second is the distinction between "hard" and "soft" rules. Hard rules are those that are never broken, that define all Renaissance music, whereas soft rules are really just style guidelines. The latter vary from one composer to another and count significantly less in grading. The distinction between types of rules permits teachers some personal preferences while clearly defining errors.

Teaching Modal Counterpoint, Renaissance Style

This book has been used successfully at all levels of higher education and even pre-college, and the material can easily be taught in a different order or with different emphases.

First-Semester College Students

At the introductory level, the focus is on voice leading in two parts, and chapters 1 through 12 should be covered at the rate of about a chapter a week. This speed reflects the view that species exercises are designed primarily to teach mastery of voice leading. They are based on what young singers might improvise, and because they have so little aesthetic content, students should work through them as quickly as possible, leaving more time for truly interesting music (the free imitative duo) later in the course. The advantage of starting students on modal counterpoint is that it trains them in basic skills, such as checking pairs of voices for errors, in a simple context. The more advanced techniques described in this book (stretto, mirror, inversion, tonal answer) are an excellent preparation for later study in tonal counterpoint. Their presentation here as purely intervallic constructions, free of any harmonic progression, provides a gentle introduction in a simple context. Students will improve in basic skills: score reading, interval identification, clef reading, and ear training. They will also gain an increased awareness of the elements of Renaissance style in general.

In spite of all the obvious techniques common to both counterpoint and harmony, however, students often fail to make the connection. For this reason, if this book is used as preparation for the study of harmony, it is necessary to insist on the relevance of counterpoint from the very beginning. After introducing passing dissonance in second species, it is helpful to look at a Bach chorale right away and find some passing dissonances; after lower neighbors in third species, find them in a Mozart piano sonata; after suspensions in fourth species, find the agent and the patient in a Brahms symphony. Doing so requires a little more preparation on the part of the teacher, but it will pay off in students' understanding.

At this level, it may be advisable to skip some sections: the introduction on Renaissance style, the section in chapter 7 on contour, the exercises in chapter 9 on writing against breves, and the section on free two-part writing from scratch at the end of chapter 12. The motivic analysis in chapter 9 and the cadences in chapter 10 can be done in a single week. Thus the course can end with adding a line to a given French chanson tune and writing three-part species, or with writing a duo from scratch.

Some teachers end the semester with three-part writing (chapter 14), which makes a good transition to four-part harmony. In order to get this far in one semester, you can skip chapters 9 and 13 entirely, condense chapters 6 and 10 (fourth species and cadences), and condense chapters 14 and 15. You can arrive at trios in mixed values easily by the twelfth week of the semester and even get to the invertible canon opening.

The book offers the option of introducing invertible counterpoint (chapter 13) at any time. The motive-spotting exercises in two-part music (chapter 9) can be supplemented with analysis exercises on music in three parts (chapter 14) and four parts (chapter 18), a good preparation for later theory courses.

Third-Year College Students

At the upper level, plan to cover two chapters of species a week. The course can culminate either with sophisticated three-part writing (a three-voice "invertible canon" opening and a canon against a cantus firmus) or basic four-part writing (skip the canon against a cantus firmus and end with adding three loosely imitative parts against a cantus firmus as described in chapter 18). With advanced, well-prepared students who know species before beginning the course, it is possible to complete the book, ending with free four-part writing. I have not included writing in more than four parts (which is largely a matter not of contrapuntal technique but orchestration), preferring to dig deeper into sophisticated techniques in fewer parts.

At the end of the course, students will have a feel for the materials of the period, as well as an understanding of how whole pieces are put together. They will be able to write in the style and analyze using Renaissance concepts. They may struggle with the conflict between their desires and the demands of the material ("I wanted this countermelody, but the combination wasn't invertible" or "I wanted to start the next point of imitation on A, but it wouldn't overlap with the cadence"), but thinking in the medium is an experience essential to majors in theory and composition and helps historians understand the compositional process.

Graduate Students in Theory or Musicology

Some readers have suggested using this book at the graduate level as an adjunct to a Renaissance survey course or as the basis for a seminar on Renaissance compositional techniques. In such contexts, the nuts-and-bolts exercises in the first chapters would not be necessary, and students could focus on the analytical and aesthetic implications of the techniques in chapters 8 through 21.

New to This Edition

Thanks in great part to suggestions by users (see Acknowledgments), this edition boasts several improvements. On the small scale, many misprints have been corrected and confusing instructions clarified; in particular, chapter 10 (on cadences) has been rewritten. More significant improvements are the overhaul of chapters 14 and 15 (on three-part writing) to include period strategies, additional repertoire examples, more explicit rules, and new exercises. Another major innovation is the improvisation activities added at the end of chapters throughout the book. This is not only historically appropriate (the word "counterpoint" originally referred to real-time singing at sight), but provides invaluable practice in ear training and musical thinking. Several teachers suggested collecting the rules in one place for easy reference, and this edition includes a summary of rules following chapter 7.

Acknowledgments

Years in the making, this book has passed through many hands. When I started using historical materials to teach counterpoint at McGill in 1990, I would assign the class to "read Zarlino's chapter 55 and write something like Example 111a." It was tough going, and it quickly became apparent that Zarlino needed to be interpreted, that words like "diatessaron" and "fusa" had to go, and that the work of many other theorists had to be brought in. I must therefore first thank the many students who suffered through the early stages of this book. I am also grateful for the suggestions of those professors who have used it: Brenda Ravenscroft, Frank Samarotto, Janna Saslaw, Les Black, Glen Ethier, John Kelleher, and Donald Patriquin. Also teaching assistants Ayal Adler, Kerim Anwar, Joe Argentino, Henry Avison, Alan Campbell, Paulin Daigle, Elizabeth Dehler, Ivan Elezovic, Angelo Emmanouelides, Paul Frehner, Scott Godin, Karen Kalliojarvi, Anait Keuchgerian, Diane Kipling, Andrew Lefcoe, James MacKay, Justin Mariner, Margaret Miner, Rod Shergold, Lois Simmons, Fran Spidle, Keiko Yamanaka, and Marcus Zagorski. These teachers helped me correct numerous (but, alas, I suspect not all) unclear instructions, inconsistencies, and typos.

For their friendly encouragement and valuable assistance I am indebted to Benito Rivera, Julie Cumming, Lars Lih, David Chodoff, Jan Beatty and the staff at Oxford University Press, and Cynthia Leive and the staff of the Marvin Duchow Music Library. Less obvious but no less tangible influences on this book came from my teachers Patricia Carpenter, Nadia Boulanger, Christopher Hatch, Norwood Hinkle (under whom I sang "O magnum mysterium" year after year in high school), and Jacques-Louis Monod. And, finally, thanks to my wife Lori, the "without which not."

Preface

The major changes to the second edition are the integration of improvisation activities into several chapters of the book and the complete rewriting of chapter 14 on three-part writing. Chapters on cadences (10) and on writing two voices in mixed values (11) have also been improved. The numerous minor changes include clarifying instructions and correcting misprints. These changes are the result of published reviews, comments of colleagues and students, questions emailed to me, and suggestions from readers commissioned by OUP, including Michael Eckert, The University of Iowa; Susan Epstein Garcia, New World School of the Arts/Miami Dade College; Rusty Jones, University of Missouri-Columbia; Jett Perry, Louisiana State University; and Anton Vistrio, New York University. I wish to thank Robert Cook, Patrick Deurtzen, Reisa Lipszyk, Ralph Lorenz, Samuel Moisan, Lionel Pike, Matthew Provost, Dominic Shann, Stephen Slottow, Van Stiefel, Jamshed Turel, and Asher Vijay Yampolsky. Special thanks to Jonathan Wild, who found many improvements to make and who let me adapt an assignment and his summary of rules, and to Catherine Motuz, whose experiments in improvising cadences were invaluable.

Note to the Student

If you are using this book at the beginning of your theory study and are not interested in Renaissance music, you still stand to learn a great deal that will be useful later on. Most important, you will learn to read and evaluate a score, and have a good idea what it sounds like. If you are a performer, you will find that this helps you to understand the composer's intentions, to shape phrases, and to break a piece up into reasonable sections.

Hard Rules

To benefit from the book at this level you don't need to become a Renaissance composer. But you do need to master the hard rules. Breaking a hard rule in counterpoint is analogous to writing a sentence without a verb—you must master basic grammar to be literate.

Soft Rules

Soft rules are just style guidelines. The difference between them and hard rules is like the difference between correct grammar and elegant, poetic expression. The exercises in species, particularly, are designed to enable you to "speak Renaissance music" the way you first speak a foreign language. The first six chapters enable you to say the musical equivalent of "Please, where is the bathroom?" Following the hard rules to the letter should get you a good grade, and you should not obsess over the soft rules—many composers break them from time to time!

If you are really interested in Renaissance music, or you enjoy the challenge of composing, and you have time to spend on subtle issues, you will want to pay close attention to the soft rules. They are often a matter of personal style, and since different Renaissance composers treat them differently, soft mistakes don't count much. It can be quite challenging to work with them, and it is possible to write a "perfect" counterpoint exercise, as many students have shown.

Renaissance Style

"Renaissance style" is of course not one uniform set of behaviors. I pulled together examples that originally served different purposes. For example Diruta, an early seventeenth-century organ teacher, will illustrate things that Sermisy, an early sixteenth-century chanson composer, would never do. I try to make it clear all along what *you* are to do, with rules that generally represent vocal style around 1570. In early chapters especially, you are to work within *very* restrictive rules, just to keep things simple. Some treatise examples appear to "break" these narrow rules, but of course that is absurd: how can a dead composer break a rule that I made in the 1990s? It's a big world; you'll stay on the main road for your exercises, but in the examples you'll take a lot of side trips to see the scenery. I will always warn you when you are *not* to use some example as a model.

The Problem with Books about Music

If this were an art history book, it would have pictures for you to look at. Then, when the text said "The small circular hole in the clouds in the upper right balances the cow on the hillside in the lower left," you could look at the reproduction of the painting and sure enough, there they'd be. This book has musical examples printed, but they don't have the power of a picture. The only thing that can take the place of a picture is *your performance* of the musical examples. To stay awake through a sentence like "The tenor-bass combination in mm. 8-10 is the inversion at the twelfth of the soprano-alto combination in mm. 1-3" you need to play, sing, or listen to Claudio Merulo's excellent organ piece in chapter 19. More than once. You need to observe technical details in the context of the whole aesthetic experience. You should read this book at a piano, or sitting around singing with friends, not at a desk.

Why Writing Exercises?

The hands-on experience of writing forces you to pay attention to details that you might miss when you read. Such close attention enables you to follow a line of thought, and to actually predict what the next note will—what word do you expect here?—be. Knowing correct writing technique enables you to spot misprints, too. If you get a faulty edition of a piece, you will be able to say, "This must be a misprint; Palestrina would never have written that." Knowing how the piece is put together makes you sensitive to the composer's intentions and helps you interpret music. Writing music helps you read music.

Improvisation

In the sixteenth century, boys learned to sight-sing and then to improvise counterpoint in the course of church services. Nowadays, although we think of counterpoint differently, primarily as a writing technique, there's a lot to be gained from trying to improvise within the rules. It's as fun, exciting, challenging, and satisfying as a fast-paced video game, and it's useful. It's the quickest way to learn to "think in music" on your feet. If you improvise your homework, you'll be playing one line while singing another (see "Introduction to Improvisation" at the end of chapter 3). Playing one part and singing another is an important exercise in basic musicianship. Knowing how a fifth "feels" from the inside (when you are singing one of the notes) is bound to be helpful in taking dictation and sight-singing in other contexts.

Counterpoint and the Computer

Many students do their work at the computer and then have the completed exercise played back by the computer (through MIDI, for instance). Playback is not a satisfactory substitute for playing and singing. Until you are very good at dictation, a mistake-filled exercise might sound all right to you. You will be much more aware of what's going on in your exercise when you are inside it, not just listening to it.

Why Study Renaissance Music?

Imagine you are an architecture student, and that you are taking a course on ancient architecture in which you design and build old Roman buildings using the techniques and materials of the period. You might start with ground plans of real historical buildings and work up from there. You would learn how big the windows could be without the walls falling down, and where to put the plumbing. In addition to finding out why Roman buildings look the way they do, dealing with ancient materials would make you aware in a general way of how materials affect aesthetic ideals.

Similarly, from this text you will learn why Renaissance pieces sound the way they do: how they are put together, beginning with the old melodies as "ground plans," and how they progress through different stages of structural planning and ornamentation. You'll start with simple materials: just two lines, white notes, and two rhythmic values—the equivalent of a pail, a shovel, and some sand—and see what you can build with them. The problems Renaissance composers faced are the same ones all composers face: how to build a climax, how to make clear beginnings, middles, and ends, how to keep the piece moving, how to vary texture and achieve the richness and complexity that comes from independent lines sounding together. Renaissance music is a laboratory for simple musical experiments that teach the laws of many musical styles.

Note to
the Instructor

Some Simplifications, Omissions, Anachronisms, and Neologisms

If you know a lot about Renaissance music, you will immediately recognize that many elements have been simplified. I have made decisions based on my experience in the classroom, where one can't introduce everything all at once. For instance, after twenty years of studying and teaching mode, I decided that the twelve-mode system is the best one to start students on, for the very reason that Glarean invented it: it is logical and easy to learn. Many other notions of mode (as expressed in the eight-mode system and melodic formulas such as *melodiae* and psalm tones) have been eliminated entirely as inappropriate at this level.

Two elements of Renaissance style were downplayed for the sake of practicality: triple mensuration and music in more than four parts. The purpose of the book is not to produce a Renaissance master, but someone who can cope with most of the principles behind the music. I traded thicker textures and other mensurations for a closer look at some interesting techniques (e.g., the effect of invertible counterpoint on mode) and a broader view of genres.

This is not a book *about* genres, however—it is about contrapuntal techniques that are common to different genres. Contrapuntally speaking, a cantus firmus ricercar is like a Lutheran chorale setting, a Lassus motet like a Morley madrigal. Thus, differences between genres are somewhat leveled, and many genres are omitted entirely. You will find no villanelle, frottole, polychoral motets, or dances in this book, but if you want to introduce them in class, your students will have the *contrapuntal* expertise to deal with them.

This book is only as historically correct as it needs to be for its audience. I believe it is efficient to refer to elements that the student may already know, even if they were not expressed at the time. These elements include "scale degree," "leading tone," "pitch class," "key," and the "II6/5" chord. Some, like "pitch class," are essential, even if they require extra explanation. All underlined terms in the text are indexed.

Whose Style?

I have assembled the rules from many sources. They do not represent the views of any one theorist or composer. Their purpose is to be an effective teaching method applicable to the widest range of actual repertoire. Because theory and practice differ from one individual to another, we run across examples that break one rule or another. For instance, similar motion to a perfect interval is not allowed when adding one part to a cantus firmus. This rule reflects the view of most theorists, and creates a simpler, more restricted context at the beginning (the rule is relaxed later). However, Zarlino *does* allow similar motion to a perfect interval. His example in chapter 3 contains one instance of it, which disturbs some teachers and students. They ask, Why include this example? The answer is that although it may be initially confusing, it's honest. It would be misleading to pretend that there aren't contradictions in practice, that Renaissance music is a monolith. Allowing some contradictions (and pointing out exactly how they differ from our rules) means nothing has had to be censored out of this book, and there is no piece you can't bring in to class to discuss. The student is expected to understand that the *rules are a pedagogical convenience*—they clarify and limit the task, level the playing field, and facilitate objective grading—but they aren't a perfect mirror of the world.

Playing and Singing

It is of the utmost importance that the students have a chance to hear, sing, and/or play all the examples in the book and their own exercises. The old idea that theory exercises train the "inner ear" is all right, but most students who will use this book need to train the "outer ear" first. They are urged to compose at the piano and to sing with their colleagues. Singing in class can provide an occasion to discuss likes and dislikes and to consider the performance implications of theory (e.g., breathing between repetitions of motives as presented in chapter 9). Another way to get the music into the ear is to give dictations of the material being studied. For this, it is convenient and helpful to use the examples in the book—in truth, few students will have taken the time to play and sing them at home; even if they have, they are not likely to remember them.

The Exercises

The heart of this book is the exercises. They have been carefully crafted to lead the student to a positive result. They begin with solutions to tiny problems, and gradually expand to allow the student more creativity and exercise of musical judgment. Some teachers will find the Warmup Exercises mechanical and unmusical, but they are comforting for students who feel awkward "composing" at first, and they encourage technical facility.

- Series A (Warmup) exercises are designed to show all possible solutions to a tiny problem (two CF notes), concentrating only on legality ("hard" rules). They are meant to be done quickly, but there are so many possibilities that they end up taking a lot of time. They may be done most efficiently by solving them in real time (see "Improvisation," later). If they are written, have different students solve different fragments in class and then exchange papers, correcting each other's. This often leads to productive class discussion.
- Series B (Find the Errors) exercises are a bit longer. They can also be done quickly in class and corrected out loud. They offer a chance to work on "soft" rules of style.
- Series C exercises give practice and feedback to help the student work up to the longer Series D exercises. They can be done in class or as short assignments. Here too students can correct each other's. Like Series A exercises, these can be improvised.
- Series D exercises should be done slowly and carefully. Show students how to check their work for mistakes and encourage them to play one part and

sing the other. It is ideal to have one student perform for the class, the others listening and commenting, but this is often impractical. Ideally, the student should do a short exercise which is corrected and handed back before doing a Series D exercise. This is easily accomplished if the course meets three times a week, but when the course meets only twice a week, the all-important feedback has to be given on a short exercise done in class.

The technical goals of Series D exercises in the first four species are clearly stated, and do *not* include beauty, elegance, grace, or a good gestalt. Since the purpose of the species exercises is limited primarily to the mastery of correct voice leading, no more than a week should be spent on each species, permitting more time to be spent on chapters dealing with repertoire (9 and up). Even in early chapters, it is a good idea to look ahead to the more interesting finished products, and you can add repertoire examples for singing and discussion.

Improvisation

To be really historically accurate, we would have to teach our students to improvise and then give them daily opportunities to sing and improvise in church, because that was the prerequisite to composition in the Renaissance. The word counterpoint in the sixteenth century referred to improvisation, not to a compositional technique. Most of the treatise examples quoted in this book are examples of what a young singer might improvise. For that reason, they are merely correct and not necessarily good music (a few observers have criticized them as bad compositional models). But they do the job—they are like sentences you learn in a foreign-language phrase book: inelegant maybe but functional.

I strongly recommend making improvisation a part of the course, at least as an activity, even if not graded. I have often put up two CF notes (on the board, overhead, or whatever), asking "Who wants to sing a solution?" Somebody is always willing to give it a try. The other students can then sing back the first student's solution and evaluate it. If it contains a mistake, I move right along to another volunteer. Eventually you can ask for a second-species solution to four CF notes, and so on. I have even offered students the opportunity to substitute an improvisation for a written assignment, but that's impractical in a large class.

If you want to pursue this tack, I recommend starting it as early as possible, after doing a few first-species Series A exercises in class. As I say in the "Note to the Student," it doesn't matter whether they quickly visualize a solution or hear it or play it on an air-guitar—the important thing is quickly to solve the problem mentally and then to sing it. Students could ultimately use improvisation to do their written homework, playing the CF and singing along and then writing down what they sang. It's actually much more efficient to hear a vertical fourth than to spot it, and nobody would ever sing the tritones that students so often write!

Repertoire Examples

Few complete pieces appear in this book, and so it will be necessary for you to bring in examples of complete pieces. For counterpoint on a CF, you could look at Costanzo Festa's collection (see bibliography). For two- and three-part music, I recommend music by Lassus, Morley (instrumental and vocal), Iean Gero, from the "Flour des chansons à 3," and those published by Rhau and by RRMR (see bibliography). For three- and four-part music there are innumerable movements from masses and magnificats, especially those by Palestrina, Lassus, and Morales. Many readers have asked for an anthology, and I still occasionally use the Soderlund and Scott collection (all these items are listed in the bibliography). The problem with some of these modern editions is the note values, which are often halved. This means that the strict correspondence between rhythmic levels (for purposes of evaluating dissonance, embellishment, text setting, etc.) gets muddled in the student's mind. I have restored original note values in the many cases where the published examples had note values halved, and I use only treble, alto, tenor octave, and bass clefs. This is in order to have all the music look the same, so the student comes to expect a correspondence between such things as dissonance and beat unit.

Initially, many students find that Renaissance music "all sounds the same." To get students to appreciate the differences between pieces, some teachers give listening tests or have students write down tunes (like the cantus firmi in chapter 1) from memory. These are especially important if the focus of the course is historical style more than theoretical nuts and bolts. For instance, a listening test on the initial points of imitation in the duos in chapters 11 and 12 will encourage the students to attend to musical qualities of the examples, not just their technical features.

The Invertible Counterpoint Option

You can decide whether and when to take up invertible counterpoint, or you can leave it to the students to decide for themselves. Some students will try it even when it has never been discussed in class, allowing them to exercise their initiative.

Writing with Text

Beginning in about chapter 9 students may write texted music in response to the exercises. They should refer to Appendix 1, which gives the rules for text setting (I have often used the Benedictus movement of the Mass, and the book contains a high proportion of examples with this text). Writing with text gives the students a feeling of contact with the real world, but it is not necessary for the acquisition of musical technique. After all, the authors of the treatises thought it unnecessary to give texted examples, even when they were explicitly dealing with the principles of vocal music.

Grading

At McGill, infractions of hard rules subtract the most, and in a "one above, one below" Series D exercise, each hard mistake counts about a third of a letter-grade, or about five percentage points. Soft mistakes in the same exercise count one point, unless the instructor feels strongly about some particular soft rule. By the same token, many infractions of soft rules can be disregarded entirely.

Introduction: Renaissance Musical Style and Notation

Variety

The most highly prized quality in music of the second half of the sixteenth century was variety. However, when we first hear pieces from that time, we are more likely to be struck by how uniform they seem. We are used to hearing much more variety in the music from succeeding periods (Baroque, Classical, Romantic, Modern). Extremes of dynamics and range, contrasting articulations and orchestral colors, and complex melodies and rhythms in the later music make Renaissance music seem fairly bland. Indeed, with the exception of minimalist music, is there any repertoire since then that seems so consistent? Many recent recordings of Renaissance music stress uniformity, with their narrow dynamic range, homogeneous blend, and smooth lines. Ironically, the present-day popularity of those recordings may be due to the value we place on consistency, even though it's the opposite of what the composers intended!

It is an interesting exercise to reconcile the Renaissance music we hear with the values of the people for whom it was written, and it helps us get inside that music. As a start, let's take an excerpt from a widely recorded piece, one of the best-known works of the Renaissance, and look closely for the elements that create variety. The piece is Tomás Luis de Victoria's <u>motet</u> for the Christmas season "O magnum mysterium."

Variety in a Single Line

Example I-1 Soprano line of "O magnum mysterium"

Sing the soprano line through m. 9. Some people think the opening four measures are kind of mysterious or solemn or even spooky. That is of course suggested by the text, but it may also have to do with the slow rhythm and the big skips. Certainly mm. 7–8 are very different, with fast, stepwise motion. Thus in the soprano line alone we find two kinds of variety: *skips vs. steps* and *long vs. short* notes. Some people think there's a kind of tension in the big skips and a kind of release in the fast scales.

The skips themselves are not just any skips the composer wants to write. They set the boundaries of the entire soprano line, low *D* to high *D*, and they set an important note in the middle, the *A*. The idea that some notes are more important than others is basic to all music. In the Renaissance, the hierarchy of notes was expressed in the system of <u>modes</u>, which you will study in chapter 1. Chapter 2 deals with which intervals to use in a melody, and where in a particular melody to place skips and steps.

Variety in a Duo

Example I-2 "O magnum mysterium" (mm. 1–22)

Sing the soprano-alto duo through m. 9. On the syllables "O ma-" the alto line descends by skip while the soprano line rises by step on the syllables "my-ste-." Here *melodic direction* makes the contrast: *ascending vs. descending* lines make the lines seem independent. Later, when the soprano has the scales, the alto is on the slower-moving repeated note, so we have a contrast of *long vs. short* notes sounding simultaneously.

If the opening measures sound mysterious, another reason might be the emphasis on perfect vertical intervals. Note the perfect fifths *D–A* before and after the minor tenth. The different *classes of interval* (*perfect consonance, imperfect consonance, and dissonance*) are an important source of variety to Renaissance composers. Theorists said these different classes should be mixed. At the end of the duo there is a dissonance between the sopranos and altos. This is a pretty striking moment because we haven't had much dissonance before. In chapters 3–7 the focus is on dissonance treatment in Renaissance music in two voice parts.

Some singers like to think of their lines in physical terms. For them, a dissonance is like the parts rubbing together and creating friction, so that the consonance that follows is a relief. Many like to sing the dissonance a bit louder, relaxing into the following consonance. The unison, a perfect interval, is also a physical sensation, as if the two voices were dissolving into one. You should get in the habit of singing one part while playing the other, or while someone else sings the other, so that you experience this music *from the inside*.

One of the effects of imitation is to offer the possibility of truly independent, *overlapping phrasing* to the different parts. For instance, while the alto finishes "mysterium," breathes, and begins "et admirabile," the soprano pushes right through on the climactic "et admirabile" (downbeat of m. 6).

Variety in a Larger Musical Space

In m. 9 the tenor repeats what the sopranos sang at the beginning, and then the basses repeat what the altos sang, so most of the duo is repeated. But the repetition is varied by register, another area for contrast: *high voices vs. low voices*. In addition, the first duo was sounded alone, but when the tenors and basses have the duo, the sopranos and altos keep singing, so we have a contrast of texture: *two parts vs. four parts*. The effect of more parts is to add more pitch classes to each vertical sonority, creating *richness of sonority*, another ideal of Renaissance music. For instance, in the opening duo when the soprano sings "et" we hear two notes but only one pitch class, *D*; in the corresponding place in m. 12, when the tenor has "et," we hear three pitch classes, *D*, *B♭*, and *F*.

When the tenors enter, they are beginning a phrase, but the sopranos and altos are finishing a phrase. Probably the sopranos and altos will breathe between "sacramentum" and "O magnum" in m. 9, creating a little silence through which the tenors will be heard in the middle of the word "magnum." Similarly, the basses and tenors will probably breathe in m. 19 between "sacramentum" and "ut," leaving the sopranos and altos holding the final notes of their phrase. This kind of overlap is discussed in chapters 12 and 15.

Some performances get louder at m. 17, as if there were a climax here. What are the performers responding to when they sing louder here? It may be partly the fact that this is the first time all the parts have had the same rhythm and words at the same time. It is as if the singers pulled themselves together to declaim the text forcefully. This texture is called homorhythm. It provides a strong contrast to the imitative texture that predominated up to that point, in which there was rarely rhythmic unison, and parts almost never sang the same words at the same time.

Another reason for treating this spot as a climax is that a fragment of the opening soprano line three whole notes long ("et admirabile") has been broken off and repeated in different parts (this fragment has been bracketed: tenor m. 12, bass m. 13, soprano m. 15, and tenor m. 16). The repetition of the text fragment creates tension that is released in the cadence at m. 19, which completes the text phrase with a longer musical phrase and marks the end of the opening section. Repetition of a short melodic fragment is the subject of chapters 8 and 9, and cadences are covered in chapter 10. Yet another reason for treating m. 17 as a climax is the change of register in the bass and alto parts. Both parts leap up an octave, so it is natural for them to sound a bit louder.

The next section ("ut animalia") begins with a pair of lines in parallel motion, answered by the same idea an octave higher. The last notes of the soprano and alto in the previous section overlap with the first notes of the new phrase. Overlap, or elision, is used to create continuity, to keep the piece going. Writing imitative phrases and elided cadences is the subject of chapters 11 and 12.

Summary

The elements of contrast that create variety in the opening of "O magnum myste-rium" include:

- long notes vs. short notes (rhythmic values)
- skips vs. steps (melodic intervals)
- ascending vs. descending melodic motions (direction)
- perfect consonance vs. imperfect consonance vs. dissonance (vertical intervals)
- a high duo vs. a low duo (register)
- two voices vs. four voices (texture)
- thin vs. rich sonorities

- imitation vs. homorhythm (texture)
- long phrases vs. short phrases
- beginning vs. ending, continuing vs. breaking (phrasing)

The means of creating variety used by Renaissance composers may seem pretty subtle, but if you can accept their "tone of voice," you will find this music very interesting. We will use this page of "O magnum mysterium" as a touchstone for the elements we study. In many chapters you will find reference to it, and eventually you may get to know this bit of a famous motet by heart. Finally, in chapter 20, we will analyze the whole piece, using terms and concepts we have developed along the way.

We will not only point out technical details in the music, we will consider their aesthetic purpose. I propose that every piece or section has some kind of climax, or point of greatest intensity, that is approached and left gradually. This is a little simplistic: not every section has to have a climax, and there are many different kinds of climax, as we will see. But this approach gives us a way into the music, to see how the parts of the piece are differentiated, to glimpse one kind of compositional intention. And it can affect our performance; climaxes are opportunities to use the many means we have to vary our performance (dynamics, articulation, tone, tempo, etc.).

Renaissance Notation

Example I-3 Original Renaissance notation (Victoria, Thomas Ludovicus. Cantiones Sacrae. Dilingae: Ioannes Mayer, 1589. Sig. A1 verso and A2 recto. Shelf No. Fétis 1714 A RP. Permission to reproduce is granted by the Royal Library of Belgium.)

Renaissance music was almost never preserved in score format. Each part was printed separately, either in a part-book (like a modern orchestral part) or on its own part of a page. If the singers got lost, they couldn't say, "Go back to measure 10," they'd have to say, "Take it from the cadence where we both say . . ."

The note values used in the Renaissance are the breve, the semibreve, the minim, the semiminim, and occasionally the fusa and smaller values. We will use these note values and rests with their modern names:

Example I-4 Note values and rests

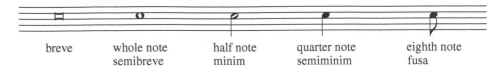

breve	whole note	half note	quarter note	eighth note
	semibreve	minim	semiminim	fusa

The basic unit of measure (comparable to our quarter note) was most often the semibreve, whose tempo should be $\circ = 60\text{--}75$.

Bar lines are almost never used in Renaissance notation. The music is organized into units a whole note long, and the "downbeat" is defined as the beginning of each whole-note unit. In the exercises and examples in this book, barring is presented in a variety of ways, for convenience of lining up the parts only. You should disregard the bar lines and remember that each whole-note unit defines a downbeat *regardless of how many are grouped in a measure.* One effect of adding bar lines, as we do in modern notation, is to create tied notes. In Renaissance notation there are no tied notes; when you look at a modern transcription, you should think of the single note value represented by the sum of the tied values.

The old notation has some advantages over our barred notation. One is that because you don't see the other parts, you are freer to express the features of your line regardless of what else is going on. You are also less likely to think in terms of vertical sonorities, or chords.

Another advantage is to let you forget the meter to some extent, and to perform the natural accentuation of the text in groups of different lengths, without the accents that come from syncopating. In these examples we can hear triple-meter groups, as indicated.

Example I-5 Barred notation and old notation: Examples from Byrd (a) and Palestrina (b)

b.

Fu – it ho - mo mis-sus a De - o

⌐ 3/1 ⌐ 3/2 ⌐ ⌐ 3/2 ⌐ ⌐ 3/2 ⌐

Fu – it ho - mo mis-sus a De - o

A third advantage is to make melodic patterns easier to spot, regardless of where they fall in the measure, so that you can perform them in a similar manner. In the following excerpt it's easier to see the five-note pattern when the whole notes look the same:

Example I-6

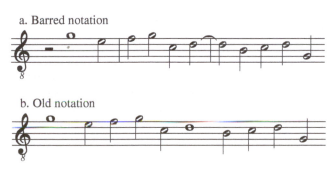

a. Barred notation

b. Old notation

Clefs

Clefs used in the Renaissance include many different placements of the *F-*, *G-*, and *C*-clefs. The purpose of different clefs is primarily to avoid ledger lines. In this book the only clefs we will use are treble, bass, "tenor octave" clef (treble clef with an 8 below, sounding an octave lower than regular treble clef), and alto clef (middle *C* on the third line), but this last only for slow-moving lines. Here is what middle *C* looks like in each of these clefs:

Example I-7 Clefs

treble   bass   tenor octave   alto

Musica Ficta

One aspect of Renaissance notation that seems bizarre to us now is <u>musica</u> <u>ficta</u>, or "unreal music" ("fictitious music"). This refers to the introduction of accidentals when none are indicated in the written music. Cadential leading tones make up one large family of musica ficta (see "Writing Your Own Cadences" in chapter 6). Another large family contains cases, as shown in Example I-8a, where a melodic augmented fourth (or diminished fifth) is "corrected" through the use of *B*♭ (sung at the asterisk). Vertical augmented fourths and diminished fifths are corrected the same way (Ex.I-8b); presumably a singer would hear the dissonant interval and correct it on the next run-through (this interval would not be corrected using *F*♯, however). In another class of ficta (Ex. I-8c), the *B* upper neighbor to the *A* is to be performed as *B*♭. The *B*♮ is avoided because it makes a tritone with the *F*♮ below in the melody.

In modern editions of Renaissance music, the editor will often show where he or she believes musica ficta should be performed by placing an accidental *above* the note. You can take what the editor suggests with a grain of salt: present-day authors are not all in agreement about musica ficta. In all your own exercises you are to indicate accidentals.

Example I-8

Treatises and Theorists

Over a dozen theorists, writing between 1558 and 1622, are cited in this book. Their treatises contain a mixture of music history, practical advice to composers and performers, illustrations of techniques, discussions of style and genre, and philosophical speculation. I have taken from them what I think you will find useful as a musician working four hundred years later.

Most of these treatises cover more or less the same techniques, so I have tried to pick the best discussions and examples of each technique. You may, however, want to compare another author's treatment of a given topic. The authors are mostly Italian followers of Zarlino, and by and large they share the same outlook. However, when they disagree, I have, for pedagogical purposes, chosen a single view on which to base the rules for your exercises.

Disagreement between theorists is normal. Why should any two thinkers in the past be more in agreement than any two university professors nowadays? In this book you will ocasionally run across conflicting opinions, examples by one author that break another's rules. When this happens I will point out the conflict and remind you what the rules for the exercises are. Outside of the exercises, outside of the classroom, you are of course free (indeed, encouraged) to experiment with principles of style that you have seen in the examples.

1

Mode

Modes function in Renaissance music the way keys do in later tonal music. In a general way, they define which notes are more important than other notes, they give a sense of direction, they give a piece a special "feel" or "sound," and they give <u>closure</u> at the end of a piece (the sense that we have come back to where we belong). A melodic line is said to be "in" a mode in much the same way that a line can be "in" a key.

Modes use the natural ("white") notes in the <u>diatonic</u> arrangement, with a few occasional accidentals. Intervals in the diatonic arrangement are measured in terms of the number of letter-named notes they contain (e.g., a third spans three notes). Intervals are further distinguished by their quality, determined by the particular size of the step (for example, a major third contains two steps of a major second, while a minor third contains a step of a major second and a step of a minor second).

The Twelve-Mode System

Renaissance writers argued about different modal systems a lot; we have chosen to use the very logical twelve-mode system here. The criteria that we will use for defining them are:

1. The <u>final</u> note in a melodic line. If the line ends on *D*, the mode is first or second; *E*, third or fourth; *F*, fifth or sixth; *G*, seventh or eighth; *A*, ninth or tenth; and *C*, eleventh or twelfth. Each mode also has a Greek name (see Ex. 1-1a).

2. The <u>range</u> of the line. It is normally an octave, built either above the final or above the fourth below the final. The former is the range of the authentic, odd-numbered modes; the latter the plagal, or even-numbered modes. In the Greek nomenclature, the names of the plagal modes begin with the prefix "hypo-" ("below"). The last note (final) in a plagal melody lies in the middle of the range; in an authentic melody, at the top or bottom. In practice the modal octave may be exceeded by a step at either end. If the melody goes farther than that, the mode is called "excessive"; if the melody covers both the plagal and authentic ranges, its mode is said to be "mixed"; if the melody covers less than an octave, it is called "incomplete."

3. <u>The species of fourths and fifths.</u> The types ("species") of fourth and fifth are numbered according to the positions of the semitones and tones enclosed within them (T = whole tone, S = semitone). For instance, the TTST fifth is called a "fourth species fifth" and it occurs in two locations in the natural diatonic system (some species of interval only occur in one location, as shown in Ex. 1-1b). When a species of interval is characteristic of more than one mode, the whole octave must be examined to determine the mode. The species of fourth and fifth give a mode its "sound," so you should learn to sing the different species and to identify them aurally. The end points of the various species of interval can be stressed by skipping to and from them or by using them as turning points in a melody.

4. <u>Characteristic notes</u>. The end points of the characteristic species of fourth and fifth are the characteristic notes of the mode. They are always the final and the fifth above (or the fourth below) the final. Thus if we hear or see a melody that is continually emphasizing the notes *E* and *B*, we can be sure that melody is either in the Phrygian mode or the Hypophrygian.

The structural features of the twelve modes are illustrated in Example 1-1a. The numbers of the modes (circled), their constituent fourths and fifths (bracketed and numbered), their finals (whole notes), and their Greek names must all be memorized. It is fairly easy if you begin by remembering that D is number one in all things (it is the first final and the lowest note of the first species fourth and fifth), that odd-numbered modes have the final at the bottom, and that B is not a final. Five of the octave spans (A–A, C–C, D–D, E–E, and G–G) contain two different modes; in order to tell them apart (the Hypomixolydian from the Dorian, for instance) you need to look at the final.

Example 1-1a The twelve modes

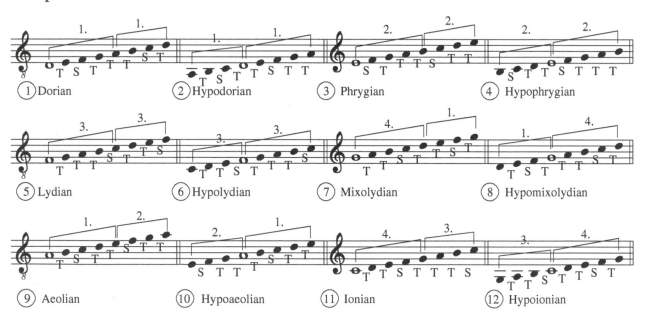

Example 1-1b The species of fourths and fifths

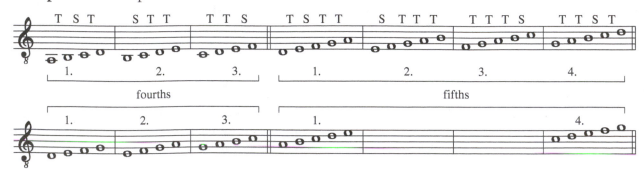

As an aid in memorization, you may find it helpful to compare scales of modes with scales of major and minor keys. For instance, the ninth and eleventh modes resemble A minor and C major, and you can think of the Dorian as a minor scale with a raised sixth degree, the Lydian as a major scale with a raised fourth degree, etc.

In a two-voice texture, the two voices must end on the same <u>pitch class</u>, that of the final, but not necessarily on the same note. The term <u>pitch class</u> refers to the group of notes that all have the same name. In Example 1-2, both voices begin on the same note (*D* below middle *C*), but they end on different notes (*D* above middle *C* and *D* below) that belong to the same pitch *class* (*D*). The two voices may lie in different modal ranges; in Example 1-2 the upper voice is authentic (Dorian) and the lower plagal (Hypodorian). These ranges are appropriate to tenor and bass vocal ranges. In this case the theorist might choose one voice from which to label the mode of the entire piece. Note the skips in the bass part that outline the characteristic species of interval.

Example 1-2 (Tigrini)

final at extreme of range

1st sp. 5th

final in middle of range

1st sp. 4th

Accidentals and Transposition

An occasional *B♭* may be used without changing the mode. As we have seen, the principal reason to use a *B♭* is to avoid a tritone skip or outline. No other accidentals are to be used except for leading tones at cadences, which are supplied for you in the early exercises.

Transposition

If a *B♭* occurs in the signature, we take this as an indication that the mode has been <u>transposed</u>. Its final note and the extremes of its range are a fourth higher or a fifth lower than in the natural system, but its characteristic arrangement of semitones is the same. The names of such modes include the name of the new final (e.g., "*F*-Ionian" or "*A*-Hypophrygian"). In a piece with a *B♭* in the signature we can expect to find *E♭* used in the same way that *B♭* would be used in the system with all natural notes: to correct a tritone without changing the mode (see Ex. 1-3h). You may not use a *B♮* in the context of the system with one flat. Key signatures other than the one with one flat are rarely used in Renaissance music, and will not be considered here.

The Importance of Mode

Range

Unlike keys, modes establish the outer limits of the <u>range</u> of a melody. The limits of melodies were based on vocal ranges, and for the most part these were limited to a tenth or twelfth. Within this range, the concept of mode further restricted melodic activity to a little more than an octave, with the notes at the extremes of the octave having a special importance (they are the final or the fifth). This aspect of mode is a little hard to grasp for us, since the range of more recent music has been expanded, and in polyphonic music it is hard to hear extremes of a single line. Mode will help you avoid lines that meander around over a great range, a common mistake in early counterpoint studies.

Skips and Outlines

A melody will tend to stress the important notes of its mode by placing them at melodic turning points or at the extremes of skips. The species of interval enclosed in the skip or outline identifies the mode, and the emphasis on these notes gives consistency to the melody. Other skips and outlines can be used for contrast (see Ex. 1-3j).

Cadences

Cadences are like punctuation at the ends of phrases. In a single line, cadences are usually made by a descending step. Mode determines the right notes on which to conclude the piece and most phrases. Then cadences can be made on other notes to provide contrast (see Ex. 1-3i).

Expression

Renaissance authors believed that the different modes were appropriate for different moods or emotional states that we call affects. The Mixolydian, for instance, was sometimes considered happy, the Dorian serious, and the Aeolian sad, although authors did not always agree with one another. This aspect of mode will play only a minor role in subsequent chapters of this book.

In Example 1-3, you are given some modal melodies from a wide variety of traditions. Sing them; identify the mode of each. Many of them were used as the basis for compositions and treatise examples, and you will use them as the basis for exercises.

Example 1-3a "L'homme armé." This tune was used in different modes by many composers; it offers a good opportunity to experience the differences between modes. Memorize the tune in the Mixolydian, and then sing it in the natural-note collection beginning on C, D, etc., up to A. You will thus sing it successively in the Ionian, Dorian, Phrygian, Lydian (you'll have to add an accidental B♭ to avoid the tritone leap), Mixolydian, and Aeolian modes. ("The armed man, the armed man must be feared. People are shouting everywhere that everyone come armed with an iron coat of mail.")

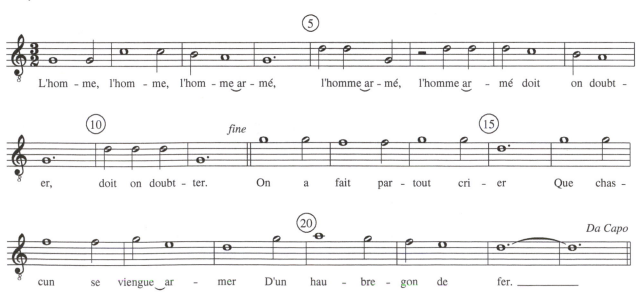

Example 1-3b Kyrie VIII (De Angelis). All the Bs in this melody are flat, but because the flat is not in the signature, we take this melody as Lydian. ("Lord have mercy; Christ have mercy; Lord have mercy.")

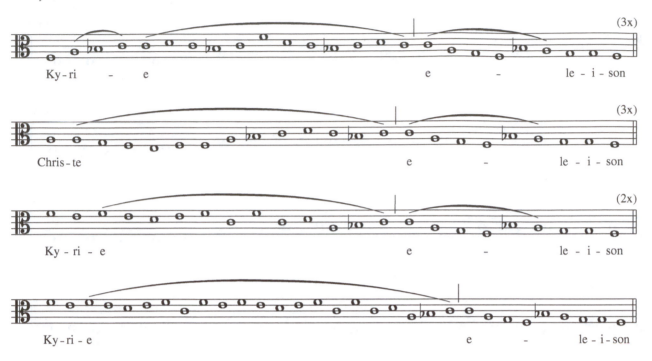

Example 1-3c Kyrie IX (BVM; Cum jubilo). In this melody the plagal and authentic ranges are mixed, so we would call it "mixed Dorian and Hypodorian."

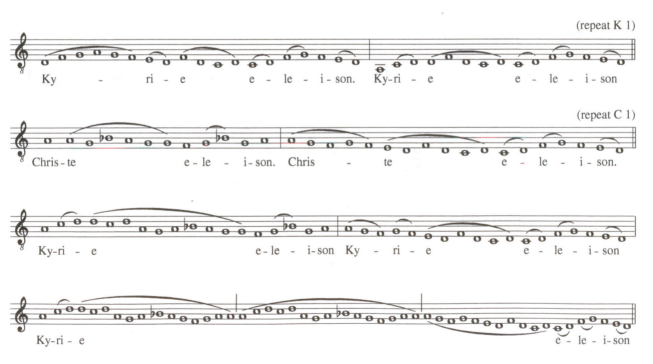

Example 1-3d Kyrie XI (De Dominica; Orbis factor). There is a lot of repetition in this Kyrie, some of it quite obvious. The repetition of the bracketed seven-note fragment in the Christe section, transposed a fifth lower in the final Kyrie section, is not so obvious on first hearing.

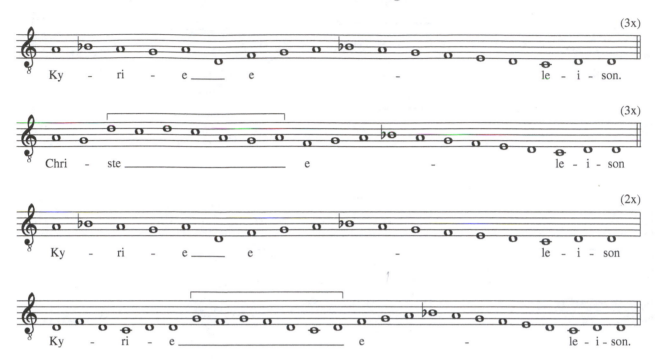

Example 1-3e "Christ lag in Todesbanden" (chorale). When chorale melodies are used as cantus firmi the note values of the original may be retained, or they may be evened out (see Exx. 14-9 and 14-10). ("Christ lay in the bonds of death, given for our sin; He is risen again and has brought us life. Then shall we be joyful, praise God and be thankful, and sing Alleluia.")

Example 1-3f "Da Jesus an den Kreuze stund" (chorale). The mode of this melody is incomplete. ("When Jesus was on the cross and his body was wounded, with bitter sorrow the seven words that Jesus spoke, ponder in your heart.")

Da Je -sus au dem Kreu -ze stund   und ihm sein Leich -nam war ver -wundt   so gar mit bit -tern Schmer -zen

die   sie – ben Wort die   Je – sus sprach,   be –tracht in   eu – rem   Her   –   zen.

Example 1-3g "Vater unser in Himmelreich" (chorale). Note that the third and fourth phrases can end with cadences using the raised leading tone. Sometimes these accidentals are retained when the tune is used as a cantus firmus, sometimes not (see Exx. 14-9 and 14-10). ("Our Father in heaven, you who call us all to be brothers alike, and to call to you, and who will receive our prayer: let us not pray with our mouths alone, but help it come from the depths of our heart.")

Va   –   ter   un – ser   im   Him – mel –reich,   der   du   uns   al – le   heis –sest gleich

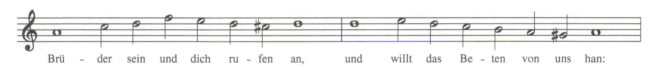

Brü – der   sein   und   dich   ru –fen   an,   und   willt   das   Be – ten   von   uns   han:

gib,   dass nicht bet   al – lein   der Mund;   hilf,   dass   es   geh   von   Her –zen –grund!

Example 1-3h "La Spagna" (basse danse). This melody is in a transposed mode.

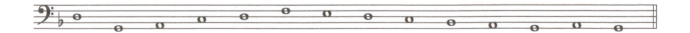

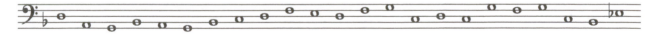

Example 1-3i "Ave Maris Stella" (hymn). The cadences to D (at "alma" and "porta") clearly organize this chant into two halves. Each half consists of two phrases, the first of which concludes on a note other than D (A at "stella" and C at "Virgo"). ("Hail Star of the Sea, fostering mother of God and still virgin, happy door to heaven.")

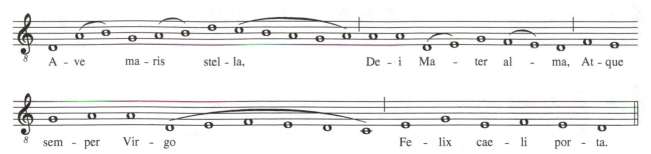

Example 1-3j "Spiritus Domini replevit" (introit). Zarlino finds this melody noteworthy for containing outlines of species of fifth that are not appropriate to the mode of the tune as a whole (the eighth mode). Find the foreign outlines. Note the gradual descent in the last phrase, with the successive high points E, C, B, A leading to the final, G. ("The spirit of the Lord fills the whole earth, and that which contains all things knows [what is said by] the voice.")

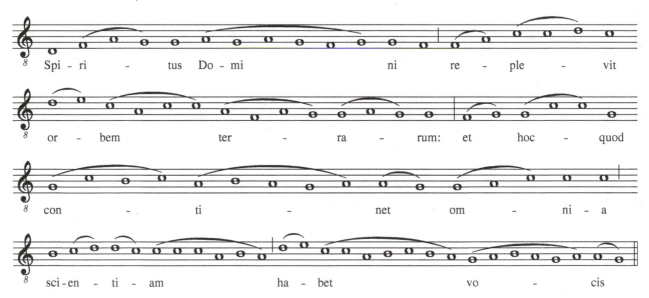

Example 1-3k "Ecce sacerdos magnus" (antiphon). When this melody is used as a cantus firmus, the falling third at the end of each line is altered to become a falling step (A–G) so as to make the standard cadence. ("Behold the great priest, who in his days pleased God and was found to be just.")

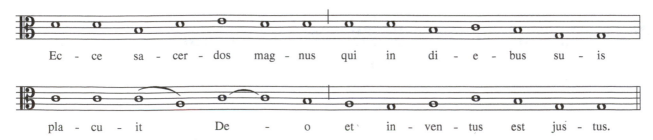

Mode in Polyphony

In a polyphonic texture each voice is governed by mode in the same way a mono-phonic melody is; in fact, it is possible to consider a polyphonic texture to be a col-lection of modal melodies sounding simultaneously. Because different voices can be in different modes, it is a more complicated affair to judge the mode in polyphonic music. Usually different voices are in the plagal and the authentic modes that share the same final (like Ex. 1-2), but sometimes different voices can be in modes with different finals.

Look back at each voice in the first page of Victoria's "O magnum mysterium" (Ex. Intro-3), and label the mode of each voice. Based on the ranges and skips, the soprano and tenor seem to be in *D*-Aeolian and the alto and bass in *G*-Dorian. The four cadences in the first section are to *D* (the falling step is in the soprano in m. 10) and *G* (falling steps occur in the tenor in m. 13, in the alto in m. 16, and in the tenor in m. 19).

On the basis of the first page we can't determine whether the whole piece is *D*-Aeolian or *G*-Dorian. This is a common state of affairs in Renaissance music, and many authors of the period tell us that you can only judge by the end. This piece ends on *G*, making it *G*-Dorian, a mode that is appropriate for the serious mood of the text.

Introduction to Two-Part Species Counterpoint

The Cantus Firmus

In Examples 2-1a and b, Pietro Pontio has written two different contrapuntal lines above the same melody. This lower line is an abbreviated version of Kyrie IX (see Ex. 1-3c). When a melody is used in a relatively slow, even rhythm, with other lines added to it, we call it a cantus firmus (abbreviated CF). For instance, if a composer wrote a setting of the Ordinary of the Mass based on the tune "L'homme armé" (Ex. 1-3a), he would add contrapuntal lines to that tune (with the words of the Mass: Kyrie, Gloria, etc.), and the finished piece would be identified as Missa "L'homme armé." The original tune might move so slowly that we would have trouble hearing and identifying it, but it would still be the basis of the piece. Any melody could be used as a CF (you could compose a Missa "Surfin' USA"), but we will follow the example of teachers around 1600 and use tunes that were well known then. These tunes share certain characteristics: they are presented in equal note values (whole notes or breves) and they end with a stepwise descent to the final. You will use the melodies in Example 1-3 as the basis for exercises and compositions just as Renaissance composers did.

The whole note (or semibreve) represents the basic pulse of this music. You should get used to thinking of the whole notes moving at about MM = 60–80. The importance of the whole note is that it is the unit by which we measure the behavior of the vertical intervals that are formed when another line is added to the CF. Remember that each whole note defines a downbeat *regardless of how many are grouped in a measure*. In subsequent chapters you will see whole notes grouped in twos or fours with no time signature, or not grouped at all, as in Example 2-1.

Example 2-1a and b (Pontio)

a.

Consonance and Dissonance

You should get in the habit of labeling vertical intervals by placing numbers between the parts until you are a confident score reader (this has been done in Ex. 2-1a). Classes of vertical interval are: <u>consonances</u>, which are divided into <u>perfect</u> (unison, octave, fifth) and <u>imperfect</u> (third, sixth), and <u>dissonances</u> (second, fourth, augmented fourth, diminished fifth, seventh). These classifications also apply to the compounds of these intervals. <u>Compound intervals</u> are simple intervals (unison up to seventh) plus one or more octaves. Thus a ninth is a compound second, and is a dissonance. Label all vertical intervals in Examples 2-1a and b as PC (perfect consonance), IC (imperfect consonance), or D (dissonance).

The rules of counterpoint relate the vertical (or simultaneous) intervals to the melodic (or linear) intervals by which they are approached. The relationship between the melodic and the vertical dimensions is called <u>voice leading</u>.

Types of Motion

There are basically two types of melodic motion: by skip (disjunct) and by step (conjunct, or stepwise). A step occurs between two notes with adjacent letter names. The types of motion between two parts are shown in Example 2-2: a) <u>parallel</u>, in which both voices move in the same direction over the same distance (measured diatonically); b) <u>similar</u>, in which both voices move in the same direction but different distances; c) <u>oblique</u>, in which one voice stays put; and d) <u>contrary</u>. Note that when both voices stay put, there is no motion.

Example 2-2

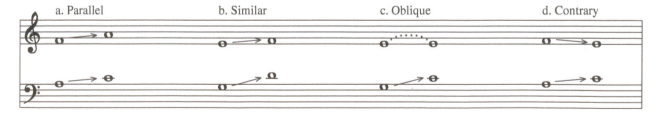

Go back to Example 2-1a and label the types of motion between the two parts as P (parallel), S (similar), O (oblique), or C (contrary). In Example 2-1b you can see that all motions made by the contrapuntal voice *during* the CF whole note are oblique—the other types of contrapuntal motions only occur at changes of CF notes. Label the types of motion at changes of CF notes in Example 2-1b (consider only the downbeat interval and the interval immediately before it). You will notice that contrary motion predominates; this is because one of the ideals of Renaissance style is independence of the lines, and contrary motion distinguishes the two lines the most.

The Four Species of Counterpoint

In species counterpoint, melodic motions and vertical intervals are related to the metric position of the notes involved. In order to show how melodic motions and vertical intervals relate to metric position, theorists devised examples in which a single note value was used at a time, providing practice in solving just one problem. A line consisting of a single type of note value (all half notes, say) is placed against a CF, and exercises demonstrate the possibilities for half-note behavior against wholes. Each different note value defines a kind ("species") of counterpoint (not to be confused with kinds of fourth and fifth intervals). In this way the focus is on one note value at a time.

In first species the added line moves in whole notes (this is also called "simple" or "note-against-note" counterpoint). In second species the added line moves in half notes. In third species the added line moves in quarter notes. In fourth species the added line moves in whole notes, but they are displaced (syncopated) by a half note. The usefulness of this system is that when a line is composed in freely mixed values, we can describe the behavior of the notes according to the rules of the appropriate species.

In Example 2-3 Gioseffo Zarlino has written a contrapuntal line above a CF, using freely mixed note values. This is the kind of piece you will compose in chapters 7 and 8. The rhythm of the added line can be broken down into the different species enumerated above. These have been labeled. Dotted halves (or halves tied to quarters) are treated as changing from second to third species at the dot (look at the downbeat of m. 6). Note that syncopated half notes (tied quarters marked with X in mm. 11-12) are not an accepted species, and will not be used in this book.

Example 2-3 (Zarlino)

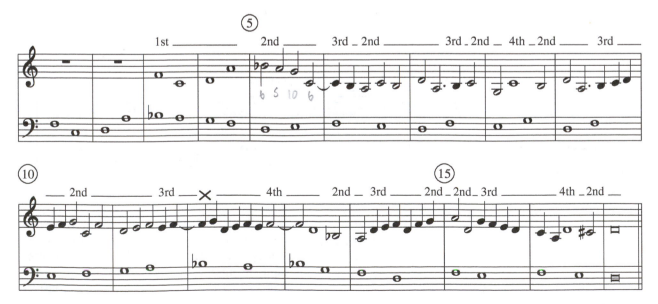

General Rules for All Species Exercises

"Hard" rules are those that cannot be broken under any circumstances. They appear in boldface type. Most hard rules are based on contrapuntal principles, and are found at the beginning of each chapter. However, some other hard rules are found in the instructions to specific exercises, and they apply only to those exercises they immediately precede.

"Soft" rules are more a matter of taste, and Renaissance authors often give them, adding that they are "not fatal." It is virtually impossible not to break soft rules, and often there is a very good musical reason for doing so; the individual professor's judgment plays a large part here. In this book, hard errors are indicated with "X" and soft ones with "(X)." Concentrate on observing hard rules first, then worry about soft ones.

Hard Rules

1. Use only natural notes and *B♭*. *B♭* is to be used as little as possible. It may be an upper neighbor to *A* or it may be used to avoid a melodic or vertical tritone (augmented fourth) or diminished fifth. (Later, when you write cadences, you will use various sharped leading tones.)

When there is a *B♭ in the signature*, *E♭* may be used in the same way as *B♭* was in the natural system (as an upper neighbor to *D*, etc.). *E♭* may never be used in the natural system, and *B♮* may not be used in the system with one flat. You may never alter a note in the CF.

When two different versions of a note (flat, natural or sharp) occur in close succession, this is called a <u>cross-relation</u>. Example 2-4 shows a cross-relation between two different versions of *B* in the upper voice. In general, you should let the raised version of a note ascend, and the lowered version descend. Cross-relations can seem awkward, but th ey are perfectly legal.

Example 2-4 Cross-relations (from Diruta)

Example 2-4 shows another cross-relation, between *F♮* and *F♯* at the cadence (the *F♯* has a lower neighbor, but it does eventually ascend as it should). At cadences, accidentals are often used as leading tones so that one of the stepwise motions to the final is a semitone; in the early exercises the cadences have been provided for you, so you won't have to worry about these accidentals.

On the use of accidentals, Thomas Morley says "Let your eare be the iudge . . . if anie man like the other waie better, let him use his discretion." The opening of Victoria's "O magnum" features several striking cross-relations between *F♮* and *F♯*. Find them. They contribute to the characteristic "sound" of the piece.

2. Skips of augmented and diminished intervals, and skips larger than a sixth are prohibited (except that octaves are allowed). This means that no chromatic motions (i.e., augmented unisons) are allowed, no leaps of augmented fourths (tritones) or diminished fifths, no augmented seconds, diminished fourths, etc. Skips of a sixth must be used sparingly, and as described in "soft" rules below.

3. Outlines of an augmented fourth are forbidden, and a diminished fifth outline must be completely filled in and followed by a step in the opposite direction. An <u>outline</u> is the interval from a temporary high point in a line to the next temporary low point, or vice-versa. In Example 2-3, for instance, the upper voice outlines the fourth from *F* down to *C*, then the seventh from *C* up to *B♭*, then the ninth from *B♭* down to *A*, etc. Zarlino's illustrations of the correct use of diminished fifth outlines are shown in Example 2-5.

Example 2-5 Diminished fifth outlines (Zarlino)

4. Begin and end with perfect consonances between the two parts. This means you may begin at the unison, fifth, or octave (and rarely, a twelfth) above or below. In exercises in the first three species, the end will be provided, so this won't be a problem.

Soft Rules

One of the goals of Renaissance style is that lines be easy to sing. This is of course subjective, but if you can sing a melody easily, it passes at least a first test. Most of the rules below address how skips are used because skips affect singability. It is not hard to find exceptions to these soft rules in Renaissance music—but following them is a surefire way to start writing in Renaissance style.

1. Use steps more frequently than skips. (In many chapters the actual proportion of skips to steps is specified as a hard rule, so you won't have to judge how much is too much.)

2. Avoid skipping a major sixth in either direction, and avoid minor sixths descending (minor sixths ascending are fine). These skips are occasionally found in late Renaissance madrigals whose texts deal with extravagant and harsh emotions.

3. It is preferable to precede and/or follow a skip with a step or steps in the opposite direction.

4. Do not use more than two skips in succession (whether in the same direction or not).

5. If you use two successive skips in the same direction, keep them small.

6. When you use skips or steps *in the same direction*, the larger intervals should be below the smaller ones. This is called the "pyramid" rule, on the theory that larger intervals are heavier and support smaller ones. (The example shows picture of pyramids right side up and upside down.) You could also think in terms of energy or momentum: you are more likely to take stairs two at a time when you start going up, switching to one at a time near the top. Going down you would be more likely to start taking the stairs one at a time, skipping nearer the bottom (Don't try doing the reverse!).

7. Avoid skipping both to and from a temporary high or low point. This leaves one note "hanging," detached from the rest of the line.

8. Accidental B♭s should be followed by descending motion.

Illustration of Soft Rules

Find the Errors

Sing and discuss the following melodies, some of which break various rules described above. Those marked with asterisks (*) are from madrigals by late Renaissance composers; these madrigals were considered radical and highly expressive—are they hard to sing? Mark hard errors with X and soft errors with (X).

| Exercises: | ## Melody Writing |

1. Compose a 36-note melody using only whole notes, covering the entire Hypophrygian range, using no repeated notes, and ending with a stepwise descent to the final (*E*). Use a text if you like. If you follow the rules in this chapter it will not be surprising if your melody turns out to sound a lot like some of those in Example 1-3.

2. Compose a short melody (12–15 notes) in each of these modes: Dorian, Phrygian, Hypophrygian, Lydian, Mixolydian, and Hypomixolydian.

Melodic Analysis

Go back to the melodies in Example 1-3. Pick one you like and find exceptions to the rules and principles given in this chapter. Are any hard rules broken? How are skips used in your chosen melody? What is the largest skip? What proportion of melodic intervals do skips account for?

Most of these melodies contain some repetition. Repetition is an essential element in all music. It creates musical logic and makes it easier to memorize music. In your chosen tune, what is the longest string of notes that you can find repeated exactly elsewhere? What is the longest string that you can find repeated in transposition elsewhere? A repeating segment in Example 1-3d has been bracketed as an illustration. Looking for patterns is essential to thinking about any music, and in later chapters we will see how Renaissance composers in particular dealt with repetition.

Try to sing your chosen line from memory. Do you think your activities outlined in the two preceding paragraphs make it easier to remember the tune?

Consider the soprano line of "O magnum mysterium." Victoria breaks our soft rule about following skips by steps in the opposite direction. Both the first and second skips are abandoned without being filled in, which gives that part of the melody an intensity that comes from incompleteness. The *D–A* span is not filled in by stepwise motion until mm. 7-8. Victoria makes the listener wait for the satisfying conclusion, and just as that tension is being resolved, the tenor enters, so there's always something exciting happening. What about the types of motion between the parts in the opening duo? Victoria uses almost exclusively contrary and oblique motion in mm. 1-9; find the only exception.

Voice Crossing and Voice Overlap

One way to distinguish voices is by having each one move in its own range. For the most part, an upper voice always stays above a lower voice. For instance, in Pontio's examples at the beginning of this chapter, the tenor's notes always sound above those of the bass. When, however, the notes of the upper voice sound below those of the lower, or vice-versa, we say the voices are <u>crossed</u>. Voices in different ranges often cross for brief periods, so you must be careful in reading the score to measure intervals up from the lowest *sounding* note—don't assume the bottom line has the lowest note (the intervals have been labeled in Ex. 2-6a). The instructions for your exercises will specify whether voice crossing is allowed, and if so, for how long.

Although most of the music in this book and most of your exercises use voices that occupy different ranges, many Renaissance pieces contain voices that occupy the same ranges. A duo for equal voices ("<u>voci pari</u>") is shown in Example 12-4; label the vertical intervals in it. Example 19-17 is a four-part piece with two alto parts and two tenor parts; within each pair the voices cross freely. Because the standard SATB texture uses the entire range of the chorus, most pieces with more than four parts are likely to have two parts in the same range. Example 19-23 has two soprano parts that cross freely.

Voices are said to <u>overlap</u> when the lower one goes to where the upper one just was, or beyond (or vice versa). It is rarely used in music in only two parts unless one voice moves by step or both voices skip a third.

Example 2-6a and b Voice crossing and voice overlap

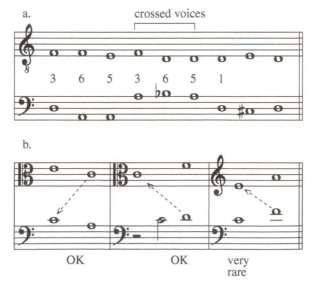

3

First Species

First species is also called "note-against-note" counterpoint. The notes of the added voice are whole notes, and the attack is on downbeats, with the CF notes. Review the hard rules in chapter 2, especially rule 4.

Hard Rules

1. All downbeats must be consonant. Since there *are* only downbeats in first species, all vertical intervals will be consonant. The rule is stated this way because it does not change in the first three species. A dissonant downbeat can be indicated with "ddb."

2. All perfect intervals must be approached by contrary or oblique motion. This means you cannot use any parallel or similar motion to approach a perfect vertical interval. Such motions are described as "parallel fifths" (successive vertical fifths made by voices moving in parallel motion, shown by "‖5") and "similar octave" (a vertical octave approached by similar motion shown by "sim. 8"—some teachers also call this a "direct" or "hidden" octave). Oblique motion is possible in first species when notes are repeated in one voice.

3. Repeated notes in the counterpoint may not occur against repeated notes in the CF. Repeated notes may occur *either* in the CF *or* in the added line, but never in both at the same time. However, you may occasionally skip an octave in the contrapuntal voice even if the CF is stationary.

4. Counterpoint may run parallel to the CF for four notes maximum. Any more, and the counterpoint ceases to be an independent line. Remember that the only parallel intervals allowed are thirds and sixths.

5. Skips must account for less than half the melodic motions. This somewhat arbitrary proportion is higher than you are likely to find in the repertoire. In other species, a higher proportion of skips will be allowed. (This rule does not apply to short Series C exercises.) In the example, nine out of twelve motions in the lower voice are skips.

6. Direct repetition of the whole contrapuntal combination (two or more simultaneities) is forbidden, and only two sequential repetitions are allowed. A combination consists of melodic motions and vertical intervals; in the illustrations below, the combinations are bracketed, with vertical intervals labeled. "Direct repetition" means without intervening material. It is legal to repeat a combination if other material intervenes, but this intervening material must last at least two whole notes. <u>Sequential</u> repetitions are those in which the combination is transposed; "two repetitions" means three occurrences: an original and two repetitions. This error occurs only when there is direct repetition of a melodic pattern in the CF, so check the CF before beginning to compose a solution.

  7. All Exercises must begin and end with a perfect vertical consonance (See hard rule 4, p. 22).

Illustration of Hard Rules

1. CF

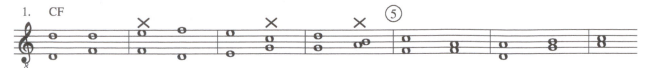

2. CF

3. CF

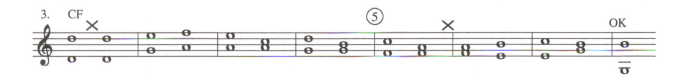

4. CF

5. CF

6. CF

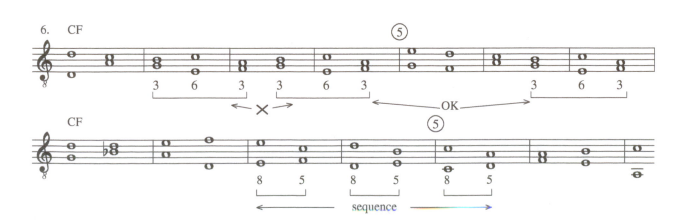

Exercise Series A: Warmups

Warmups are the first exercises in each chapter. They are mechanical drills that can be done very quickly. They are designed to make you more comfortable at finding solutions to a CF problem. In the warmup exercises on the first four species, you are asked to find **all possible legal solutions,** above and below, to a two-note fragment of a CF. Your **solutions must lie within the given range, and just for this exercise, voice crossing is not allowed** (see Ex. 2-6). You are to assume that the fragment is neither the beginning nor the end of a piece, so perfect vertical intervals are not necessary as stated in chapter 2, rule 4. If a $B\flat$ occurs, assume it is accidental, not in the signature, so you can't use $E\flat$.

One way to go about this is to stack up all vertical consonances (unison, third, fifth, sixth, octave, and their compounds) against each of the two notes and then "connect the dots" (or, more accurately, "connect the sounds"). In Example 3-1a, you are given a two-note CF fragment A–C and the range of the added voice above and below:

Example 3-1a

Within these ranges six notes are possible above the A and five above the C, and five are possible below the A and five below the C; in Example 3-1b they are sketched in as black noteheads:

Example 3-1b

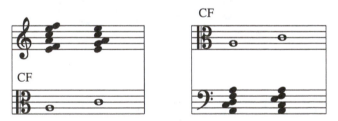

If we could connect every possible note above the A to every possible note above the C, we would have $5 \times 6 = 30$ possible solutions. However, because of the voice-leading rules not all of these connections are legal. Example 3-1c shows all the thirty possible connections between contrapuntal notes above, and Example 3-1d shows all the twenty-five possible connections between contrapuntal notes below. Xs show hard mistakes and (X)s show soft mistakes, as described in chapter 2. Make sure you know which rule is broken at each X.

Example 3-1c

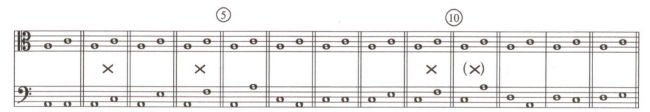

Exampel 3-1d

Why Look for All Possibilities?

This admittedly tedious technique was known to Renaissance theorists, and it is good practice. If you memorize the legal solutions you will acquire "voice-leading chops." Later on you can consider a longer CF as many two-note successions. This method may seem to be at odds with the notion that counterpoint is writing nice lines, but the example we just did gives you material to choose from to make a nice line when the CF moves up a minor third. The example may contain some attractive solutions that you would not have thought of if you hadn't looked for all possibilities. Without these new solutions, you might fall back on a small number of tricks you happened to know, not exploring all that the style has to offer.

When you do the exercises below, you needn't go to the lengths shown in Example 3-1, writing down all possibilities and crossing out the bad ones. You can run through possibilities in your head, jotting down only the good ones. This will help you develop the skill of *imagining music that is not written down*, a skill that is basic to all contrapuntal activities.

You can cover more ground in less time if you and another student each write against a different pair of notes, then exchange papers and correct each other's. You can also save a lot of time by improvising, discussed at the end of this chapter.

Warmup Exercises

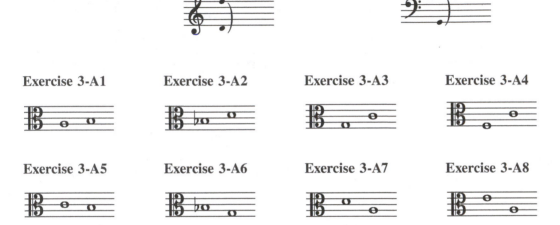

The Invertible Counterpoint Option

Some teachers like to introduce invertible counterpoint early on. At any point in chapters 3–6 you can skip to chapter 13 and study invertible counterpoint at the octave. Then you can use it in your species exercises. For instance, in the exercises above, you could first make it a point to find those solutions that are invertible at the octave. These solutions should be displayed lined up vertically with the CF in the middle. Then you could find all other solutions. Use this option in series A, C, and D exercises. Both your original duo and the inverted one must conform to the rules for each exercise. Save invertible counterpoint at the twelfth for chapter 7, mixed values.

Soft Rules

1. Avoid more than two perfect vertical intervals in a row (see Ex. 3-4). Use a mixture of perfect and imperfect, or mostly imperfect intervals.

2. Avoid unisons, except on the first and last notes. One of the voices appears to vanish.

3. Avoid skipping simultaneously in both parts (in any direction); this is not so serious if both voices move only a third.

4. Widely separated voices (more than a twelfth) should be avoided, and should be done as briefly as possible.

5. It is generally better to change direction after a large skip (bigger than a fourth), and move in steps.

6. It is best to connect extremes of register with smooth, mostly stepwise motion; even if skips are not immediately filled in, try to fill them in before or after.

7. In first species you should try to cover the whole modal octave approximately every 10–20 CF notes (except for octave skips). This will ensure that your line keeps moving and doesn't get bogged down in a narrow range or leap about wildly.

You can see now that some of the legal solutions in Examples 3-1c and d break some of these soft rules (especially the ones about simultaneous skips and avoiding unisons).

Note: Sometimes it is impossible to "fix" a tritone or diminished fifth by using B♭; in these cases it's best just to compose something new.

Illustration of Soft Rules

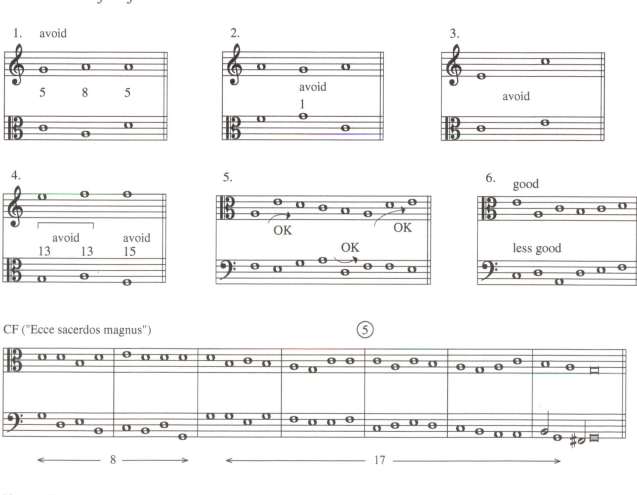

CF ("Ecce sacerdos magnus")

Note: d5

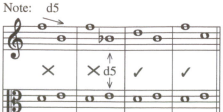

Exercise Series B   Find the Errors

Mark hard errors with X and soft errors with (X). You may find it helpful to write in the vertical intervals between the parts as has been done in the line below the CF in B2.

Exercise 3-B1

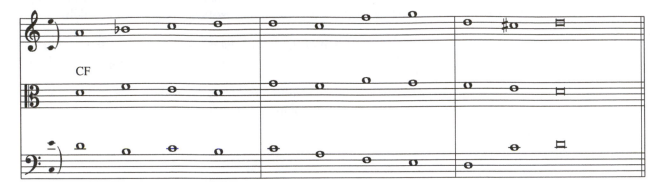

Exercise 3-B2

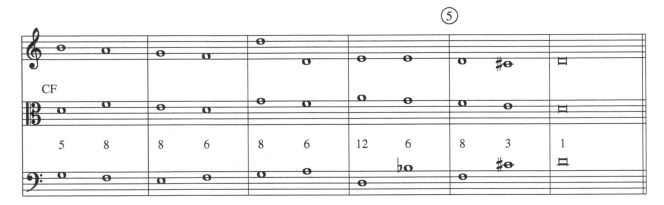

Exercise 3-B3 Counterpoint on a CF used by Diruta

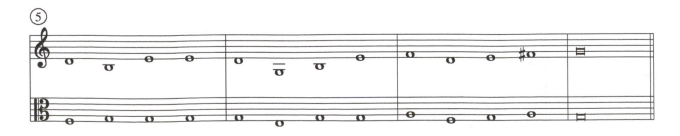

Study of Examples from Treatises

Example 3-2 (Diruta)

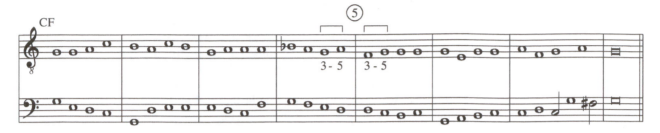

Look for repeating patterns in Girolamo Diruta's CF (Ex. 3-2) and see how they are handled. Note the two-note <u>sequence</u> in mm. 4-5; in a "harmonic" sequence, a whole combination, both vertical and melodic intervals, is transposed and repeated. Diruta covers the modal octave four times in the course of twenty-eight CF notes.

Remember that all of these treatise examples were intended as models for young improvisers who were not composers yet. Therefore we will often find unstylistic and awkward moments. For instance, Diruta's skip down to the G in the lower voice in m. 2 is not filled in until m. 6. The purpose of studying species is to master dissonance treatment, not to write great music.

Example 3-3 (Banchieri)

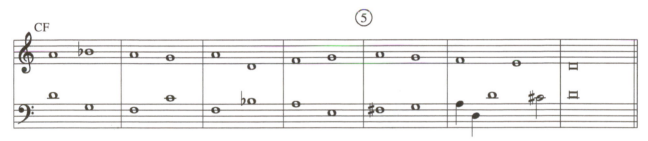

Adriano Banchieri's CF (Ex. 3-3) is one of the melodies in Example 1-3. Which one? Which soft rules does he break? What is the range of the added voice? Disregard for now the *F#* at the ninth whole note (you are not allowed to use accidentals other than B♭).

Example 3-4a (Morley)

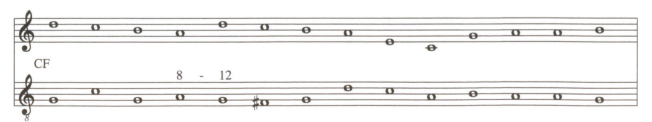

Thomas Morley's 1597 treatise is a dialogue between two pupils and a teacher.

MASTER: "Let me see what you can doe on the same playnesong agayne."

PUPIL: "Heere is a way; how like you it?" (Ex. 3-4a)

MASTER: "Peruse it, & see how you like it yourselfe."

PUPIL: "I like it so well, as I thinke you shal not find manie faultes in it."

MASTER: "You live in a good opinion of yourselfe, but let us examine your example. This is indeed better then your first, but marke wherein I condemne it. In the first and second notes you rise as though it were a close [an ending], causing a great informalitie of closing when you shoulde but begin. [He means the motion to the octave makes it seem like the piece is over.] Your third note is good; your fourth note is tollerable, but in that you goe from it to the twelfth maketh it unpleasing, and that we commonly call hitting the octave on the face, when we come to an eight [octave] and skip up from it agayne to another perfect concord, but if it had beene meeting one another [exchanging], the playnesong ascending and the descant [soprano] descending, it had bin very good, thus":

Example 3-4b (Morley)

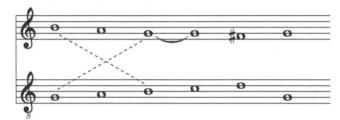

Then the teacher criticizes the diminished fifth on the sixth note ("I doe utterly condemne it as being expresly against the principles of our art"), and the repeated note in both voices at the end ("in your penult and antepenult notes you stande still with your descant, the plainsong standing still, which is a fault not to be suffered in so fewe as two parts, especiallie in eightes"). The teacher then proposes the following improvement:

Example 3-4c (Morley)

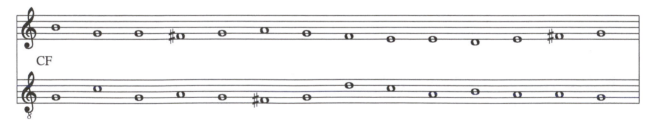

Example 3-5 shows four counterpoints by Zarlino to a CF, two above and two below. The CF, placed in the middle, is to be played and/or sung with any *one* of the other four voices (this is a compressed presentation of four little two-voice pieces). Zarlino breaks one of our hard rules. Which? What soft rules does he break? What can you say about the modes of the added voices? In a couple of these examples, Zarlino has written a bit of the CF tune in the added voice—where? with what alterations?

Example 3-5 (Zarlino)

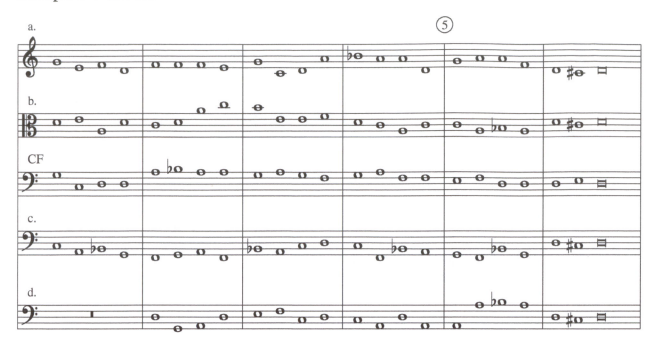

Exercise Series *C:*   CF Fragments

We will use Zarlino's example as a model for our exercises, in which we will add different counterpoints to the same CF. In the following exercises, you are given a four-note CF fragment, the range of the added voice, and one note that must be included in the counterpoint. As in the warmups, each fragment is neither the beginning nor the end, so you may use an imperfect consonance against the first and last notes. In this exercise, however, voice crossing is allowed for two notes maximum. You are to find three **different** solutions above, and three below. "Different" means that **no two consecutive notes are the same from one solution to another.** It is possible for a counterpoint below to be the same as one above. The purpose of this rule is to encourage you to find different alternatives, and to appreciate their unique qualities (sometimes beginners write the same thing twice without even noticing!). Put a checkmark on the one you like best of the three. Because these exercises are so short, you may be forced, in one of your solutions, to use more than 50 percent skips. Therefore **first species hard rule 5 is downgraded to a soft rule** for these Series C exercises only. As preparation, look back at the Zarlino (Ex. 3-5); check to see how many duplications Zarlino has between his two counterpoints above, and between his two below. You will find it easier to spot duplications in your own exercises if you line up the solutions vertically as Zarlino did.

Example 3-6 is a sample working-out.

Example 3-6

Given this CF fragment: and this range above: and this given note:

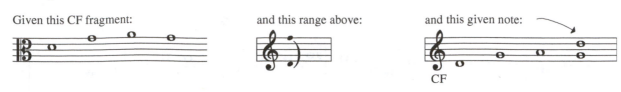

CF

you could write these different solutions (the given note is circled):

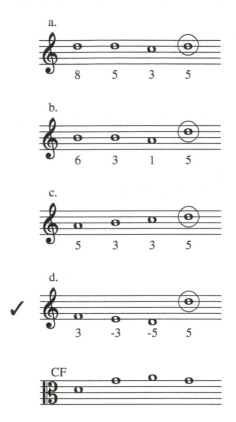

Vertical intervals between each solution and the CF have been labeled; "−3" means the upper voice sounds a third *below* the CF. Solutions a and c contain a duplication, so you must pick the better one to hand in. We have checked d as the one we like best because of its contrary motion and the octave skip against the step in the CF. Note that solution d, played on the piano, sounds like parallel fifths. It doesn't when sung.

CF Fragment Exercises

Exercise 3-C1   **Exercise 3-C2**   **Exercise 3-C3**

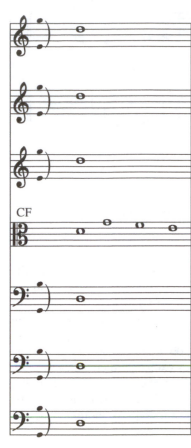  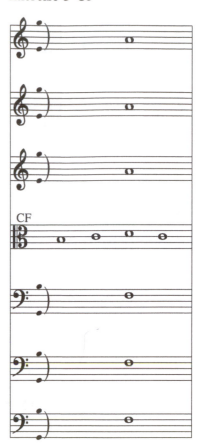

Exercise Series **D**	Complete CFs

Finally you are given a complete CF, the range of the added voice, and the final cadence. You are to find two **different** solutions above and two below. As in the foregoing fragment exercises, "different" means no two consecutive notes of the counterpoints above can be the same, nor of those below; however, a counterpoint below could use some (or all) of the same melodic material as one above. The added melody must begin on a perfect consonance with the CF, it **must include the notes at the extremes of the octave of the mode**, it may include the extra step beyond the extreme at either end, and it need not touch on every note in between the extremes. When the CF is shorter than about fifteen notes, it is difficult to cover the range without a lot of skips. **You may cross voices for a fifth of the notes maximum per solution.**

One way to approach these longer exercises is to plan first for the specific obligations you must meet in the exercise: the first perfect consonance and the high and low points. A sample working-out is proposed in Example 3-7, where we are to write above "Christ lag in Todesbanden" in the Hypodorian range. A good way to ensure different solutions is to pick different high and low points (as shown with arrows) for each one before beginning; then you will be heading in a different direction in each solution.

Example 3-7a and b Two possible solutions

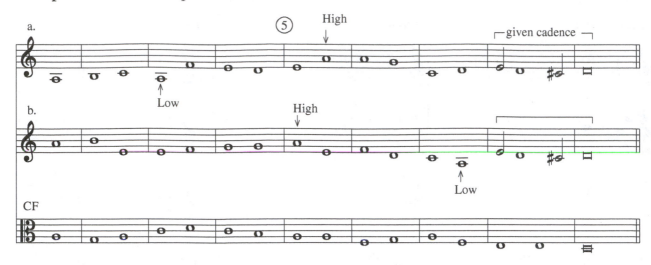

In the next examples, we write an authentic (Dorian) line against the same CF. The first solution (Ex. 3-7c) has no hard errors, but it is a *truly terrible line*. It shows what is meant by "no sense of direction." The beginning isn't a melody, it's (as one of my teachers used to say) a slow trill! Then, in order to meet the assignment of filling out the octave, the author has made five leaps in a row, none filled in. An improvement is Example 3-7d, although the end is a bit precipitous, owing to the brevity of the CF. The dotted arrows show <u>exchanges</u>, in which the voices exchange their notes or pitch classes. In this example the notes are a third apart, and the exchanges are made either by skip or by crossing on an octave, as Morley suggested above. It is useful to be conscious of such two- or three-note fragments that permit contrary motion.

Example 3-7c and d

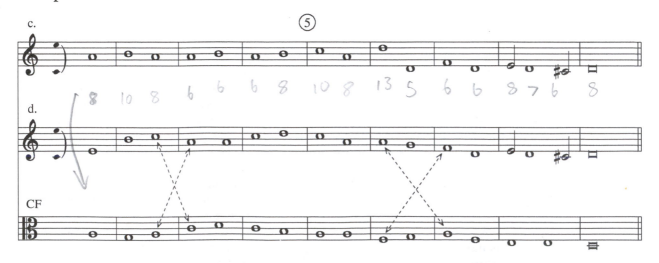

Exercise Series **D**   Complete CF Exercises

Exercise 3-D1   Write two different first-species G-Hypodorian lines above "La Spagna" and two below,
   linking up with the given cadence. The given ranges are D–D with a step added at either end. If you are
   taking the invertible counterpoint option, indicate which lines are the same.

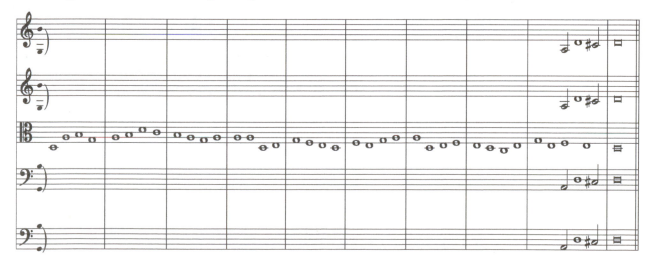

Exercise 3-D2   Write two different first-species Hypodorian lines above "Ave Maris Stella" and two below,
   linking up with the given cadence. The given ranges are A-A with a step added at either end. If you are
   taking the invertible counterpoint option, indicate which lines are the same.

The Invertible Counterpoint Option

If you are taking the invertible counterpoint option in these long exercises, one of
your counterpoints above will be the same as one below. Since you are writing in ic8
(invertible counterpoint at the octave), as described in chapter 13, your counterpoint
should have no fifths in positions that require consonance. If you have an octave in
the original, it will invert to a unison, breaking a soft rule. However, when you are
doing invertible counterpoint, this rule is waived. Renaissance writers often permitted

some small infractions when a more difficult contrapuntal challenge was being met. Your other lines (one above, one below) should be different from the invertible line and from each other. The exercises you hand in will have three different solutions (please label the invertible one).

Invertible Counterpoint Option

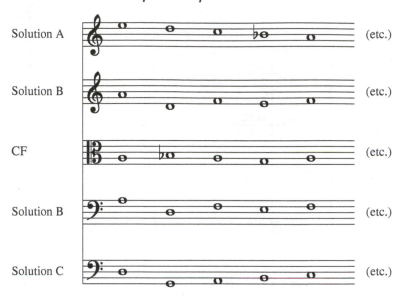

Introduction to Improvisation

In the Renaissance, contrapuntal improvisation was the basic preparation for composition. Adrian Petit Coclico wrote a treatise in 1552 in which he described how much value the great composer Josquin Desprez placed on improvised counterpoint for future composers:

> There are many who pride themselves on being composers because they have composed many pieces, having followed the rules and types of composition but making no use of counterpoint; my master Josquin thought little of them and held them as a laughing-stock, saying they wish to fly without wings. The first requirement of a good singer is that he should know how to sing counterpoint by improvisation. Without this he will be nothing. Secondly, he should be led to composing by a great desire, and by a certain natural impulse he will be driven to composition, so that he will not taste food nor drink until his piece is finished, for, since this natural impulse so drives him, he accomplishes more in one hour than others in a whole month. Composers to whom these unusual motivations are absent are useless.[1]

Musical training began with improvised singing in church. Coclico describes in a bit more detail how counterpoint was taught. Once the pupil knows all the vertical consonances (from a third to a triple compound sixth, or a twenty-seventh), he then

[1]*Compendium Musices*, translated as *Musical Compendium* by Albert Seay (Colorado Springs; CO: Colorado College Music Press, 1973), p. 24.

provides himself with a slate on which one may write and erase; he takes a tenor from plainchant and at first writes note against note, using these intervals. Whenever he has gotten used to making note against note by improvisation and has become practiced in it, then he can go on to florid counterpoint. In this, when he has become trained, he will put aside the slate and learn to sing in improvising on a plainchant or on figured music printed in a book or copied on a sheet of paper. But this is a task for continual exercise.[2]

Most treatises that teach counterpoint are really teaching improvisation. The examples in this book that are taken from treatises illustrate what a ten-year-old boy might do on the spot. They aren't supposed to be particularly elegant or artistic, but simply correct and roughly within the style. **If you improvise, concentrate at first on not breaking hard rules.** Once you get fast and proficient, you can worry about being stylish.

If you want to try this (or your teacher insists), you should be aware that improvising is just very fast composition. If your teacher says, "Who wants to try improvising against these two notes?," it's OK to raise your hand. In the few seconds before you are called on, you can be thinking about what notes you will sing in your solution. If you need more time to think, stand up, adjust your collar, cough, etc. Remember, there are a lot of correct solutions (there were 37 in Ex. 3-1c–d). You're almost bound to get one of them. If you make a mistake, it's no big deal; remember: it's "a task for continual exercise."

Visual, Auditory, Tactile, or What?

How will you do this? I remember a student who came to audition for my chorus. When I asked him to sight-sing, he held the music in his left hand, and as he sang he moved his right forearm up and down. He was a trombone player, and he was pretending he was moving the slide in and out. He sang correctly and very in tune! He was using what is called a "physical referent"; i.e., he associated the sounds of the notes with his arm position. We often see pianists or trumpet players moving the fingers of their right hands as they take dictation, for the same reason. The problem for singers is that they don't have such a reference: There is no "place" in the throat where a *D* is.

When you improvise, you are doing something like sight-singing, and you need to use whatever works. If it helps you to imagine a keyboard, so much the better. I believe, based on Coclico's description cited earlier, that the referent for singers has to be musical notation. After you have seen some series A exercises, you may be able to visualize both the CF and the counterpoint. Some authors recommended a staff with more than five lines for this purpose so that the student could really "see" both the CF and the added line in the same space.

For instance, Ornithoparchus, an early sixteenth-century author, says: "It is necessary for yong beginners to make a Scale of ten lines, then to distinguish it by bounds [add bar lines], so that they may write each time within each bound, by keyes [clefs] truly marked, least [lest] the confused mingling together of the Notes hinder them." His example shows a ten-line staff with five clefs: low *G* (*Gamma ut*), *F* (bass), *C* (alto), *G* (treble), and high *D* (written *dd*). This pretty much covers the entire space in which Renaissance music lies! The CF is written in breves and the improvisation in black notes below. Play one voice and sing the other (note that there are two flats in the signature).

[2] Ibid., p. 23.

Example 3-8 (Ornithoparchus/Dowland)

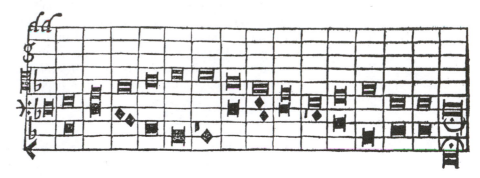

This corresponds to the slate of Coclico. Only after using a visual aid for a while could the student "put away the slate" and look at any line from any source, without all the extra lines, and imagine an added part. Eventually you will just "hear" in your head what's about to happen, and your "inner ear" will develop.

Improvisation and Ear Training

Improvisation is an excellent adjunct to ear-training courses. You will learn the physical sensation of being inside a fifth and how different it "feels" from a fourth or a third. Playing one line and singing the other is the best ear training there is, because you are in control of both voices, even though they may be moving independently. Your fingers do one thing, your voice another; if you can control two voices, you will be that much better at two-part dictation.

Solfège and Improvisation

The question of solfège syllables is a difficult one. Fixed *doh* works fine in modal music, but movable *doh* is a problem, since in each mode the semitone positions are different, and no single *doh* can be defined by semitones. It will work to sing English note names (*F*, *G*, etc.) or even just nothing ("la la la") because you are already so busy figuring out where the next note will be.

Step by Step

1. The first thing is to decide if you will do this alone or with another singer (or player). If you have a colleague and you are doing first species, you can indicate with a wave of the hand when he/she should change notes, giving you time to figure out your next move. In other species, however, the rhythm has to be steady and unyielding (and slow!). If you are doing it alone, you can play the CF on a keyboard or guitar (or cello or marimba—any instrument that you play with your hands).

2. Choose an exercise from Series A, C, or D.

3. Range: You must be able to improvise both above and below a CF. If you are a baritone and you are improvising above, you will have to move the CF down to where it will be below you when you are in a comfortable range. Do not play the CF where it is written in "Series A Warmups" and sing below it, thinking you

are above. Thus if the CF has middle *C* and you mean to sing *G* a fifth above and instead sing *G* a fourth below, you are making a serious mistake.

4. The first move: When you get right down to it, a kind of geometry is at work here. Let's say the CF starts on *C* and moves to *D*, and you start a fifth above the first note (singing *G*). Then you must ask yourself, where can I go? How far and in what direction? You might remember from your Series A Warmups that *F* would be safe above the *D* (*thirds are always safe to approach*); then you have to know how to get from *G* to *F*. This mental process can be summed up: "How far down do I have to go to get to a note a third above the *D*?" The answer: a whole step down.

5. An alternative to the mental process described in step 4 is quickly to choose any note, evaluate its legality, and accept or reject it. You might do this if you need to go in a specific direction (you are at the bottom of your range, you don't want to cross voices, etc.). Then you might start with a nearby note in that direction. In our example, if you didn't want to go down for some reason, you would say to yourself: "Can I stay on *G*? No. Can I move up to *A*? No. Can I move up to *B*? Yes."

6. Moving forward (stepping stones): The initial *C–G* fifth was like one rock in a river. You got to a second rock, the *D* and the *F* you're on now. Now from the *D–F* rock you have to move to the next one. Suppose the *D* moves down to *B♭*; if you go up, there are a lot of places you can go, because *contrary motion is always safe*. Each second rock becomes the first of a new pair, and a new "first move" is required. Don't bother looking ahead more than one rock until you have had some experience!

Improvising Homework

Series A and C Exercises can be improvised in class, but you should at first improvise Series D Exercises at home at your own pace. Remember to play the CF in an octave that makes your singing fall into a comfortable range. In first species, there is a requirement that the added line cover the modal octave, so you should mentally mark in advance your high and low points (a good plan is to put your high point near the lowest point of the CF, and vice versa, to facilitate contrary motion). Now you need to look a little more than one note ahead. Take your time—savor each vertical interval, harmonize with the piano! After you have done a few notes you like, see if you can remember them and write them down. Memory training is an important side effect of this whole process.

4

Second Species

Two half notes sound against each whole note. The downbeat is the first half of each whole-note value, the upbeat the second. The following hard rules from first species continue to apply:

1. **All downbeats must be consonant.**

2. **All perfect intervals must be approached by contrary or oblique motion.**

3. **Skips must account for less than half the melodic motions.**

4. **Direct repetition of the whole contrapuntal combination (two or more simultaneities) is forbidden, and only two sequential repetitions are allowed.**

Hard Rules

1. **The upbeat half note may be dissonant if it is passing.** A <u>passing</u> <u>tone</u> (p.t.) is one that is approached and left by step in the same direction. This means that there are no dissonant <u>neighbor</u> <u>tones</u> (u.n. = <u>upper</u> <u>neighbor</u>, l.n. = <u>lower</u> <u>neighbor</u>).

If you have a consonance on the weak beat, you connect it to the next strong-beat consonance using the same principles as in first species. It is possible to have perfect intervals of the same type (e.g., two fifths) on two successive downbeats if contrary motion to the second is caused by the weak beat. We say the weak beat "breaks up" the parallel fifths.

2. **Skips to or from dissonances are prohibited.** These are indicated with "std" (skip to dissonance) and "sfd" (skip from dissonance). When you skip from the strong to the weak beat, you must skip to a consonance. (This rule is a necessary consequence of rule 1.)

3. **Repeated notes are not allowed in the added voice.** But octave skips are allowed.

4. **You may begin with a half-note rest, but the first sounding note must form a perfect consonance with the CF.**

Illustration of Hard Rules

Exercise Series **A:**	Warmups

There are more possibilities in second species than in first because even though the number of consonant possibilities for the downbeats is the same, the upbeats can skip or step to consonances or pass through dissonances. Because of the preference for stepwise motion in Renaissance style, we will focus in this exercise exclusively on possibilities that move **stepwise in one direction.** One method is to start with all consonances against the two notes of the fragment, and see which two consonances are a third apart. The second-species line will always span a third from one downbeat to the next, so you will learn how these spans can fit against various CF motions, and you will have these formulas at your fingertips for later exercises. Example 4-1a shows all possible starting notes above and below the *A* and the *C* of the CF, and Example 4-1b shows all solutions that connect notes a third apart. Those that break voice-leading rules are marked with X. Be sure you understand what is wrong with each.

Example 4-1a

Example 4-1b

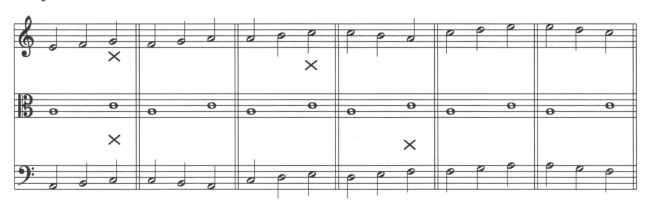

Warmup Exercises

a. range above   b. range below:

Exercise 4-A1   **Exercise 4-A2**   **Exercise 4-A3**   **Exercise 4-A4**

Exercise 4-A5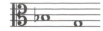

Exercise 4-A6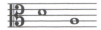

Exercise 4-A7

Exercise 4-A8

If you are doing the invertible counterpoint option, follow the instructions on page 39.

Soft Rules

1. First-species soft rules about simultaneous skips, widely separated voices, change of direction after a leap, and prevalence of stepwise motion still apply. (See soft rules in Chapter 3.)

2. Unisons are acceptable on the weak beats, but should still be avoided on downbeats.

3. First-species rule 4, about counterpoint running parallel to the CF, was designed to prevent the counterpoint from following the CF too closely. Now, because other intervening consonances can give a different emphasis or contour, we use the following soft rule: The same vertical interval should not be used in more than four successive whole-note units. (Note that it makes no difference on what beat the repeated interval falls.)

4. The first-species soft rule about avoiding more than two perfect vertical intervals in a row still applies, but now in half notes.

5. Try to cover the modal octave every 4-8 whole notes. (See first-species soft rule 7.)

Illustration of Soft Rules

Soft Rule 2.

Soft Rule 3.

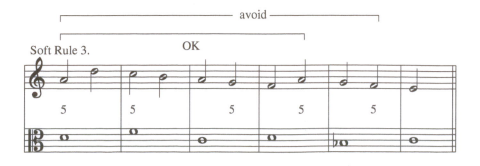

Soft Rule 4.   avoid

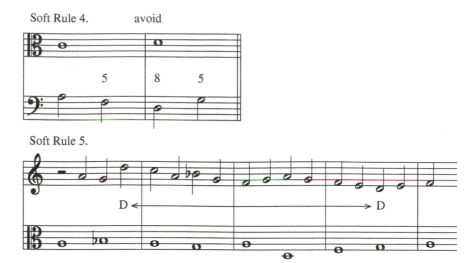

Soft Rule 5.

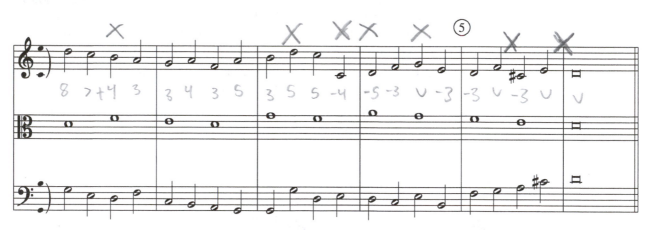

Exercise Series **B:**   Find the Errors

Mark hard mistakes with X and soft ones with (x).

Exercise 4-B1

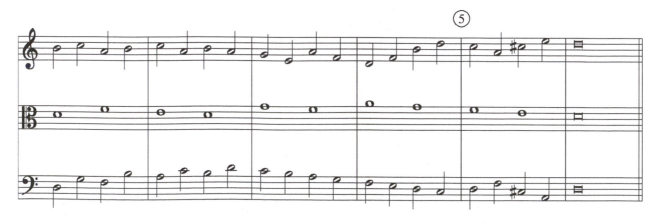

Exercise 4-B2

Study of Examples from Treatises

Example 4-2 (Diruta)

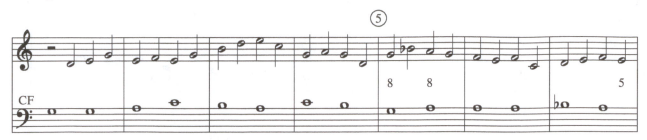

Fifths or octaves on consecutive downbeats have been labeled in this example by Diruta. They are legal on the principle that any intervening consonance a half note long "breaks up" perfect intervals on consecutive whole notes. Diruta covers the Hypomixolydian octave (*D-D*) four times in twenty-eight CF notes, and nearly half the melodic motions are skips.

Example 4-3a (Banchieri)

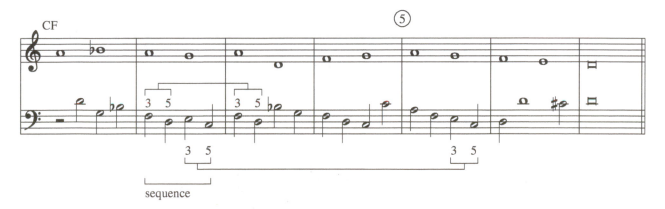

Banchieri covers an octave or seventh six times in twelve CF notes. His added line is all consonant and too full of skips for our purposes. Note that the third and fifth whole notes have the same counterpoint, and the fourth and tenth whole notes have the same counterpoint, as shown with brackets; this is OK because there is intervening material. Also note that the third and fourth whole notes have the same combination but transposed; this is OK because it is within the limit of two sequential repetitions.

Example 4-3b (Banchieri)

Second species can be considered as an embellishment of first species with notes in smaller values (diminutions) added. Compare Banchieri's solution to his first-species example on the same CF (from Ex. 3-3, printed on adjacent slaves in Example 4-3b). In five of the first six whole notes it is as if he had inserted skips to consonant notes between his original first-species notes (checked) to make the second-species line. The effect is more like arpeggiated chords than an independent line.

Example 4-4 (Thomas de Sancta Maria)

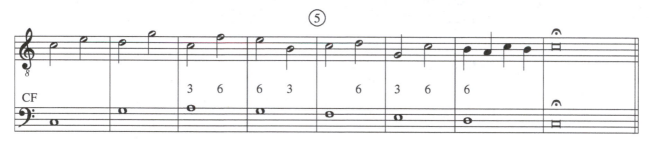

Thomas de Sancta Maria is illustrating organ improvisation, not vocal composition, so he has broken some rules of vocal style. Like Banchieri, he uses only consonances right up to the cadence, making a line with too many skips, suggesting broken chords. Also, he has broken our soft rule about following the CF too closely: he has used one too many sixths in consecutive measures. Alternating sixths and thirds is a tempting formula, but it must not be overused.

Example 4-5 (Tigrini)

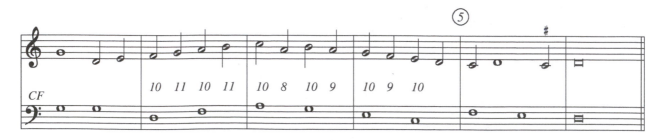

Orazio Tigrini, illustrating his discussion of passing weak-beat dissonance against skips of a third in the CF, has also paralleled the CF too closely (in tenths) for our purposes.

Exercise Series C: CF Fragments

In these exercises, you are given a three-note CF fragment (not the beginning or end of a piece), the range of the added voice, and one note that must be included in the counterpoint. You are to find three **different** solutions above, and three below. "Different means that **no three consecutive half notes can be the same in any two added lines.** It is possible for a counterpoint below to be the same as one above. You are to add four half notes, always ending on the downbeat of the last whole. Voice crossing is allowed for two notes maximum. Because these exercises are so short, you may be forced, in one of your solutions, to use more than 50 percent skips. Therefore **first species hard rule 5 is downgraded to a soft rule** for these series C exercises only. Check off the one you like best. Here is a sample working-out:

Example 4-6

Given this CF fragment: and this range below: and this given note:

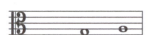   

You could sketch the following (the given note is circled):

Solution d duplicates three notes of a, so we must choose one of them. Solution d is too skippy, so we would hand in a, b, and c, our favorite being c because it has the fewest skips.

CF Fragment Exercises

Exercise 4-C1   **Exercise 4-C2**   **Exercise 4-C3**

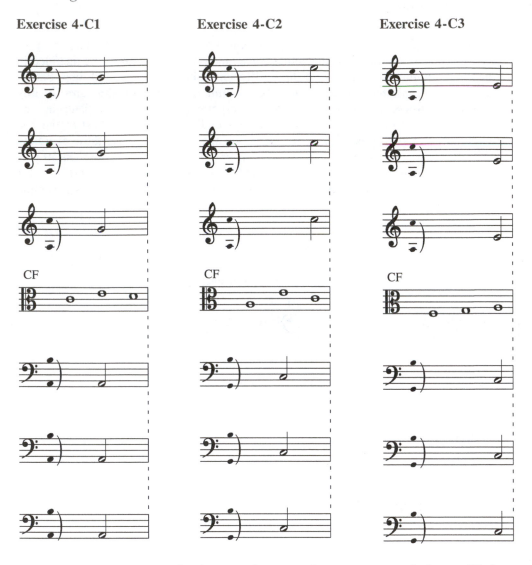

In the next four exercises you are to find one CF fragment that can be placed legally above or below the given second-species lines. One of these only has one solution—which?

Exercise 4-C4   **Exercise 4-C5**

Exercise 4-C6   **Exercise 4-C7**

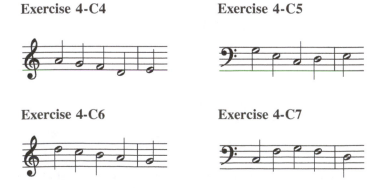

Exercise Series **D:**　　Complete CFs

Finally, in these exercises, you are given a complete CF and the final cadence of the counterpoint. You are to fill in the rest, finding two different solutions above and two below ("different" as defined in Series C Exercises). In these exercises you must **include at least one skip characteristic of the mode**; identify this skip with a bracket. (See chapter 1 to review characteristic modal skips.) The purpose of this small added challenge is to get you thinking about how these skips affect the *sound* of the added line, confirming the mode. Obviously, there will be many other skips in the added line, but even one appropriate skip helps keep the line from sounding random and disorganized. As in first species, voice crossing is allowed 20 percent of the time, and **you must sound the notes at the extremes of the modal octave.**

As a sample, here is the beginning of "Da Jesus an dem Kreuze stund" in the third mode; we are to write a line below in the fourth. One way to approach this exercise is to sketch in all the places it's legal to put a skip of the mode. In Example 4-7a we have sketched in all possible places to put a skip between an *E* and a *B*. There are so many, how can we choose? The best way is just to pick one and run with it. Examples 4-7b and c are two of many solutions.

Example 4-7a

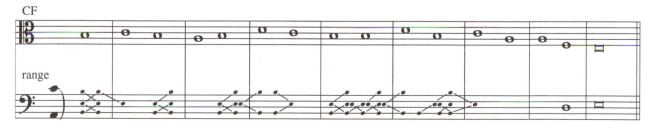

Example 4-7b and c

Second Species as a Diminution of First

Another systematic approach to second species is to regard it as a diminution of a first-species line, as we observed in Example 4-3 from Banchieri. For instance, in Example 4-8 we have taken a sample first-species solution (Ex. 3-7a) and added a half note in each measure. We filled in the skip of a third with a passing tone (asterisk), in this case making an exchange with the CF, and we embellished stepwise motion with consonant skips (†). In several cases we put the original first-species note on the weak half of the measure (arrows) and put the consonant skip first. Once we had to abandon the framework (at X). That was because it is difficult to embellish a repeated whole note using second species. Right after that is where we put the Dorian skip, since the first-species framework had none to begin with.

Example 4-8 (based on Ex. 3-7a)

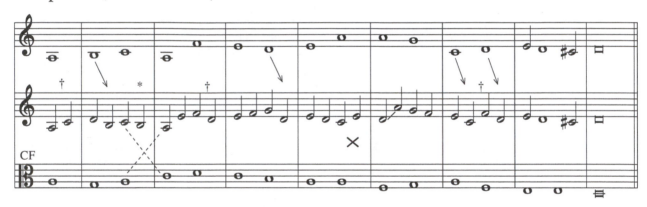

Try adding half notes to this first-species counterpoint:

Example 4-9

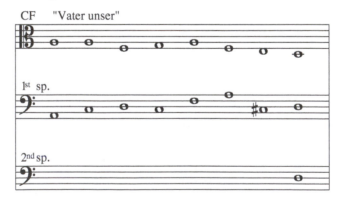

The Invertible Counterpoint Option

If you are taking the invertible counterpoint option when you do these long exercises, you should deliberately plan to make one of your counterpoints above the same as one below. Since you are writing at ic8, as described in chapter 13, that line should have no fifths in positions that require consonance. Your other lines (one above, one below) should be different from the invertible line and from each other. The exercise you hand in will have three different solutions:

Invertible Counterpoint Option

Improvising Second Species

You can follow all the suggested steps outlined in the "Introduction to Improvisation" section at the end of chapter 3, but second species is surprisingly more difficult. You will find yourself falling back on skips to consonances, as in the examples by Banchieri (4-3a) and Sancta Maria (4-4). To use dissonant passing tones, you must look ahead for a legal note on the next downbeat is a third away from the downbeat you are on. That target note must not make a perfect interval with the CF unless you are moving to it by contrary motion. You can be very pleased with yourself if you can get five notes stepwise in the same direction!

Exercise Series **D:**   **Complete CF Exercises**

Exercise 4–D1 Write different second-species Hypodorian lines above the "Christe" phrase from Kyrie XI and two below, linking up with the given cadence. Remember to include and label one skip characteristic of the mode in each added voice. If you are taking the invertible counterpoint option, indicate which lines are the same.

Exercise 4-D2 Write different second-species *G*-Hypodorian lines above the beginning of "L'homme armé" and two below, linking up with the given cadence. Remember to include and label one skip characteristic of the mode in each added voice. If you are taking the invertible counterpoint option, indicate which lines are the same.

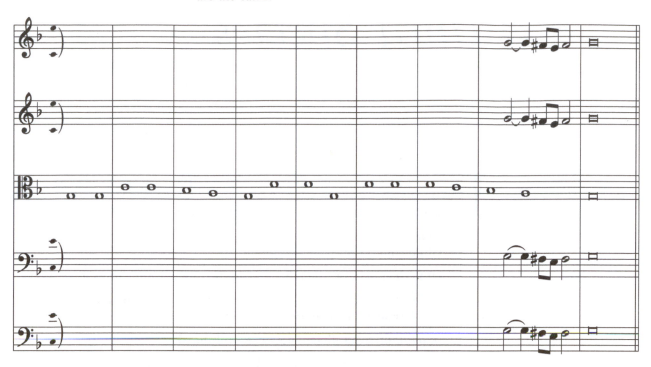

5

Third Species

Four quarter notes sound against each whole. Quarter notes should feel to you, at the tempo suggested earlier (whole note = 60–72), the way sixteenths do in a Bach allegro: lively! The following rules from first species still apply.

Old Hard Rules

1. All downbeats must be consonant.

2. All perfect intervals must be approached by contrary or oblique motion.

3. Direct repetition of the whole contrapuntal combination is forbidden, and only two sequential repetitions are allowed.

4. Skips to or from dissonances are prohibited.

5. Repeated notes are not allowed in the added voice.

6. You may begin with a half-note rest, but the first sounding note must make a perfect consonance with the CF.

Hard Rules

1. The first and third quarters must be consonant. These are the "strong" quarters, one on the downbeat, the other halfway through the measure. (A dissonant third quarter in the examples is indicated with "d3q.") Note that ascending four notes from a third to a sixth above the CF is not the same as descending four notes from a sixth to a third, because of d3q.

2. The second and fourth quarters may be dissonant if they are passing or lower neighbors. A lower neighbor is a tone that is approached by step from above and is followed by the note that preceded it. Dissonant lower neighbors were not allowed in second species, but are now allowed in the faster motion of quarter notes. No dissonant upper neighbors are allowed.

3. Skips must account for less than a quarter of the melodic motions.

4. Do not use the same neighbor twice in a row, and do not change direction more than three times in six quarters. Changes of direction are marked with ∧ and ∨. The effect of changing direction is intensified by the use of more and/or larger skips, which must be taken into account as well.

Illustration of Hard Rules

"Because not everyone knows how to use the . . . rules, nor all who wish to learn counterpoint are naturally gifted for it . . . they may learn the following simple rules, since every beginner has to learn his alphabet." Thus the Spanish theorist Pietro Cerone introduces examples and descriptions of the most common formulas for putting quarter notes against whole notes. He intends the beginner to memorize these formulas for improvising. Of the first examples shown here he says, "If the plainchant rises a step, the counterpoint will go down stepwise from a tenth, or from an octave."

For the second pair of examples shown here he says, "If the plainchant goes down a fourth, the counterpoint will ascend scalewise from a unison or a third." The rest of his examples show every possible CF motion, and for the most part the quarters move stepwise in a single direction, contrary to the CF motion. He uses some half notes in his examples, but we will stick to quarters for now.

Exercise Series A: Warmups

In these warmups, **you are to find all possible solutions using stepwise motion.** These exercises differ from those in second species because the motion does not have to be all in one direction: dissonant lower neighbors and consonant upper neighbors are allowed. You will write five quarters, stopping after the new downbeat. In Renaissance music there is only a very small number of commonly used quarter-note figures. Cerone's examples span a fifth from downbeat to downbeat. Third-species formulas that span other intervals *using only stepwise motion* are:

Example 5-1

a. unison, 2 p.t.s (fairly common)

b. unison, 2. l.n.s (out of the question; see rule 4)

c. ascending third, l.n. + p.t. (very common)

d. descending third, p.t. + l.n. (very common)

e. descending third, u.n. + p.t. (rare; see soft rule 1)

f. ascending third, p.t. + u.n. (rare; see soft rule 1)

There are two other possibilities for spanning a unison, but these consist entirely of neighbors and have a weak high point. The only possibility for a consonant upper neighbor above a CF is 5–6–5, and the only possibility below is 6–5–6 (because the fifth and the sixth are the only consonances that are a scale step apart).

It is *not possible* to span a second or fourth in four stepwise quarters. The examples in 5-2a and b begin, as previously, with all legal consonances above the two CF notes. Example 5-2a shows all five possible starting notes above the *A* and the *C* of the CF, and Example 5-2b shows all solutions connecting the downbeat notes a unison, a third, or a fifth apart. Those that break voice-leading rules are marked with X. Be sure you understand what is wrong with them. **Limit yourself to**

the most commonly used formulas: five steps in the same direction, or formulas
a, c, and **d** from Example 5-1.

Example 5-2a

Example 5-2

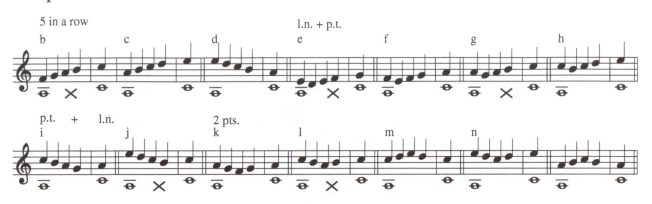

Warmup Exercises

Exercise 5-A1   **Exercise 5-A2**   **Exercise 5-A3**   **Exercise 5-A4**

Exercise 5-A5   **Exercise 5-A6**   **Exercise 5-A7**   **Exercise 5-A8**

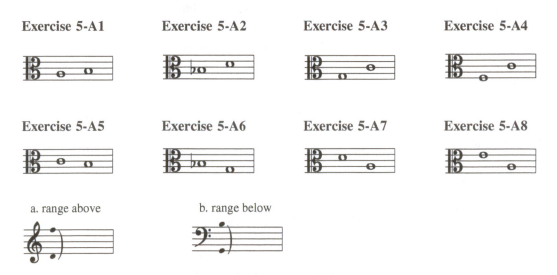

a. range above   b. range below

If you are taking the invertible counterpoint option, follow the instructions on p. 30.

Other Third-Species Formulas

In order to span a second or fourth in five quarters, it is necessary to skip. Below
are the most common formulas for covering a second or fourth from downbeat to
downbeat. They use skips no larger than a fourth. "(X)" indicates a skip up to a
weak quarter, an infraction of soft rule 1 following.

Example 5-3

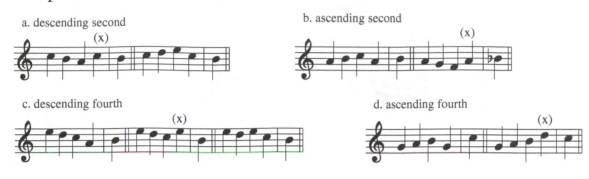

a. descending second

b. ascending second

c. descending fourth

d. ascending fourth

Soft Rules

1. Avoid skipping up to a weak quarter. Also, avoid having a temporary high point on a weak quarter, even in stepwise motion. This is very rare in Renaissance style because it creates a sense of syncopation that results from the conflict of a <u>tonic</u> <u>accent</u> (i.e., a relatively high note) with a relatively weak metric position. This effect is intensified if the motion up to the weak quarter is by skip. However, we often find weak-quarter high points in instrumental music (see Exx. 13-8a & 13-9 and the Morley fantasias).

2. Unisons are acceptable on the second, third, or fourth quarter but should still be avoided on downbeats.

3. Skips, at this faster speed, should be kept small, only rarely exceeding a third.

4. As in second species, the same vertical interval should not be used in more than four successive whole-note units (to avoid following the CF). Note that it makes no difference which beat the repeating interval occurs on.

5. Avoid breaking up parallel perfect intervals with only one quarter.

Illustration of Soft Rules

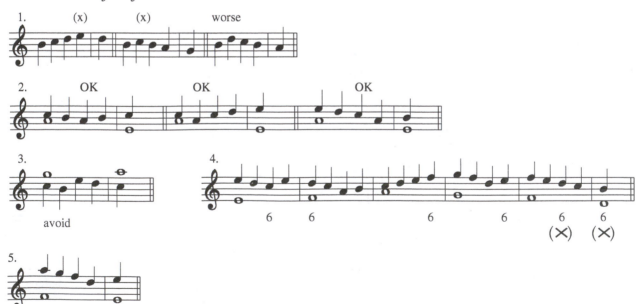

Idioms

<u>Idioms</u> are specific patterns in which a rule may be broken. In the following melodic figures, a skip from a dissonance is allowed.

Cambiata

The dissonance in the <u>cambiata</u> must be approached by descending step and must be on the second quarter; the skip from the dissonance must be a descending third to a consonance, and it must be followed by at least two ascending steps, making a five-note figure minimum. The cambiata spans a descending second from one downbeat to the next.

The only possible dissonant cambiatas above make vertical intervals 8–7–5–6, as in Example 5–4, or 6–d5–3–4; below, only 3–4–6–5. You must label dissonant cambiatas. The consonant cambiata (6–5–3–4 above or 5–6–8–7 below) is not an idiom because all its intervals are consonant, so it need not be labeled. (The cambiata beginning on the third quarter and the inverted cambiata, a later invention, are not allowed here.) This example ends with an unusual evaded cadence, discussed in chapter 10.

Example 5-4 (Tigrini)

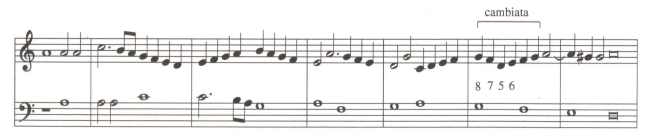

Echappée

The <u>echappée</u> is a figure in which a descending step is delayed by a step up to a dissonance on a weak beat. It is completed by a skip of a third down. This figure may occur in a variety of rhythmic values, as shown in Example 5-5 with asterisks. It is fairly infrequent in the music of this period, and we will not use it.

Example 5-5a (Zarlino)   **Example 5-5b**

Double Neighbor

The <u>double</u> <u>neighbor</u> involves skips from and to dissonances; it consists of four quarters, starting on the downbeat. It may be inverted (step up, then skip down). We will only use it, as in Example 5-7, at the cadence.

Example 5-6

Exercise Series **B:**   Find the Errors

Mark hard errors with X and soft errors with (x).

Exercise 5-B1

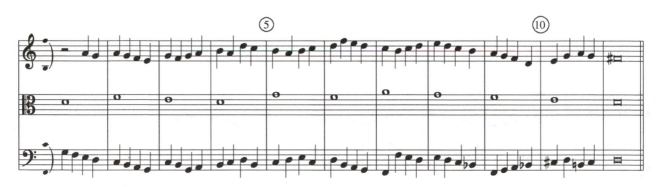

Exercise 5-B2

Study of Examples from Treatises

Example 5-7 (Sancta Maria)

double neighbor

In this example by Thomas de Sancta Maria, you will notice repeating patterns; does he exceed our limit for sequential repetitions? How many different melodic four-note patterns are there?

Example 5-8 (Cerone)

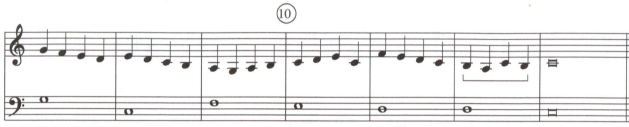

Cerone knew how hard it was to write counterpoint against a repeated note in the CF, and he gave several examples of long scalar spans against a repeated note followed by a step.

Example 5-9 (Diruta)

Eighths occurring in this example by Diruta should be ignored for now (you will use eighths later). Also ignore the repeated quarters in m. 6 (this is an idiom that will be described and used in chapter 11). Find repeating patterns in Diruta's example. While he mostly favors long spans in a single direction, which are typical of vocal writing, the example becomes more idiomatic for organ at the end, where we find too many skips and changes of direction.

Example 5-10 (Banchieri)

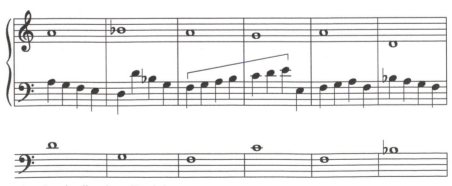

First-Species line from Ex. 3-3

Note that beneath CF notes *A–G* Banchieri has used the same solution both times, shown with brackets (remember, you can repeat within an exercise as long as there is intervening material). Compare this line to Banchieri's first-species solution to the same CF (from Ex. 3-3, printed here below the bass staff). Like his second-species line, this one may be considered a diminution of the first-species one.

Renaissance writers were aware that third species could be a diminution of first or second; here are some examples showing how a simple original is ornamented through the use of quarter notes. Zarlino reduces some third-species motion (Ex. 5-11a) to its second-species framework (Ex. 5-11b—the two halves of these examples are interesting; see "Mirror Inversion" in chapter 19). Diego Ortiz shows singers and players how to ornament simple step and third motions written in long values (Ex. 5-12—Ortiz doesn't use clefs because his examples can be transposed anywhere).

Example 5-11 (Zarlino)

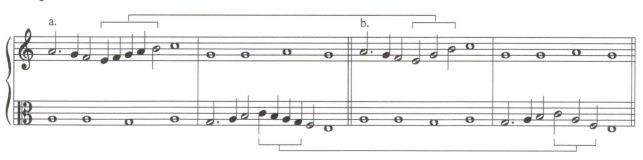

Example 5-12 (Ortiz)

Here are some examples by Thomas Morley of some other "species" in which three notes, five notes, or $1\frac{1}{3}$ notes sound against each CF note. They illustrate that any rhythmic pattern could be considered a species, and they are only presented here for their novelty. They are rhythmic games that might have been improvised, so "correct" metric notation is ignored in the CF.

Example 5-13a–c (Morley)

Exercise Series C: CF Fragments

In these exercises, you are given a three-note CF fragment (not the beginning or end of a piece), the range of the added voice, and one note that must be included in the counterpoint (now your range may extend as far as *two steps beyond* each end of the modal octave). You are to find three **different** solutions above, and three below. "Different" means that **no five consecutive quarter notes are the**

same from one solution to another. It is possible for a counterpoint below to be the same as one above. You are to add eight quarter notes, always ending on the downbeat of the last whole. **The only idiom you may use is the cambiata (if it is possible), and you must bracket and label it.** Voice crossing is allowed for three quarter notes maximum. Check off the solution you like best. Here is a sample working-out:

Example 5-14

Given this CF Fragment: 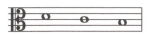 and this range below: and this given note:

You could sketch the following (the given note is circled):

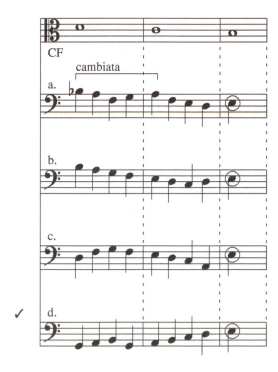

Solution b duplicates five notes of c, so we must choose one. We would hand in a, b, and d; our favorite is d, with its strong contrary motion.

CF Fragment exercises

Exercise 5-C1   **Exercise 5-C2**

Exercise 5-C3

In C4–C6 you are to find one CF fragment that can be placed legally above or below the given third-species lines. Remember, you may repeat whole notes in the CF. One of these has very few solutions—which?

Exercise 5-C4   **Exercise 5-C5**

Exercise 5-C6

Exercise Series D: Complete CFs

In these exercises you are given a CF and the final cadence of the counterpoint; you are to fill in the rest, finding two "different" solutions above and two below. In these exercises **you must include at least one *outline* of an interval characteristic of the mode, and it must be completely filled in.** An outline is the interval from one temporary high point to the next temporary low point or vice versa. As with the inclusion of characteristic skips in second species, this requirement is meant to make you aware of the way outlines contribute to the modal sound of a melody; naturally, you may have many other outlines as well, given the problems of writing against a CF.

As with skips in second species, you can sketch in the modal outlines first, then compose the rest. Example 5-15 is the end of the first phrase of "Ecce sacerdos magnus" in the seventh mode, with a few Mixolydian outlines (between *D*s and *G*s) sketched in. **Bracket your modal outlines.**

This will help your teacher to identify any misunderstandings you may have. As in previous species, voice crossing is allowed a quarter of the time, and **you must sound the notes at the extremes of the modal octave.** However, now your range may extend as far as *two steps beyond* the end of the modal octave. This will give you more ground to cover, making it easier to avoid a kind of roller coaster between the ends of the modal octave.

Example 5-15 Bracketing modal outlines

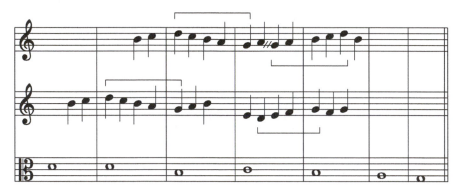

Another approach to third species is to regard it as a diminution of a first-species line, as illustrated by Banchieri. Take this first-species line and embellish it with quarters.

Example 5-16

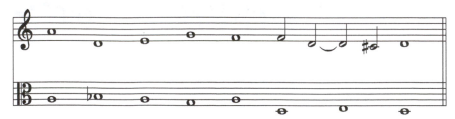

If you are taking the invertible counterpoint option, follow the instructions on p. 39.

Exercise Series *D:*   Complete CF Exercises

Exercise 5-D1   Write two different third-species Hypolydian lines above the "eleison" phrase from Kyrie VIII and two below, linking up with the given cadence. Remember to include and label one outline characteristic of the mode in each added voice. If you are taking the invertible counterpoint option, indicate which lines are the same.

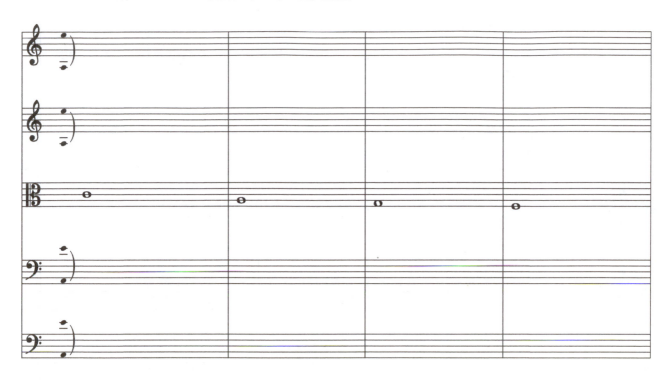

Exercise 5-D2   Write two different third-species Hypomixolydian lines above the word "continet" (from "Spiritus Domini replevit") and two below, linking up with the given cadence. Remember to include and label one outline characteristic of the mode in each added voice. If you are taking the invertible counterpoint option, indicate which lines are the same.

Improvising Third Species

Again, you may want to review "Introduction to Improvisation" at the end of chapter 3. Improvising third species for any length of time can be very taxing. Finding all possibilities can be slow-going too. As in second species, where skipping a third was reliable, you can always fall back on the outline of a third, but this time you can fill it in with a dissonant passing tone (like m. 2 and several others in Sancta Maria's Ex. 5-7). If you see a rising step in the CF and you are an octave or tenth above the first note, you know from Cerone's example (in the illustration of hard rules) that you can go straight down stepwise for eight notes. It is probable that young improvisers knew many such patterns by heart.

6

Fourth Species

In fourth species the added voice is in syncopated whole notes. Each whole note' is displaced by a half note, so it can be written as tied half notes. **Rules from earlier species that continue to apply are all those from second species (chapter 4) except that in fourth species, under special circumstances, downbeats may be dissonant.**

In *consonant fourth species,* all parts of the syncopated whole are consonant; this is also called consonant ties or consonant ligatures. The 6–5 interval succession is easy to use, but like all patterns, it is limited to three occurrences.

Dissonant fourth species is the only situation in which downbeats are dissonant! The dissonance occurs when the CF note moves on the downbeat, while the note in the added line is tied over. The CF note is called the agent, the note that acts on another. The voice that is tied over is called the patient, or note that is acted upon. This terminology is a bit unusual, and requires some explanation. Renaissance writers thought of music as a science as well as an art, and much of their thinking was modeled on that of Aristotle, who is often referred to in treatises merely as "the Philosopher." Aristotle originally used the terms "agent" and "patient" to describe cause and effect in the natural world. Artusi borrowed them to describe the notes in a dissonant suspension. We can see that Artusi applied them metaphorically: one note doesn't really *push* the other, *causing* it to resolve, but even now that seems like a nice way to think about this figure, called a suspension.

The agent may move by skip or step to cause the dissonance. This is the only situation in which a voice skips to a dissonance, but it is OK because the CF note, the agent, is always "right"; it "wins," and the other note, the patient, must resolve to accommodate the CF. The consonant weak half before the dissonant downbeat is called the preparation. The dissonance is resolved when the patient descends stepwise to an imperfect consonance. This means that only sevenths and fourths (perfect or augmented, it makes no difference) can be used above, and only seconds below: these and their compounds are the only ones that are a step above imperfect consonances. The whole figure is three half notes long. The dissonance we noticed at the end of the soprano-alto duo in "O magnum" mysterium is part of a dissonant suspension.

76

Consonant Ties

CF   (etc.)

Parts of the Suspension

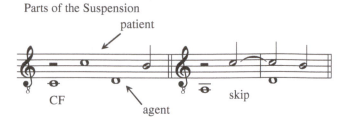

CF   agent   skip

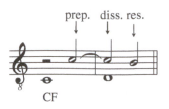

prep. diss. res.

CF

Illustration of Hard Rules

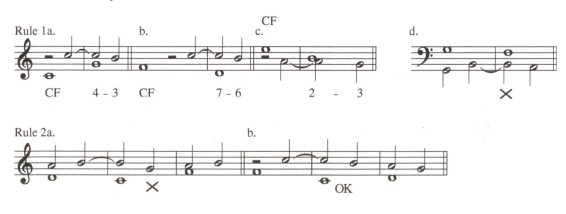

Rule 1a.   b.   CF c.   d.

CF   4 – 3   CF   7 – 6   2 – 3   ✗

Rule 2a.   b.

✗   OK

Rule 3.

1   2   3   ✗

The only legal dissonant suspensions above are the 7–6 and the 4–3 (and their compounds); below is the 2–3 (and its compound). When you are writing or improvising in fourth species, som etimes you get into a situation where you simply can't prepare a legal suspension or a consonant tie (that is, when the next downbeat would be a ninth or second above or a fourth or seventh below). At that point you have to abandon the rhythm of tied notes altogether. Instead of tying, you move to a consonance on the next downbeat, moving in second species, in effect.

Hard Rules

1. **Dissonance on the downbeat is allowed in syncopated whole notes if the first half of the whole note is consonant** (perfect or imperfect) **and the dissonance is followed by a descending step to an imperfect consonance on the second half-note beat.** Thus it is illegal to tie from a dissonance (this mistake is

abbreviated "tfd") or to skip from the dissonance ("sfd"). **The interval succession in which a diminished fifth resolves down by step to a minor sixth is an exception, and cannot be used.**

2. The dissonant fourth-species suspension must be completed with an imperfect consonance on the weak beat before second species begins. However, a consonant tie can be followed by a dissonant passing tone as if it were a second-species downbeat (Illustration b).

3. Two sequential repetitions is still the limit. In a descending stepwise CF, you may get caught in a chain of suspensions, with each resolution becoming the next preparation. Use second species to break out of the chain.

Idiom: The "Fake" Suspension (or "Dissonant Preparation")

In this idiom (Ex. 6-1) the effect is of a dissonant suspension, but the dissonance is not prepared correctly from a consonance. It consists of intervals 5–4–4–3, 3–4–4–3, 8–7–7–6, or a 6–7–7–6 figure above a breve or repeated wholes or 1–2–2–3 or 3–2–2–3 below. It is sometimes used in the middle of a counterpoint against a CF (as in Ex. 6-5), but we will use it only in cadences.

Example 6-1 Fake Suspensions

| *Exercise Series* **A:** | Warmups |

You are to find all possible tied whole notes followed by a descending step. As in earlier chapters, you can start with all consonances against the two notes, then see which consonances against the first note are a step above those against the second note. As you can see there are very few possibilities. For each pair of CF notes, **find all possible suspensions above and below** (don't bother duplicating solutions an octave apart). The added part is to be in this rhythm: [♩, o, ♩], with the second note of the CF fragment acting as the agent. Label which are dissonant suspensions, which consonant. Example 6-2 shows the slim pickings when the CF rises a third.

Example 6-2

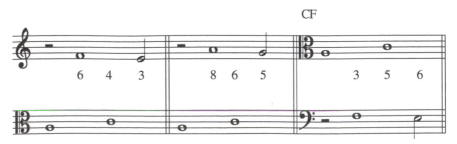

Using only tied half notes, how can you set up this suspension? What you learn from Ex. 6-3 is that some suspensions cannot be made because the preparation is not consonant with the first given CF note.

Example 6-3

Warmup Exercises

Exercise 6-A1   **Exercise 6-A2**   **Exercise 6-A3**   **Exercise 6-A4**

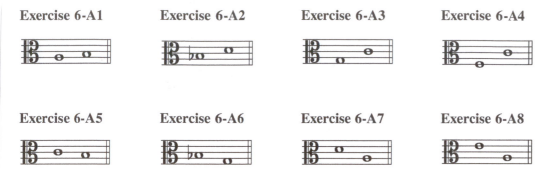

Exercise 6-A5   **Exercise 6-A6**   **Exercise 6-A7**   **Exercise 6-A8**

If you are taking the invertible counterpoint option, follow the instructions on p. 39.

Soft Rules

1. Use more dissonant than consonant fourth species, and break into second species as little as possible (say, once in every four to six CF notes).

2. Unisons are OK not only on weak beats, as in second species, but on downbeats. This is because the general principle is that when both voices move to a unison at the same time, one seems to disappear. In fourth species, since the two voices never move at the same time, one voice never seems to disappear suddenly on the downbeat.

Illustration of Soft Rules

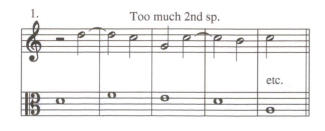

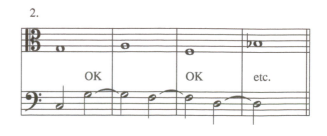

Exercise Series *B:*   Find the Errors

Mark hard errors with X and soft errors with (x).

Exercise 6-B1

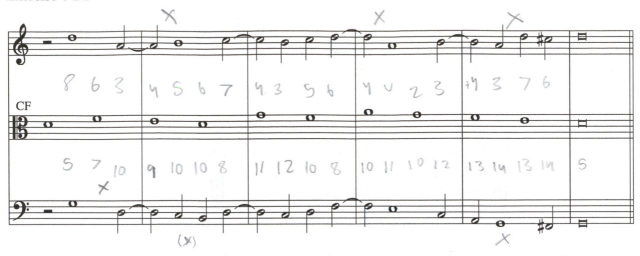

Study of Examples from Treatises

Example 6-4 (Diruta)

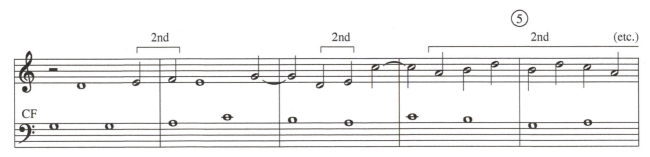

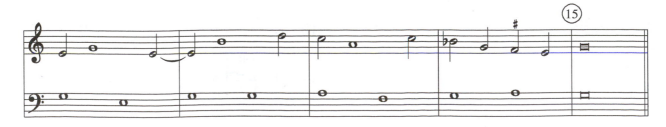

Example 6-4 illustrates only consonant ties. Diruta often breaks out of tied notes and goes into second species, as marked in the first line. The asterisk at the *B* in m. 9 marks an echappeé, a figure we are not using. In m. 3 Diruta has composed a very awkward line; the only justification for it might be to consider the low *E* the end of one phrase and the high *C* the beginning of another, even though no rest intervenes. In chapter 9 we will see that lines like this can be justified by phrasing; for now you should continue to avoid such disjunctions.

Example 6-5 (Diruta)

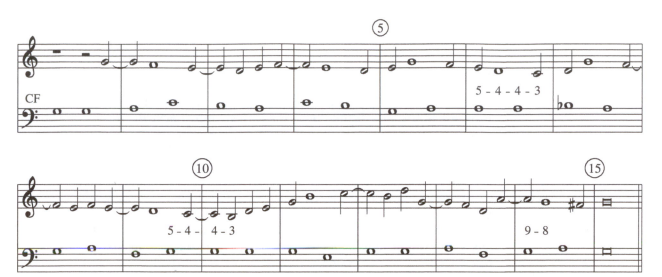

In Example 6-5 Diruta illustrates dissonant ties. The "fake" suspensions give the effect of setting up cadences in the middle of the piece that are deceptively resolved (the first, in m. 6, seems to want to go to *D*, the second to *C*). We will use the "fake" suspension only at cadences for now. This example also contains a 9–8 suspension near the end—the 9–8 suspension is illegal for you, and very rare in two parts. Morley offers one reason: "After the discord we do not set a perfect concord, for the perfect concordes doe not so well beare out the discords as the unperfect do, and the reason is this. When a discord is taken it is to cause the note following be the more pleasing to the eare. Now the perfect concords of themselves being sufficiently pleasing, neede no helpe to make them more agreeable, because they can be no more of themselves then they were before." We will use them later, in writing for three and more parts.

Example 6-6 (Banchieri)

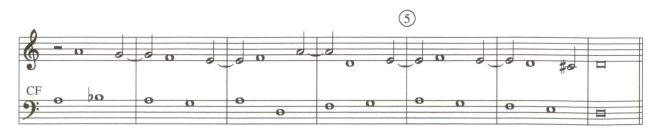

Banchieri never breaks into second species, but uses both consonant and dissonant fourth species (as you will); mark which tied notes are consonant, which dissonant. Unlike his second- and third-species lines, this line is not a diminution of his first-species line. Dissonant fourth species can only be a diminution of a first-species line that descends by step, for that is the essential melodic element of dissonant suspensions; consequently, consonant fourth species rarely works as a diminution of first species.

Go back to the first page of Victoria's "O magnum mysterium" (Ex. I-2). Find the agent and patient in the following suspensions: m. 13; m. 16; and m. 19. (Disregard for now the suspension in m. 8; it will be explained in chapter 9.)

Exercise Series C: ## CF Fragments

For each CF fragment in these Series C exercises, **find all possible dissonant suspensions above and below, then work them into lines.** Begin with a half rest and fill all the measures (you will write three syncopated whole notes and a final half note). Use reasonable ranges, and don't bother writing down solutions that are duplications at the octave. Use second species when necessary. Given the CF fragment in Example 6-7a, only four dissonant suspensions are possible above, and two below; these are collected in Example 6-7b. Finally they are worked into lines in Example 6-7c–g. You can work more than one suspension into a line if you like, as in Example 6-7c. You can expect to find fewer dissonant suspensions below because there are two possibilities above (7–6 and 4–3 and their compounds) and only one below (2–3 and its compounds).

Example 6-7

a.

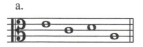

b.   (above)   (below)

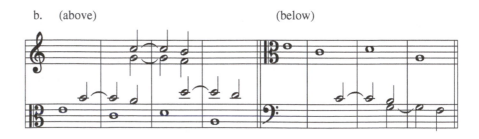

c.

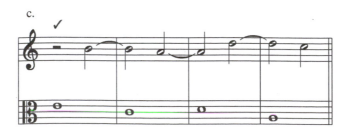

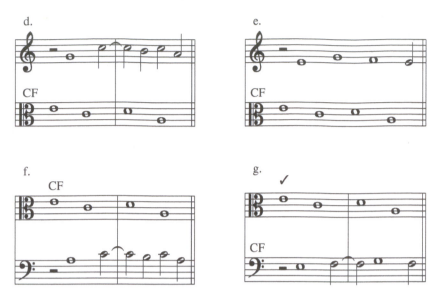

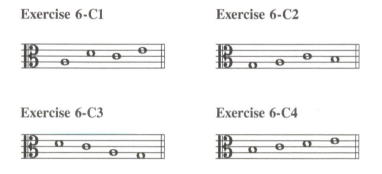

Choosing a favorite among the solutions above, we find that c seems the most elegant, with contrary motion (d has to break into second species and e circles around in a narrow range). Neither f nor g seems very exciting, but the 6–5s followed by the sudden dramatic leap to the dissonant *A* make g the winner among the solutions below.

CF Fragment Exercises

(Note that there can be different numbers of answers for each exercise, depending on how many dissonant suspensions there are, and how many can be worked into a single line.)

Exercise 6-C1   **Exercise 6-C2**

Exercise 6-C3   **Exercise 6-C4**

Exercise Series *D:*   Complete CFs

A sample working-out is shown in Example 6-8, where Hypodorian lines are added to the "Christe" phrase of Kyrie IX. Dissonant suspensions have been bracketed. In these series D exercises, write two **different** solutions above and two below. "Different" here means **no suspension is the same from one exercise to the next.** You can use the same suspension at different points along the CF (as at *) or you can have suspensions at the same point in the CF if different intervals are involved (as at †). As in previous species, you must sound the notes at the extremes of the modal octave; however, it may not be feasible to include skips or outlines of the mode. **Use at least five dissonant suspensions above and three below.** Your priorities should be: (1) use as much dissonant fourth species as possible; (2) when you can't do dissonant suspensions, use consonant ties; (3) break into second species as little as possible.

Example 6-8

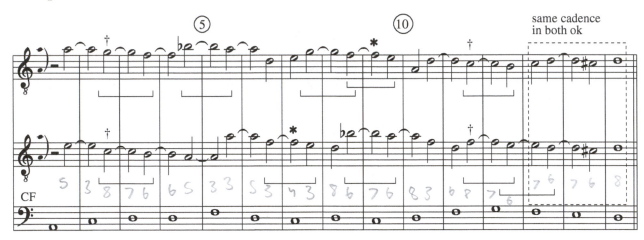

If you are taking the invertible counterpoint option, follow the instructions on p. 39; check the instructions for suspensions in chapter 13. If you want to use fourth species to write your own cadences, consult chapter 10.

Exercise Series *D*:   Complete CF Exercises

> **Exercise 6-D1**   Write two different fourth-species Hypophrygian lines above the
> last two phrases of "Da Jesus an dem Kreuze stund," and two below (treat the
> first given note as the beginning of a piece). Only the cadences, which you
> compose, will be the same. If you are taking the invertible counterpoint option,
> indicate which two lines are the same.

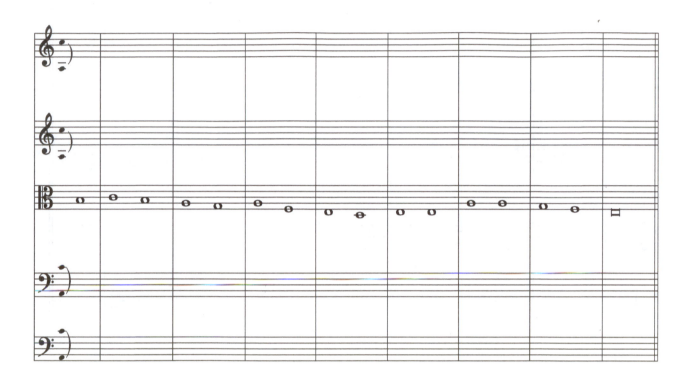

Exercise 6-D2   Write two different fourth-species Hypodorian lines above the last two phrases of "Vater unser," and two below (treat the first given note as the beginning of a piece). Only the cadences, which you compose, will be the same. If you are taking the invertible counterpoint option, indicate which two lines are the same.

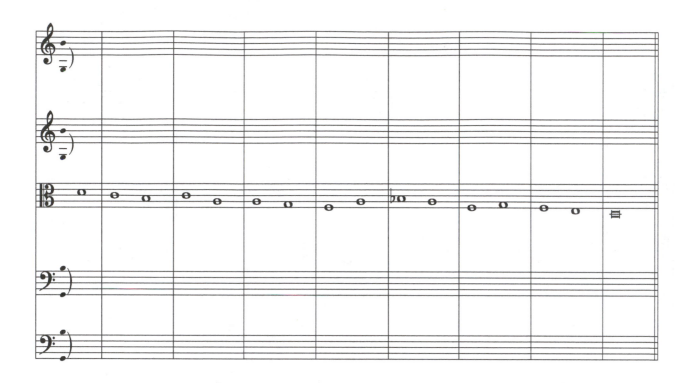

Improvising Fourth Species

Improvising fourth species above is surprisingly easy if you leap up to a consonance on weak beats. The obligatory motion of the added line is descending, so you are always safe if you skip up. If, after having skipped up, you realize that to tie would lead you into a 9–8 or some other illegal suspension, then move to a consonance on the downbeat and start all over. Improvising fourth species below is a bit more difficult because of fewer dissonant possibilities.

7

Mixed Values

The mixing of the note values is also called "fifth species" or "florid" (embellished, flowery) counterpoint. When different species "meet," the following rules apply.

Hard Rules

1. When a consonant half note on a downbeat (attacked or tied) is followed by two stepwise descending quarter notes, the first may be dissonant. This may be because at the moment of attack the first of the two quarters sounds like a dissonant second-species passing tone. The relaxed quality of descent may compensate for the tension of the accented dissonance. We can think of this as a "legal d3q." It is possible for both quarters to be dissonant (at *) and eighths may rarely substitute for the fourth quarter.

2. When two quarters on a downbeat are followed by a half, the half must be consonant. This may be because at the moment it is attacked, the half sounds like a third quarter, which must be consonant in third species. This works well treated as the start of a syncopation.

3. The dotted whole may only occur on a downbeat. Its dot represents a half note on the following downbeat. This half note may be treated as the tied-over half in fourth species (it must resolve if dissonant). Or it may be treated as a consonant half in second species, and may be followed by dissonant or consonant second species. If it is followed by two quarters, see rule 1. Such a long value is rarely used other than at the beginning of a counterpoint.

4. The dotted half may occur only on the downbeat or the second half-note beat, and it must be consonant. The dot must also be consonant, and should be thought of as a strong quarter in third species. (Do not confuse this with fourth species in which the resolution is embellished by an anticipatory quarter; see Idioms below.) If we are writing with bar lines every whole note, we can rephrase rules 3 and 4 as: **Never tie from a shorter to a longer value.** You may tie from longer to shorter, or between two equal values.

5. Never tie from a weak quarter. This is because we do not use syncopated half notes, although you will occasionally see examples of this in the repertoire.

6. No single value equivalent to 5, 7, or 9 quarters may be used. In duple meter, these can only be notated using ties, and in most Renaissance notation, ties were not used.

7. **Eighth notes may be used in pairs on the weak quarter beats in stepwise passing or lower neighbor motion.** Either may be dissonant (both may be dissonant in a single case marked with *). **Neither eighth may be approached or left by skip, and neither may be used in an upper neighbor figure.** You may only use one pair per four quarters. The illustration shows all possible ways to use eighths. They are less frequently used ascending. A dotted quarter and eighth may occasionally substitute for two quarters.

8. **The suspension figure may be embellished by an <u>anticipation</u> of the resolution, but the note of resolution must be heard on the second half-note beat.** The anticipation constitutes an exception to the rule prohibiting repeated notes in third species. However, you must never move away from the anticipation (otherwise it's not anticipating anything!). The anticipation may itself be embellished by a lower neighbor.

Illustration of Hard Rules

Idiom: Dissonant Upper Neighbor

A dissonant upper neighbor may be used on the second quarter note of the whole-note unit if it precedes a long value (a dotted half or longer). The long value can be the preparation of a dissonant suspension. See also the illustration of Hard Rule 7 in chapter 14 (7a).

Example 7-1

Soft Rules: Rhythm

The ideal Renaissance rhythm is based on rhythmic variety and lack of metric accent. This means:

1. Avoid repeating rhythmic patterns.

2. Avoid changing note values on the beat twice in a row. The coincidence of metric accent and change of note value sounds clunky.

Pietro Cerone says in "an elegant and fully polished composition" that it is bad to start a run of quarters in one direction on the downbeat when the other part stands still (in his example, you can think of the whole notes as CF notes that move from one part to the other): There are two ways to avoid the coincidence of metric accent and change of note value: one option is to tie through the downbeat, using a syncopation or a dot (do not use a rest for now), or you can continue "through" the downbeat with the same rhythmic value. Here is an example of good rhythm:

3. If you use first species, do so only at the beginning of a counterpoint.

4. In general, begin melodies with longer values and gradually speed up.

5. Use a maximum of fourteen quarters, seven halves, three syncopated wholes in a row. These rather arbitrary quantities will keep variety foremost.

6. Use dotted quarters and eighths very rarely.

7. The note of resolution should sound for the full weak half of the measure—avoid moving away from the resolution.

Soft Rules: Melody

1. Try to cover the modal octave roughly every four to eight CF notes.

2. Avoid the coincidence of rhythmic pattern *and* melodic pattern.

3. Don't use quarter notes or eighth notes to break up parallel perfect intervals.

Illustration of Soft Melodic Rules

2.

OK

OK

(Zarlino)

Exercise Series *B*: Find the Errors

Mark hard errors with **X** and soft errors with (x).

Exercise 7-B1

Exercise 7-B2

Study of Examples from Treatises

In the following examples, be sure you know which species is in operation at any moment (you could label the various species in the examples as we did in Ex. 2-3). Also note cases of rule 1 above. Rhythmic variety is a stated goal of Renaissance writers on music. In these examples, look at the rhythmic patterns in the added voice from the point of view of variety. How many rhythmic patterns two whole notes long are immediately repeated? Example 7-2a has twelve changes of species on the beat, but these changes succeed each other immediately only three times.

Example 7-2a and b (Zarlino)

Note in this first pair of examples that the CF doesn't start on the important notes of the third mode; the added lines begin at perfect consonances with *G*, so the mode is unclear until the end. Zarlino compensates for this by occasionally using the characteristic skips or outlines of the mode. Note the syncopated half note at X (illegal for us).

Example 7-2c and d (Zarlino)

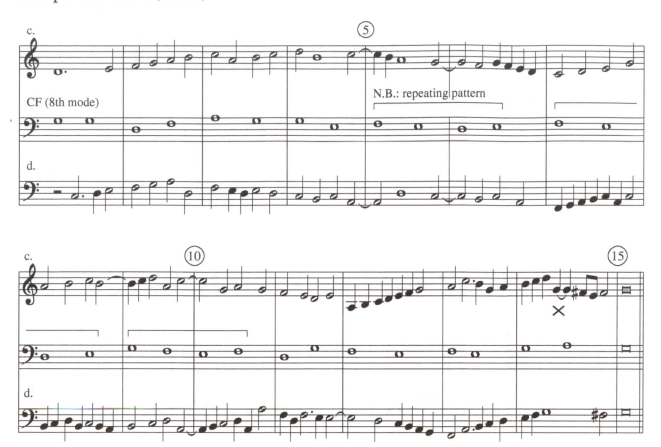

Rhythmic variety in the added voice can help in obscuring repeating melodic patterns in the CF. In mm. 4–10 of these three examples by Diruta, the pattern has been bracketed. Sing them fast enough that you can hear the repetitions!

Example 7-3a (Diruta)

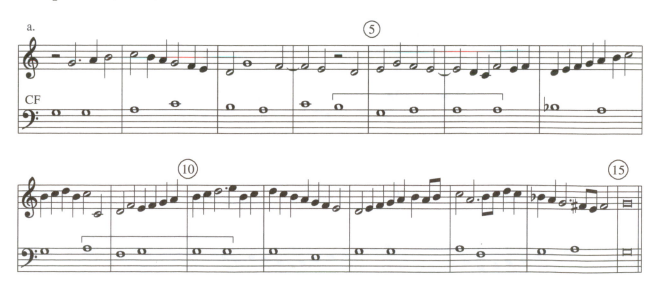

Example 7-3b and c (Diruta)

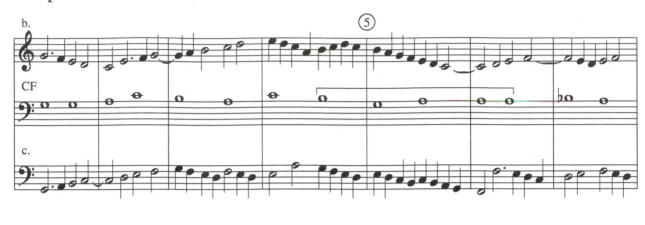

In each of these three Banchieri counterpoints on the hexachord (see Appendix 3), note where the octave skips occur. He has placed them at different points (at the 3rd, 4th, or 5th note of the CF), creating different contours.

Example 7-4a–c (Banchieri)

c.

Exercises Series **C:**   Given Rhythms

In the short exercises that follow, you are given a fragmentary phrase of characteristic Renaissance rhythm and a CF. The exercise is to write the contrapuntal line against the CF using the given rhythm, as shown in Example 7-5. Sing and comment on each solution.

Given this rhythm:

Example 7-5a

and this CF:

Example 7-5b

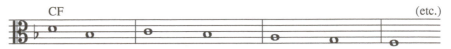

you could write the following solutions:

Example 7-5c

Given Rhythm Exercises

Pick one of the given rhythms and one of the CFs and write a counterpoint above and below the CF in the given rhythm. Assume each one *is* the beginning of a piece. A good way to start is to figure out the consonance and dissonance requirements and possibilities for each rhythmic value. This has been done for rhythmic pattern 1. Consonance and dissonance are indicated with c and d. Be sure you know under what circumstances each dissonance can be used. For instance, the third note can only be dissonant if it is passing (the d has been circled). In the third measure the third half-note beat (represented by the dot on the half note) can only be dissonant if it is treated as a fourth-species suspension; the quarter immediately following must then be an anticipation, the same note as the last half note in the measure (d-c-c circled).

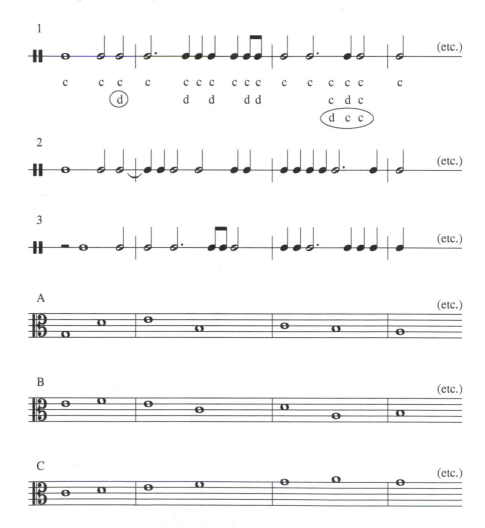

Contour

The fifth-species examples from treatises do not meander around at random within the modal octave; they are shaped in interesting ways. One of the most valuable means of expression and variety available to the Renaissance composer is the exploration of the range. Using range, the Renaissance composer can build sections out of large arches with melodic climaxes.

Take for instance Diruta's two examples (7-3a and b). Both counterpoints are written above the same CF in the same (Hypomixolydian) range, yet they are quite different. We can describe the differences in terms of change of direction, high and low points, and the rate of speed at which the melody covers range and changes direction.

Examples 7-6a and b are schematic representations of Diruta's counterpoints, showing only high and low points (high points are circled). Examples 7-6c and d show the contour of two of Zarlino's counterpoints (Ex. 7-2a uses the same CF Diruta used, with a different ending). All the notes that have been removed between high and low points are uniformly ascending or descending (such motion in a single direction is most often by scale, but occasionally skips intervene). We thus reduce the line to a succession of high points connected by means of large and small dips. We include the first and last notes in the added line, and we do not specify exactly where during the CF whole note the high and low points occur.

These <u>reductions</u>, based on the simple feature of melodic turning points, enable us to notice things we might not have noticed otherwise. For instance, that Zarlino has far more changes of direction than Diruta. Also, we can quickly spot immediate repetition of high points. These have been marked with asterisks, and we see that Zarlino uses them far more than Diruta. A look at the high points of Zarlino's example (7-6c) reveals a remarkably symmetrical structure—it is possible that Zarlino planned his high points in advance.

Our reduction of Zarlino's Example 7-2c (Ex. 7-6d) makes apparent three occurrences of a single large-scale pattern: a scalar ascent to high points *C* and *D*. The time interval between these high points is about the same, so the piece has a very even consistency. At first hearing Zarlino's example may appear similar to any of the other examples, but it has a remarkably regular structure. Does this feature make Zarlino a better composer than Diruta? a more boring one? A theoretical observation like this one is only a single frame in the motion picture of aesthetic evaluation. Maybe these contour reductions reveal a small difference in the personal styles of the two composers.

These reductions look a little like first-species exercises. However, they contain many impossible things (parallel or similar fifths or octaves, marked in Examples 7-6c and d). We must understand that this kind of reduction is only an abstraction. The mistakes disappear when we consider the details of timing and the material that has been reduced out.

Example 7-6a (reduction of Diruta's Ex. 7-3a)

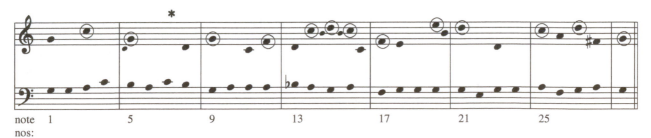

note nos: 1   5   9   13   17   21   25

Example 7-6b (reduction of Diruta's Ex. 7-3b)

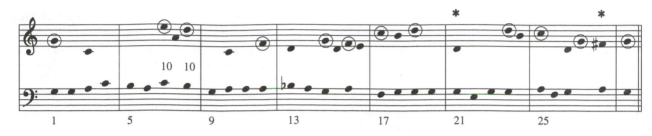

Example 7-6c (reduction of Zarlino's Ex. 7-2a)

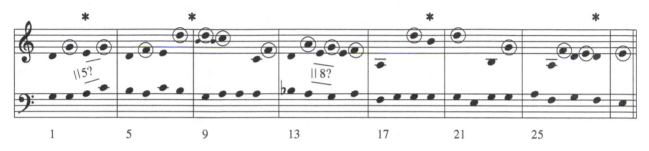

Example 7-6d (reduction of Zarlino's Ex. 7-2c)

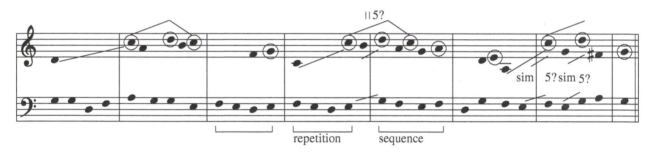

repetition   sequence

Exercise Series C: Contours

Here is a way to structure long exercises that is similar to one we used in first species, where we chose high and low points first and connected them (see Ex. 3-7). Again you are to compose a contrapuntal line that integrates the given notes (appearing as black noteheads.) The given notes may appear anywhere in the measure in which they are notated, and be of any duration. If they have a ∧, they must be high points (approached from below and followed by downward motion). If they have a ∨, they must be low points (approached from above and followed by ascending motion). If they have both symbols, they may be used as high *or* low points. You may add high and low points in between, but you must use the ones that are given. Remember that every high point should be preceded and/or followed by stepwise motion. Cadence on the given note.

Example 7-7

Given this CF:

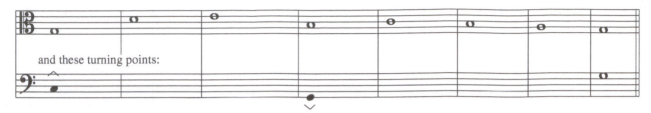

and these turning points:

You could write:

CF

Which one do you like best? One thing you might learn from this exercise (and the given rhythm exercises earlier in this chapter) is that it is very difficult to work within such narrow restrictions—after all, rhythm and contour are not separate in melody. However, you might also learn that the restrictions force you to invent surprisingly good solutions that you might not have thought of otherwise.

Contour Exercises

Exercise 7-C1

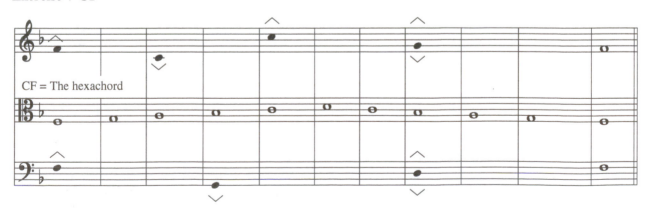

CF = The hexachord

Exercise 7-C2

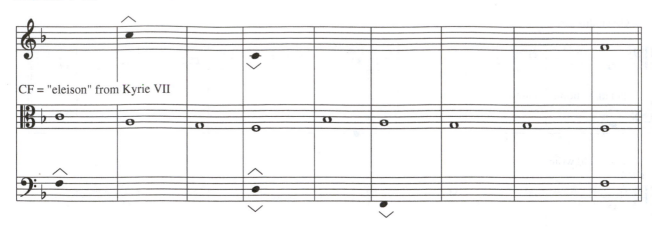

CF = "eleison" from Kyrie VII

Exercise 7-C3

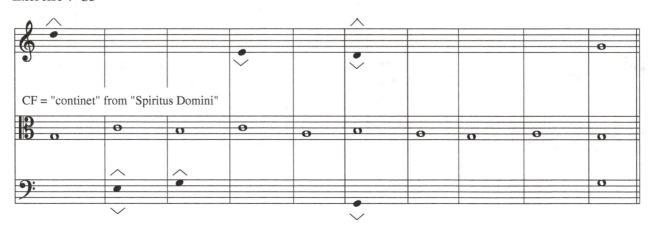

CF = "continet" from "Spiritus Domini"

Exercise Series **D**:   Complete CFs

In these exercises, compose two **different** lines in freely mixed values above, and two **different** lines below the given CFs. "Different" means that in each added line above and below: (1) **the rhythmic patterns should not be the same, and** (2) **the high and low points should not be the same.** (Remember that a line above can be the same as one below.)

The added line must have the same final as the CF. If the CF is plagal, the added line must be authentic (a fourth above and a fifth below), and vice versa (a fifth above and a fourth below). **Label** the mode of the added voice. As in third species, your melody may extend two steps beyond the ends of the modal octave.

The added melody is to sound the extremes of the octave of its mode, and include characteristic skips or outlines (one fourth or fifth at least) of the mode. **Label** each skip or outline as well. In these exercises you write your own cadences, using the appropriate cadential suspension, ornamented if you like. Remember that cadences are not an opportunity for originality, they are standard formulas that signal the ending.

Exercise 7-D1   Use the first 16 notes of "Da Jesus an dem Kreuze stund" as CF (Ex. 1-3f). Write out the tune in whole notes, omitting rests. Note: It is impossible to make a cadential suspension in a line added below this CF; instead, use a double neighbor against the penultimate note.

Exercise 7-D2   Use the first 19 notes of Kyrie IX as CF (Ex. 1-3c).

Exercise 7-D3   Use the first 25 notes of Kyrie VIII as CF (Ex. 1-3b). Because the CF ends with a repeated whole note, you must write the idiomatic "fake" suspension at the cadence (see chapter 6).

Exercise 7-D4   Use the first 32 notes (omit the repeated last *G*) of "Spiritus Domini replevit" as CF (Ex. 1-3j).

The Invertible Counterpoint Option

If you want to keep writing in invertible counterpoint at the octave, proceed as in the instructions on p. 39. However, if you want to try invertible counterpoint at the twelfth, keep these three things in mind: exact transposition (do you want the part that goes down a fifth to have a flat in the signature?); range (you will not be able to follow the instructions for range given in the instructions to Series D Exercises above); and cadence (if the original counterpoint ends with a proper cadence, you will have to alter the cadence in the inverted combination).

Improvising in Mixed Values

When you improvise in mixed values, you can always change values if you see yourself getting into trouble. For instance, suppose you're headed downward in third species and you realize that if you continue you'll land on a dissonance on the next downbeat. You can do two things to arrange for your downbeat note to be a step away from where it would have landed: You can halt on a half note and wait; or you can add eighth notes to cover a little more ground downward faster or to go back up a step; or you can skip a third to gain more ground. It's like a soccer player who, seeing four steps ahead that it's his/her left foot that's about to kick the ball, does a little skip to readjust the feet so it'll be the right foot that kicks. The hard part is maintaining rhythmic variety.

Summary of Rules

Here, the rules are divided up in such a way that you can look through your added lines, focusing on one musical aspect at a time. Thus when evaluating your line according to the melodic rules, you need not look at the rhythm or the vertical intervals; likewise, when considering your use of rhythm, you need not think about dissonance. Of course this implies that you will take the time to go over your work several times from several points of view.

Because this is a summary, the rules are not numbered as they appeared in the various chapters. (Teachers and teaching assistants may want to use this numbering as a code.) Hard rules are numbered in capital boldface type because they are so much more important. Soft rules are indented and numbered in lowercase regular type. They should be consulted only *after* it has been established that all hard rules have been observed. Your teacher will tell you how important each soft mistake is, but soft rules are always less important than the hard rules—you should not obsess over them. As we have seen in examples, sometimes it is necessary to break a soft rule in order to achieve a musical line.

"Assignment" rules are those that are purely pedagogical. Thus in second species exercises, you are asked to include a skip of the mode; this is just to get you used to thinking along those lines—it does not reflect anything about second species in Renaissance style. Likewise, some teachers insist that vertical intervals be labeled; this is to make sure you are aware of what you are writing—not all teachers will insist on this all the time.

All of the following rules apply when writing against a CF as of the end of chapter 7, and many continue to apply. Some, however, are altered later in the book, for writing under different circumstances. These include writing with a repeated motive, as discussed in chapter 9, writing cadences (ch. 10), and writing in two parts in mixed values (2pmv), discussed in chapter 11. The rules that are altered later are marked in the main list with asterisks, and the new rules are given in the section headed "Rules for Chapters 9, 10, and 11."

Melodic Mistakes

M1: motion by an augmented or diminished interval

M2: skip of a seventh, or skip greater than an octave

M3: outline of a diminished or augmented interval (diminished ok if filled in & followed by step inwards)

M4: repeated note (except in anticipation idiom, i.e., weak consonant quarter)*

M5: same neighbor twice in a row

M6: too many changes of direction

M7: does not fill modal octave/exceeds modal octave by more than allowed

m1: pyramid rule

m2: leap not followed by step inward

m3: local high point registrally disconnected from line

m4: two consecutive skips adding to more than a sixth

m5: line too skippy (more than two consecutive skips in any values; two consecutive skips in third species)

m6: stagnant line

m7: unjustified use of B♭ (or E♭ in transposed system)

m8: leap up to weak quarter

m9: leap down of a minor sixth; leap in either direction of a major sixth

Mistakes in Dissonance Treatment

D1: Simultaneously attacked dissonance*

D2: skip to or from a dissonance (except in a cambiata and when the agent in the CF skips to cause a legal suspension on a strong beat)*

D3: dissonant third quarter (legal in the stepwise-descent half-quarter-quarter against a whole note or repeated halves)

D4: unresolved suspension or resolved too early/late

D5: illegal suspension (e.g., suspended ninth above; suspended 4th or dim. 5th or 7th below)

D6: tie from a dissonance

D7: suspension placed on weaker beat than its resolution

D8: illegal neighbor (no d.n.'s in 2nd sp.; in 3rd, d.l.n. only; d.u.n only as per the d.u.n. idiom or fake suspension)

Voice-Leading Mistakes

V1: parallel perfect intervals (OK between end of one phrase and beginning of next)

V2: similar motion to perfect intervals*

v1: unison attacked simultaneously (OK at beginning and end or when doing invertible counterpoint)

v2: simultaneous leaps of more than a third

v3: in first species, repeated notes in both voices

v4: parallel perfect intervals insufficiently broken (i.e., second-species reduction has parallels)

v5: distance between voices too wide (no wider than a twelfth; thirteenth for one note only)

Rhythmic Mistakes

R1: illegal rhythmic value (e.g., five, seven, or anything greater than eight quarters)

R2: illegal rest value (e.g., quarter note)

R3: dotted rhythmic value placed illegally (e.g., dotted half or dotted quarter on second or fourth quarter; dotted whole not on downbeat)

R4: eighths used wrongly (must be on weak quarter; each one passing or lower neighbor; not more than one pair per whole)

R5: duration shorter than half note before/after rest

r1: too many consecutive notes of same value

r2: consecutive changes of species on downbeat

r3: syncopated half

r4: rhythmic unison between voices for too long

r5: repeated rhythmic patterns

r6: first species elsewhere than the beginning

r7: resolution of dissonant suspension not long enough

Formal Mistakes

F1: direct repetition of a chunk (contrapuntal combination) a whole note long or longer without intervening material.

F2: more than two sequential repetitions of a chunk

F3: no perfect consonance at beginning (or end if cadence is not provided)*

  f1: more than two perfect consonances in succession

  f2: parallel motion (or "broken-up parallel motion") for too long

"Assignment" Mistakes

A1: no vertical intervals labeled

A2: solutions insufficiently different

A3: required element missing (e.g., skip of mode in second species)

  a1: one wrong or missing interval label

Rules for Chapters 9, 10, and 11

As of chapter 9

*M4 relaxed: Repeated half notes can be used for the sake of the text, or as part of an instrumental motive, or between phrases, or to avoid an illegal duration.

As of chapter 10 (Cadences)

C1 anything other than M6 or m3 leading by step in both voices to 8ve or unison (e.g. not raising leading tone when you should, or raising when you shouldn't, or skipping to the final)

C2 doubled leading tone

As of chapter 11

*D1 relaxed: In 2pmv,[1] dissonance may be attacked simultaneously when a longer value is rearticulated (broken into repeating notes) in a suspension or against D3q as described in Ex. 11-3 and also according to the idiom in Ex. 11-5.

*D2 relaxed: The agent in a suspension may skip or step to a consonance on the weak half-note beat while the patient is resolving.

*V2 relaxed: in 2pmv, similar motion to a perfect interval is legal if one voice moves by step and the preceding sonority is consonant and lasts a half note or longer.

*F3 relaxed: The first-sounding vertical sonority need not be a perfect consonance in 2pmv imitative openings.

---

[1]2pmv = two parts in mixed values.

8

Counterpoint with Repetition of a Motive

In chapter 7, your counterpoint in mixed values was governed by the modal octave, the characteristic skips and outlines of the mode, rhythmic variety, and a general awareness of contour. But there is another way to organize music in the Renaissance—by using a repeating motive. The <u>motive</u> is a fairly short melodic fragment, identified by its rhythm and melodic intervals, that is placed repeatedly against a cantus firmus. Although repetition of the motive negates the ideal of constant rhythmic variation that was held up in the last chapter, Zarlino coined a rule that ensures variety in other ways: he says that **repetition can be used if at least one of the three elements that make up the combination is varied: the rhythms, the vertical intervals, or the "notes"** (by varying the notes he means changing the *names* of the notes of the motive—that is, by transposing it, changing its pitch level). As you know from earlier exercises, there is only a danger of illegal repetition of the whole combination if the CF contains a segment that repeats. Here are some examples written by Zarlino and his followers to show incorrect use of repetition; put a circle around repeating chunks.

Example 8-1 (Zarlino)

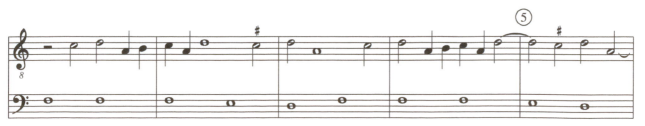

Example 8-2 (Cerone)

NB: diminished "fake" sus.

Example 8-3 (Morley)

Giovanni Maria Artusi, illustrating Zarlino's rule, devised a wonderfully systematic flow chart that exhausts all the possibilities (Ex. 8-4, with Artusi's commentary). The first in the series is like those above, and all the others contain acceptable repetition. The vertical intervals have been labeled in 8-4b, which maintains both notes and rhythms. In c, vertical intervals are varied as well as rhythms (you should disregard the last notes in c, which are not the "same notes"); 8-4e maintains rhythms and vertical intervals, but the three-whole-note combination is transposed up a fourth, which makes a <u>harmonic sequence</u>; 8-4f is like b (the vertical intervals have been labeled); in 8-4g, both the notes and the vertical intervals are different. These examples are short schematic illustrations. Once you get the idea, you apply it to longer lines of better quality.

Example 8-4

There are some melodies used by composers which, when repeated, make the composition either

poor and languid, as when the counterpoint is not varied. Such a melody is found to use the same notes, vertical intervals, and rhythm

or rich in invention and somewhat ingenious. But to be so, if the melody uses

the same notes, then it must not use the same

vertical intervals

rhythms

the same vertical intervals, then it must not use the same

rhythms

notes

the same rhythms, then it must not use the same

vertical intervals

notes

Repeating a motive against a CF is sometimes called "counterpoint with an obligation," where the obligation is repetition. Renaissance music always maintains a tension between repetition and variation. For now we are going to concentrate on leaving the rhythm and the melodic intervals intact. In the following examples, for the most part only the "notes" (transposition level) and the vertical intervals are varied. Initially, only a few transpositions of the motive will be used (at the fourth, fifth, or octave). Later, other variations may be used.

Example 8-5 (Cerreto)

Compare these two examples by Scipione Cerreto with Artusi's: which elements in each are repeated, which varied? The similar fifth in the first example reflects the liberty that some composers took when writing with an obligation (see Morley's comments on Ex. 9-2). You should not take such liberties now.

Example 8-6 (Pontio)

Pontio gives an example of acceptable repetition: which elements are repeated, which varied? The metric shift of the motive by a half note is perfectly normal, and does not constitute a variation.

Example 8-7 (Zarlino)

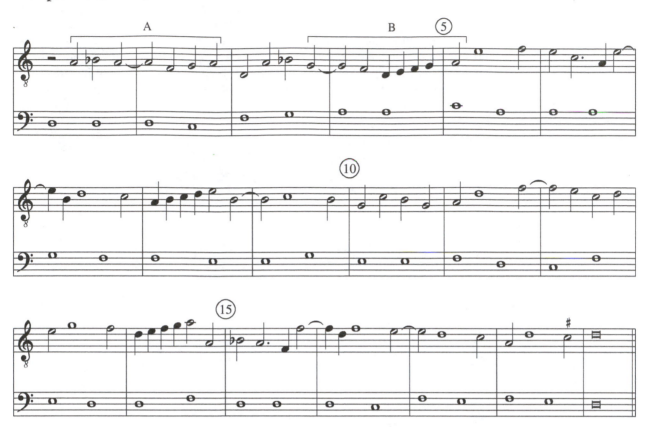

Here, Zarlino uses two different motives and connects them with freely composed material. The motives have been labeled at their first occurrences in the example; **label the recurrences of the two motives** (some are incomplete). Because rests are not used to set off the beginning of each motive, the motives are sometimes hard to find. How many different transpositions of each does he use? Note the variations in rhythm and dissonance treatment of the two motives. In mm. 4-5 you will notice a serious infraction of the "pyramid rule." Here it is because the *A* is the end of the B motive, and a new phrase is beginning on the high *E*. You may now write lines that are more difficult to sing if the phrasing is clear.

Composers use the various transpositions of a motive to build large-scale designs. Circle the high points in Zarlino's example and connect them the way we did in chapter 7. You will see that the high points make a very clear large-scale arch with a long rise, a single climax, and a brief descent.

Example 8-8 (Morley)

Thomas Morley says, "if you would maintain a point, you must go to worke thus:" The "<u>point</u>" is the melody in short values, and it has been bracketed in Example 8-8. He warns against using too many rests, but says a short rest is good before the repetition of the point. Note that an instance of "augmented fourth species" (i.e., in longer note values) and a fake suspension in diminished values occur at the end of the example. These are discussed at the beginning of the next chapter and may be ignored for now.

Rests

You may use a half-note rest in the course of a melody just before the recurrence of the motive (do not use whole-note rests). The rest may fall on the strong or the weak half-note beat. It may not be syncopated. The hard rules for rests are:

1. **The notes preceding and following the rest must be a half note long and must be consonant.**

2. **You may not use the same perfect vertical interval both before and after the rest.** That is to say, rests do not break up illegal parallels.

Illustration of Rests

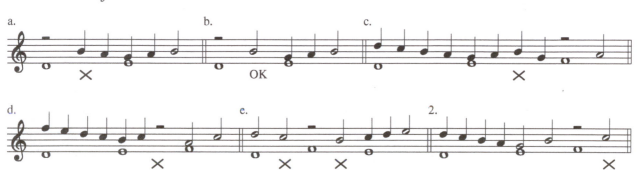

Note: In this chapter the "all possibilities" warmup exercise and the "complete CF" exercises are combined on p. 113. You should probably hand in the warmup as a first step to have it checked before proceeding.

Exercise Series A: Warmups

In these exercises you are given a CF and a motive to place against it. **The motive may be shifted metrically and transposed only as shown.** Arrows point to the strong part of the whole-note unit. Begin by finding the consonance and dissonance requirements of the motive. Thus, if the motive shown in Example 8-9a begins on the downbeat, then both the *D* and the *E* must be consonant. From this you know that the only CF note *below* that meets that requirement is *G*. If the motive is transposed to *G*, then the only CF possibility is *C*, etc. If the motive starts on the upbeat (weak) half, then there are many more possibilities.

Then find **all legal** places to put the motive against the CF using only the given transpositions and metric positions. You could imagine the motive written on a piece of clear plastic that you slide around over the CF. Many attempts to place the motive and its transpositions above the CF are shown in Example 8-9b. Some of these are illegal: what is wrong with numbers 1, 5, and 7? When you do the exercise you needn't write down wrong solutions—this is another case where you *imagine music that is not written down,* only writing down the good solutions. In this way you approach the skill of the Renaissance musician, who could improvise counterpoint with a motive!

Exercise Series **D:**   Complete CFs

Once you have found all possible legal placements, pick out some of the possibilities and connect them using freely composed material. In Example 8-9c possibilities 2 and 8 have been strung together in a Hypomixolydian line. In Example 8-9d, a couple of the "outtakes" (possibilities 3 and 6) have been elided in a Mixolydian line. In picking from among possible placements of motives, you have an architectural problem. By how much time should two occurrences at the same pitch level be separated? Can you write contrasting rhythms around the motives? Can you connect the motives smoothly in the modal octave? Can you use the transpositions to build climaxes and coherent large-scale contours?

Example 8-9

a. the motive   other metric positions   2 transpositions available

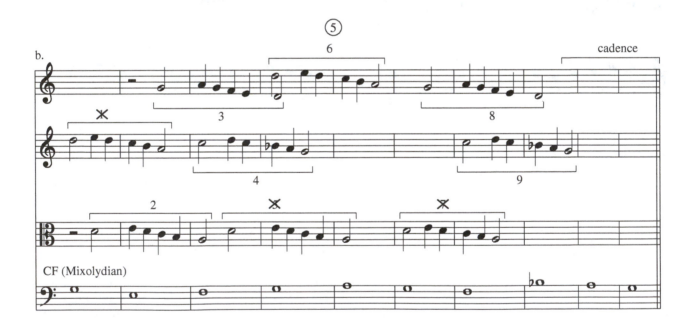

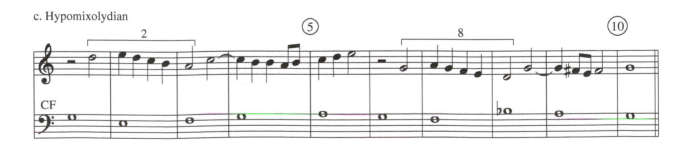

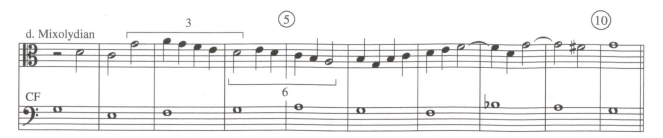

The Invertible Counterpoint Option

If you are taking this option, you may make one of the lines above the same as one below, as described in the instructions on p. xx. You should begin by making sure that the possible motive placements that you identified in the preceding Series A exercise are invertible at the interval you have chosen (in the preceding example, placement 8 is invertible at the octave, and 3 and 8 are invertible at the twelfth using $B\flat$). You will have to alter the melody so that the inverted combination makes a proper cadence.

Exercise Series **A** *and* **D**:	Two-Step Complete CFs

First find all possibilities as described for the warmup exercises above. All motives have been factory tested against the CF they go with in each exercise, and are guaranteed to fit at least five times above and below it. Ties are used instead of dots only to clarify metric position. No rhythmic alterations are allowed, but the last note of the motive (indicated with an X-shaped note) may be of any rhythmic value. Once you have found all possible legal placements, you are to write two **different** lines above and two below, each of which contains **at least two occurrences** of the given motive, connected with free material, as described for the complete CF exercises above. "Different" means that the motives occur against different segments of the CF and/or in different transpositions.

Write out the CF in alto clef. If the CF is authentic, the added line should be in a plagal mode; if the CF is plagal, the added line should be authentic; **label the mode of the added voice.** You may begin with a half rest as in previous exercises, and you may use a half rest during the exercise as specified under "Rests" above. End with a standard cadence.

Exercise 8-D1   Use the first 20 notes of "Ave maris stella" (Ex. 1-3i) or the first 19 notes of Kyrie IX (Ex. 1-3c) or the last 16 notes of "Vater unser" (Ex. 1-3g) as CF, with this motive (NB: All possible placements of this motive against the first 20 notes of "Ave Maris Stella" are given in Appendix 4. You can find the placements first and check yourself, or just look for them there to save time.):

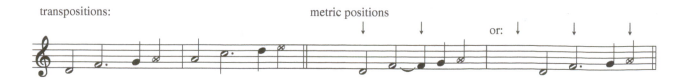

Exercise 8-D2   Use the first 14 notes of "Ecce sacerdos magnus" as CF (Ex. 1-3k; be sure to change the penultimate note to *A*), with this motive:

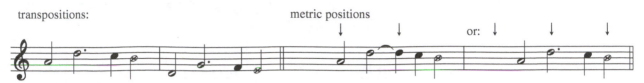

Exercise 8-D3   Use the first 15 notes of Kyrie XI (Ex. 1-3d) or the first 20 notes of "Ave Maris Stella" (Ex. 1-3i) with both motives X and Y (at least one of each); do not shift metrically.

Exercise 8-D4   Use the first 16 notes of Kyrie VIII (Ex. 1-3b) as CF, imagining it to be the first part of a longer piece, this part cadencing on the fifth degree, *C*. Note that the motive is derived from the chant.

Exercise 8-D5   Use the first 19 notes of Kyrie IX (Ex. 1-3c) as CF, with this famous motive ("la sol fa re mi"):

Exercise 8-D6   Use this segment of "Silent Night" as CF with this phrase from "Joy to the World." This last exercise will give you the experience of working with familiar tunes, associating the text with the notes, etc., as Renaissance composers did. If you are writing below, you must end with a fake suspension.

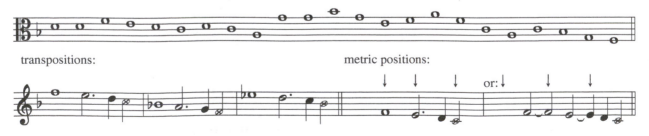

Writing with Text

This is a good time to start composing with text. You can look in the next chapter at the improvised motet by Banchieri (Ex. 9-4) or the Benedictus by Jacquet (Ex. 9-12) for models. The repeating motive always sets the same short phrase of text. The rhythm of the motive should correctly reflect the word accents of the text (see Appendix 1). In between the statements of the motive you can write free counterpoint that contains a melisma and sets a long or accented syllable of text.

For instance, in mm. 1–2 of the Banchieri, the first syllables of "Ecce sacerdos magnus" are set with repeated half notes (**repeated notes may be used in half notes or whole notes only**), and then, on the first syllable of word "magnus," a little free melisma develops. In mm. 4 and 8 the melisma is on the accented syllable of "sacérdos." Likewise in the Jacquet Benedictus, each motive begins with a relatively long value and then the accented syllables are strung out in a melisma. In each of Jacquet's three phrases, the longest melisma is the last and leads into the cadence. The last syllable of text always falls on the goal note of the cadence.

In the preceding exercises, you should see if there is a text phrase that is suggested by the notes. For instance, the motives in 8-D1 and 8-D2 could accommodate "Magni-" (from v. 1 of the Magnificat—see Appendix 1), or you could make the motive set the whole word "Magnificat" if you have declamation on the quarter note (as discussed by Zarlino). The motive in 8-D5 could accommodate "Kyrie elei-," with that last syllable extending into a free melisma ending later on "-son." Other texts for these motives are shown in Appendix 1. If you want to use your own motive and text, then before continuing be sure to show it to your teacher to see if it is appropriate.

Improvising with a Motive

In order to improvise any of the foregoing exercises, you have to do a little advance planning, along the lines of "all possibilities." But in this case, instead of taking the CF as given and placing a motive against it, you have to start with the motive and see what CF motions it can be placed against. That way whatever CF they throw at you, you will know where your motive can fit. You can organize these possibilities by cataloguing all possible two-note CF motions, the way they did in the Renaissance: unison, step up, third up (etc.), then second down, third down (etc.). Then you will have to evaluate whether your motive can fit against those two CF notes and starting on which vertical interval. In Example 8-10, a very common motive (taken from Ortiz' Ex. 9-16) is shown against a few CF motions. If the CF stands still (melodic motion of a unison), the motive has two possible placements: starting on a unison (crossing below) and starting a third above. If the CF rises a step, only one placement above is possible: starting a fifth above. This may seem like a lot of things to memorize, but in this case it's a little easier because if the CF rises a fourth or falls a fifth, *no* placement is possible!

Modal Counterpoint, Renaissance Style

Example 8-10 a–e

You can make life a little more complicated for yourself if you allow the motive to start on the weak half note. This produces that rhythm so characteristic of the Renaissance, the dotted half starting on the weak beat. With different metric placements you will get more results and be generally more impressive in your improvisation. Two possible motive placements above a stationary CF, starting on the weak half note, are shown in Example 8-10d–e.

Once you have memorized some possibilities, look at the CF and spot a few places where you can put the motive, mentally "checking them off." Remember where these mental checkmarks are, and then improvise freely until you get to one of these places. To make it clearer, you may put a rest before the motive (as long as you are on a consonance right before). You can forgive yourself some less than wonderful lines in between the motives, since the repetition of the motive will make the music seem as coherent as if it had been composed.

Motivic Variation

The composer's fascination with fitting things together is at the heart of all Renaissance music. In the last chapter, the motive was varied only by transposition, and only occurred from time to time. In this chapter, we observe more obsessive repetition of motives made possible by rhythmic variation. Zarlino says, "Because this style of counterpoint is very difficult, certain liberties are permitted. One may at times write lines not easy to sing which would not be written in ordinary circumstances." Occasionally you will see that in his enthusiasm for playing the game, the Renaissance composer not only writes difficult lines, but permits himself infractions of rules. One way to gain greater flexibility for this type of challenge is to syncopate in half notes as described below.

Augmented and Diminished Fourth Species

In some of the following examples we see fourth-species-like figures taking place at other rhythmic levels than we expect (i.e., in other note values). In m. 7 of Example 9-2 we find syncopated half notes (written also as tied quarters) in which the preparation, the dissonance, and the resolution are half as long as they are supposed to be in "normal" fourth species. These have been labeled "PDR" in some of the examples that follow. Because the note values are smaller, we call this "diminished" fourth species. When the note values are larger, as in Example 9-3, we call the fourth species "augmented." In diminished fourth species the anticipation and lower neighbor are almost never used (they would be sixteenth notes), while in augmented fourth species the anticipation and lower neighbor are twice as long.

Both augmented and diminished fourth species occur often, sometimes in the same place, as in the cadence of Morley's Example 8-8, where the real suspension is in augmented values and the resolution is embellished with a diminished fake suspension.

Study of Treatise Examples

The term contraponto ad imitatione means that the short rhythmic motive in the counterpoint imitates the CF; usually the motive is a faster version of the initial CF notes (some of the foregoing Series C exercises were examples of this). In the following two examples, the principle of imitating the CF is carried to the extreme: *all* the notes in the added line come from the CF! Tigrini presents two such examples, using the opening of Kyrie XI (slightly altered at the end). In the first example he has permitted himself similar motion to a fifth at the twelfth CF note. In the second, he has managed to place all nineteen notes of the CF twice against itself, transposed up a fifth. He can do this by fiddling with the rhythm, squeezing the tune into a shorter time span, so that the notes that are dissonant occur in legal metric positions. Note the illegal similiar octave in Example 9-1b.

Example 9-1 (Tigrini)

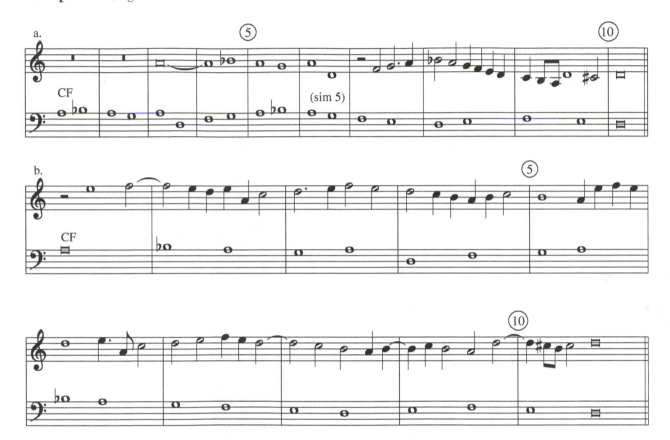

Thomas Morley acknowledges that this kind of exercise doesn't necessarily sound so good, even if it is a technical tour de force: "You may also upon this plainesong make a way wherein the descant may sing everie note of the ground twise, which though it shew some sight and maistry, yet will not be so sweet in the eare as others." Note his extensive use of diminished fourth species.

Example 9-2 (Morley)

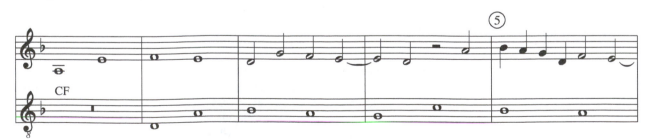

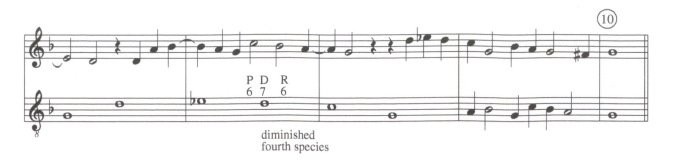

diminished
fourth species

In Morley's other examples of imitating the CF notes, the two voices are actually in a first-species canon for a while (see chapter 12).

Example 9-3 (Morley)

Note the unusual cadence in the first example, and rhythmically augmented fourth species in both. Regarding the second example, Morley tells the Pupil that he is allowed to substitute the ascending fifth for the fourth, adding, "But there is a worse fault in it which you have not espied, which is, the rising from the fift to the eight in the seventh and eight notes, but the point excuseth it, although it be not allowed for anie of the best in two parts, but in mo [re]parts it might be suffered." In other words, the similar motion to the octave is grudgingly allowed because of the obligation of imitation.

Example 9-4, by Banchieri, is really a little motet on a slightly different version of a chant tune we have used: "Ecce sacerdos magnus." Here some of the short motives in the added line are derived from successive phrases of the CF, while others are original. Notice which are which. The short motives are repeated over the slower-moving CF so that the phrases in the two lines keep pace with each other. Rests, rhythmic alterations, and transpositions at intervals other than the fourth, fifth, or octave make the job easier. The note on the downbeat of m. 6 should be considered part of a fourth-species dissonant suspension, but with the patient rearticulated instead of tied (we will use repeated notes in chapter 11). You might find it interesting to look at Palestrina's four-part mass on the same CF (an excerpt appears in chapter 18).

A particularly nice feature of this piece is the way the third statement of "et inventus est justus" is extended with a <u>melisma</u> into the final cadence. It makes a little climax on the last word "justus" in the same way that the repetitions of a short phrase in Victoria's "O magnum mysterium" lead to a climax at the cadence.

Example 9-4 (Banchieri) (Note values in this example have been doubled.) ("Behold the high priest, who in his time pleased the Lord and was found to be just.")

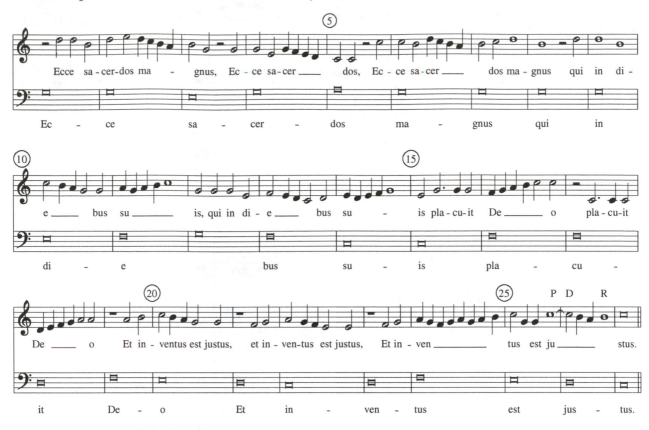

In Example 9-5a, which repeats the la-sol-fa-re-mi motive, Pontio permits himself an exceptional 9-8 suspension (at *). Of Example 9-5b he says, "Notice how the counterpoint uses the same notes as the plainsong; notice likewise how re-mi-fa-sol-la appears in different ways." In mm. 5-7 of the CF he has used direct repetition of the whole combination (intervals labeled). While this might be interpreted as a mistake according to Zarlino and Artusi, the repetition contributes to a nice series of ascending high points, marked in the example by ∧s.

Example 9-5 (Pontio)

a.

b.

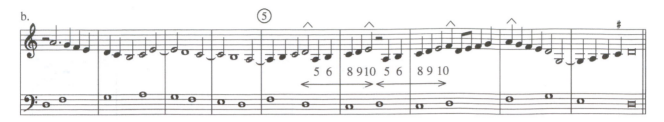

For another example of counterpoint that imitates the CF, look back at Example 2-3 by Zarlino (used to introduce species). As in Banchieri's little motet, Zarlino picks up successive groups of notes from the CF to use as motives. The notes may be the same pitch classes as those in the CF, or they may be transposed in such a way as to maintain the same interval succession. You can go through and bracket other segments of the contrapuntal line whose notes are derived from the CF.

In Banchieri's example of <u>contraponto</u> <u>ostinato</u> (Ex. 9-6), he puts repetitions of ut-re-mi-fa-sol-la over the same Kyrie he used for all his species examples. He says that outside of the special case of this "artifice," it is bad to repeat the same passage over and over in the same pitch location. Note also that the rule against the major sixth descending is a casualty of the ostinato artifice.

Example 9-6 (Banchieri)

Zarlino gives one example (Ex. 9-7) in which the added line consists entirely of repetitions of a single original six-note pattern. Although most often all three elements (notes, rhythm, and consonances) are varied, you can find some places where all three are repeated (for two or three whole notes). We have said that this is OK as long as there is intervening material. In m. 12 the motive seems to have been abandoned. This is a solmization trick; the motive consists of la-sol-fa-re-fa-mi. The first four notes of the motive are la-sol-fa-re in the hexachord on *G*, and the last two are fa-mi in the hexachord on *C* (see Appendix 3). Diminished fourth species is marked with an asterisk.

Example 9-7 (Zarlino)

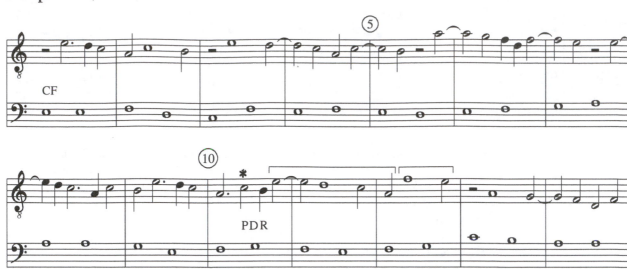

Here are two freer examples from Banchieri (Ex. 9-8). In both, the "motive" actually consists of two smaller motives that are connected in different ways. In the second example the repeated-note motive is more characteristic of instrumental writing than of vocal writing. (Note the illegal dissonant downbeat at "X.")

Example 9-8a (Banchieri)

Example 9-8b (Banchieri)

Melodic Inversion and Retrograde

Melodic inversion is a common means of varying a motive, as you will see in the examples below. Inversion can be made in many ways. The preferred methods are: 1) make the inversion replicate the tone-semitone positions, in order, of the original (Ex. 9-9a and b); 2) start the inverted melody on the same note as the original (Ex. 9-9c); 3) make the inversion fill the same space as the original (that is, it has the same high and low points—Ex. 9-9d); or, less preferable, make the inversion have as little as possible to do with the original (Ex. 9-9e).

Example 9-9a (Rodio)

Example 9-9b (Angleria)

Example 9-9c (Rodio)

Example 9-9d (Angleria)

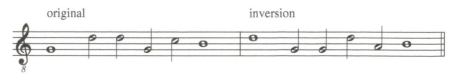

Example 9-9e

another inversion of Ex. 9-9c.

Rocco Rodio also gives examples of crab repetitions, that is, the theme in retrograde:

Example 9-9f

Here is how Morley describes melodic inversion: "The reverting of a point…is, when a point is made rising or falling and then turned to go the contrarie waie as manie notes as it did ye first" (Note that the inverted form of the melody in Example 9-10 is also rhythmically altered. Note also the cadence; such similar motion to the octave is normal in mixed values or three or more parts, but unusual in one part added to a CF).

Example 9-10 (Morley)

Study of Repertoire Examples

The treatise examples presented above should help us to analyze and understand repertoire examples. Although counterpoint with a motive against a CF is a staple of the Renaissance musical diet, it occurs mostly in four parts. Two-voice counterpoint with a motive is found very rarely in the repertoire of the second half of the sixteenth century, probably because it was no big deal: once they had studied the techniques you have worked on in the preceding chapters, good musicians could improvise a line against a CF. Morley calls such improvisation done by singers "descanting" and says it is a preliminary basic skill necessary to a composer.

Benedictus from Josquin's Missa "Hercules dux Ferrarie"

Our first example is from the generation before Zarlino, and it contains some features Zarlino would like and some he wouldn't. Josquin's Benedictus is based on a CF that is derived from the vowels of his patron's name and title: Hercules Dux Ferrarie (see Appendix 3). The text has been left out so you can focus on the musical techniques Josquin uses.

This movement of the mass is divided into three little duos in the Dorian mode. In each duo the CF starts on a different note: it is transposed up from the final to the fifth, and then to the final of the mode an octave higher. The added voice in each duo is in a different range: the first is excessive Dorian above, the second excessive Hypodorian below, and the third is mixed Dorian and Hypodorian above. In each there is a little bit of crossing. Note that the first two duos use the "fake" suspension at the cadence, and the third uses augmented fourth species at the cadence. There is a dissonant <u>appoggiatura</u> (an unprepared accented dissonance) in the first duo (asterisk), rare for Josquin and never used later in the century.

In the first two duos, short motives appear in transposition (they have been bracketed). These motives follow Zarlino's rule about varying repetition, but the motive in the third duo does not. The repetition in the third duo is of the kind Zarlino decries: two and a half times the same combination with no intervening material. The principle of repeating a short segment before a longer, climactic, third statement is one we have seen in Victoria's "O magnum mysterium" and in Banchieri's Example 9-4, but here the repetitions are not varied.

Example 9-11 (Josquin Desprez)

Benedictus from Missa "Ferdinandus dux Calabriae" by Jacquet of Mantua

The CF of this Benedictus by Jacquet of Mantua (Ex. 9-12) is also based on the vowels in the name of the dedicatee, in this case Ferdinand, Duke of Calabria:

Fer	di	nan	dus	dux	Ca	la	bri	ae
re	mi	fa	ut	ut	fa	fa	mi	re

Published in 1540, this piece is similar to the Josquin example from Missa "Hercules dux Ferrarie" above. For a discussion of text underlay in this piece, see Appendix 1. The CF is repeated three times, each time in a higher part of the mode (starting on final, fifth, and final), each time with a different voice added in a different range. What is different here is that the sections are run together (<u>elided</u>), and Jacquet varies the repetitions of the motives.

In the example, the motives have been bracketed and labeled. Each of the three sections is characterized by a different motive (A, B, and C). A fourth motive appears in all of the sections (Z), and free material leads to the cadence. In the cadences of the first and third sections a "fake" suspension is used, and in the second, augmented fourth species.

In the first section, the link between motives A and Z is varied, and in fact this link is like an abbreviated A itself (step down in quarters, skip up). In the second section, motive B is slightly varied at the end, the last note turning up the first time, down the other times. The third B is labeled B′ because the first skip is a minor sixth up instead of a minor third up (however, the syllable names of the first two notes are the same: re-fa). In the third section, motive Z is slightly altered; why do you think Jacquet used this altered version of Z (labeled Z′)? Motives C and Z′ are always connected the same way, but we don't consider them a single longer motive because Z has appeared by itself earlier. Note the too-short resolution of the suspension in m. 20 (asterisk).

Example 9-12 (Jacquet of Mantua) ("Blessed is he who comes in the name of the Lord.")

"Vater unser" by Caspar Othmayr

The particular mix of breves and semibreves in the CF of the next example, by Caspar Othmayr, is the conventional presentation of "Vater unser." The piece has one brief use of a repeating motive over the fourth phrase of the chorale tune (bracketed in mm. 18–23). You have already seen this kind of repetition, which allows two statements of the words in the added voice over only one in the CF, in Banchieri's little motet (Ex. 9-4). The repetitions here allow for a remarkably long ascent in the added line (note that the voices are crossed in m. 18, at the start of the ascent), leading through the high *F* on "hilf" (help) to the high *G* on "bitt" (pray). This use of transposed repetition for an expressive purpose is quite common in the Renaissance. You may want to look at three-part settings of this same chorale tune by Praetorius in chapter 14.

Note a few voice-leading mannerisms: Othmayr uses a quarter-note *D* echappée in m. 11. Two other mannerisms, normally not found in writing against a CF, are commonly found in writing two parts in free rhythm: the d3q in m. 16, and the similar motion to a fifth on the downbeat of m. 26. We will study these in chapter 11. Note also that voice-leading rules seem not to apply after a fermata: the new phrase starting on m. 31 has to be understood as unconnected to the preceding phrase.

Example 9-13 (Othmayr) ("Our Father in heaven you who call us all to be brothers alike, and to call to you, and who will receive our prayer: let us not pray with our mouths alone, but help it come from the depths of our heart.")

Analysis and Performance

The labeling of motives is a preliminary technique for the analysis of any music. It is also useful in preparing a performance of a piece. For instance, in the Cabezón hymn setting (Ex. 9-17), there is repetition in mm. 5–8. In order to bring out the repetitions, we need to know what the motive consists of, where it begins and ends. Then we can "breathe" or lift slightly between statements of the motive. Here are three interpretations students have made in class:

Example 9-14

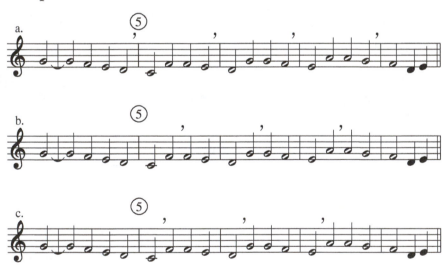

Sing these examples, breaking slightly at each comma. Which one do you like best? It is not necessary to say one is right and the others are wrong: each one feels different. The first coordinates phrasing with meter (we break right before the downbeat), but has the problem of "lifting" right after a dissonance in m. 6. The second coordinates phrasing with the repeated note, and the third coordinates phrasing with the skip. The second and third carry the phrase across the bar line, so the phrasing doesn't coincide with the attacking breves. This makes b and c more independent of the CF, probably a good thing.

Sometimes, even when there is clear repetition of motives, breathing or otherwise articulating the beginning and end of the motive is out of the question. In such cases the motive is more of a structural building block than an occasion for phrasing. Take the motives that have been labeled in Example 9-15: there is no way to break after the bracket that identifies motive A in m. 15, or the bracket that identifies motive B in m. 23. In the analysis exercises that follow, you are asked to identify motives that repeat and, in a separate activity, to think about slight breaks between phrases.

The identification of motives in Renaissance music is an important activity because it will train you to see beneath the surface of the never-ending flow of the line. When you have made decisions about exactly what it is that repeats, then you can decide how to perform the repetitions. You can divide the piece into long sections on the basis of register, modal emphasis (exact vs. inexact transpositions), and predominant motive. For now you have only one line to look at, but you will encounter similar exercises in three- and four-part music.

Analysis of Repertoire Examples

These two ricercars by Diego Ortiz (Exs. 9-15 and 9-16) are probably examples of how viol players improvised on a CF (in this case a famous tune originally used for dancing called "La Spagna"). However, Ortiz's settings are artfully worked out and can teach us a lot about principles of composition. The repetition of motives can create many expressive effects: a sense of section if they are repeated directly for a while, of starting over again if something different has intervened, of building up if transposed successively higher, or of relaxing if transposed down.

Example 9-15 (Ortiz)

Two short motives (A and B) have been labeled the first time each occurs.

1. Bracket and label other occurrences of A and B in Example 9-15. These short tunes are sometimes embedded in longer segments that repeat.

2. Bracket and label the longest segments that repeat. If motives A and B are contained in longer repeating segments, you will have to put longer brackets over the short ones. It seems unlikely that anyone could improvise such long segments.

3. You will have noticed that the motives are transposed at intervals other than the fourth, fifth, and octave, and that they occur inverted; **distinguish exact from inexact (diatonic) transpositions, and note inversions.** The very striking direct repetitions in the upper part at the end are legal according to Zarlino and Artusi—why?

4. Decide where small "breaths" could be taken to articulate phrasing. Specifically, what's the right place to breathe in m. 26? why? in m. 28? why?

Example 9-16 (Ortiz)

The next counterpoint on "La Spagna" is quite different from the preceding one. It contains several instances in which a whole contrapuntal combination is repeated exactly after intervening material. Note hard mistakes in m. 24 (a too-short resolution) and m. 35 (a dissonant upper neighbor, characteristic of instrumental music).

1. Identify and label repeating motives in Example 9-16. Find the longest segments that repeat, bracket them, and tag them with letters.

2. Decide where small "breaths" could be taken to articulate phrasing.

3. Compare the two Ortiz ricercars. Imagine that Ortiz had the same kind of assignment you have had: to write different solutions to the same CF (in fact, he wrote four more ricercars on the same CF). Note where the same motive occurs in the same location; where it occurs in different locations; where new motives are introduced and how they are repeated. You could use the reductive method explained in chapter 7 to show the large-scale patterns of contour in these examples. How do recurring motives interact with high and low points?

Example 9-17 (Cabezón) (From Antonio de Cabezón, *Obras de Musica para tecla, arpa, y vihuela* (1578). Edited by Felipe Pedrell, revised by H. Angles. *Monumentos de la Musica Espanola*, vol. 27. Barcelona: Instituto Espanol de Musicologia, 1966).

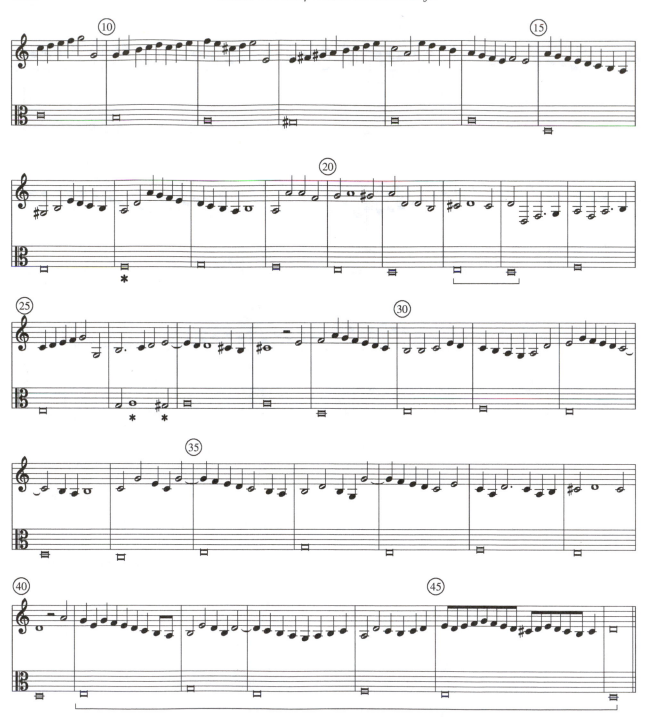

In this setting of "Ave Maris Stella" for organ (Ex. 9-17), Antonio de Cabezón has departed slightly from the version of the tune given in chapter 1. Changes of single notes have been marked with asterisks; repetitions of CF segments have been indicated with brackets. Because this is an instrumental piece, the composer can permit himself an unusually wide range.

1. Label different motives that predominate in successive sections. Try to find the longest segments that repeat. Several motives are repeated with different metric placement. Note the metric shifts.

2. Decide where small "breaths" could be taken to articulate phrasing.

Repertoire for Further Study

In addition to more ricercars by Ortiz on "La Spagna" and more organ hymns by Cabezón, you will find interesting two-part music on a CF in *Musica Rinascimentale Siciliane* listed in the bibliography. In addition, you might want to look at the 125 counterpoints on "La Spagna" by Costanzo Festa. These have been written up in an article by James Agee. Some of Festa's counterpoints contain motives whose solmization syllables are derived from someone's name, some consist of quodlibets of popular tunes, and some are ostinati.

Writing Against Breves

You can now write out your CF in breves, as in the preceding repertoire examples. There are in effect two downbeats in each breve, as if the CF were in tied whole notes, and you need to consider the species in those terms:

    1. Each breve contains two whole notes, and both must be consonant.

    2. Each breve contains four half notes, of which the second and fourth may be dissonant if passing, and the first and third must be consonant.

    3. Each breve contains eight quarters, of which the second, fourth, sixth, and eighth may be dissonant if passing or lower neighbors; the odd-numbered ones must all be consonant (to d3q we must add d5q and d7q). The dissonant cambiata may only begin on the fifth quarter; the double neighbor can only begin on the fifth quarter.

    4. Ordinary dissonant fourth species can only be used from the end of one breve to the beginning of the next (but see below for exception).

    5. The general rule for unisons is still to avoid having both voices move to a unison at the same time.

    6. Hard rule relaxed: From now on you may use augmented and diminished fourth species at cadences. You *must* **use augmented fourth species or a fake suspension at the final cadence when writing against breves.** In augmented fourth species the rhythmic values are all doubled, resulting in a sort of written-out ritardando.

Example 9-18

a. (from Ex. 9-4)

b. (from Ex. 9-12)

c. (from Ex. 9-15)

Sometimes the leading tone (i.e., the resolution of the suspension) is itself embellished with a fake suspension in diminished values (half as long as normal):

Example 9-18d (from Ex. 9-16)

You can use augmented fourth species anywhere in the course of a CF to suggest a cadence; see for instance Example 9-12, mm. 10–12. Do not use diminished fourth species unless you are dealing with some other very challenging obligation. In such a case, explain to your teacher the nature of the obligation.

Repeated Half Notes

In this chapter we have seen several examples of repeated half notes, which have been forbidden in the counterpoint you have done until now. Repeated half notes are simply a rearticulation within a whole note, and treatise examples seem to avoid whole notes in the middle of a counterpoint. However, repeated notes are widely used in Renaissance repertoire, mostly for two reasons:

1. to support text syllables in a natural rhythmic declamation, usually in the opening of a soggetto (see Ex. 9-4 by Banchieri and Ex. 9-12 by Jacquet);
2. to build a characteristic rhythmic motive in an instrumental context (see Ex. 9-17 by Cabezón);
3. to start a new soggetto on the same note as the end of a previous phrase (see Ex. 9-13 by Othmayr, at mm. 20 and 35);
4. to break up an illegal duration (e.g., a single note five quarters long is impossible, but a half note and a dotted half note on the same pitch solves the problem neatly).

Hard rule relaxed: You may now use a half note on the same pitch as the one preceding under one of the foregoing circumstances. You might want to write your teacher a note of explanation.

Exercise Series **D:** Complete CFs in Breves

You may choose from the Series D exercises on pp. 113–114, altering the CF by putting it in breves, and using not only the motive as given, but inversions of the motive as well. While the uninverted motive should occur only in the transpositions given, the inverted motive may start on any note. You should be aware of whether the inverted motive replicates in order the tone-semitone positions of the original (label those that do not). Because the CF has now expanded to twice its length, and because of the new freedom afforded by the use of the inverted motive, you must make **at least five placements** of the motive in each of the lines above and below.

Other Modeling Exercises

You may now draw your materials from other sources. For instance, the CF could be another chant melody, some other popular tune, or "carved" out of the letters of someone's name. The requirements for a CF are that it end with a step descending to the final and (less important) that it be modally clear. My name, for instance, does not make a good CF because although it is pretty clearly Dorian, it doesn't cadence properly: Peter Norman Schubert = re re sol fa (or la) ut re.

For the faster-moving motive you could:

1. derive a short motive from the first notes of the CF
2. fit all the notes of the CF *twice* (or more times) against the CF (see Exx. 9-1 and 9-2)
3. derive new motives from *successive* phrases of the CF (see. Exx 9-4 and 2-3)
4. compose the counterpoint using exclusively repetitions of a short motive, like the hexachord or la sol fa re mi ("ostinato"—see Exx. 9-5a and 9-6), transposed or untransposed
5. use a short bit of a popular tune ("la sol fa re mi" or "Surfin' USA")

For any of the preceding you need to decide with your teacher how much freedom to allow yourself: Can you use transpositions other than those at the fourth, fifth, or octave? Can you replace a skip of a fourth with a skip of a fifth (cf. Ex. 9-3 and Exercise D4, p. 111)? Can you present the diminished subject in inversion? Can you alter the rhythm of the diminished subject? Can you use intermediate cadences (ones that occur during the course of the CF, like those in Example 9-17 by Cabezón or those in Example 9-13, Othmayr's "Vater unser")? If you are to include intermediate cadences, do the exercises in chapter 10 as practice.

Finally, can you, in the name of some "obligation," commit errors knowingly? You should restrict yourself to similar motion to perfect intervals (as in Exx. 9-1 by Tigrini, 9-10 by Morley and 9-13 by Othmayr), and the use of diminished fourth species in the course of the example. In these cases you should write the teacher a note explaining that you are aware of the infraction and that *the point excuseth it!*

10

Cadence Formulas in Two Voices

Y ou have seen how the CF provides opportunities for using motives; it also provides opportunities for making cadences, which have until now been used only at the ends of pieces. It is possible to make cadences during the course of a piece, as we saw in the longer pieces by Ortiz and Cabezòn.

The word <u>cadence</u> comes from the Latin *cadere*, "to fall," referring to the falling of the voice at the end of a sentence. It is usually an opportunity for a relaxing of intensity, but not always. In a single line of chant, the fall is usually by step, occasionally by third, to the final. In two parts, we accompany the cadential descent to the final by a line that moves in contrary motion toward the same pitch class.

Proper Cadences

Cadences (called *Closes* in Renaissance England) are melodic formulas that end phrases. In proper cadences, each of the two voices heads for a goal note of the same pitch class (i.e., both voices head for a *D*, whether an octave apart or a unison). At the end of a piece this note should always be the final, but during the course of a piece we may encounter cadences to other notes than the final. The standard model cadence inherited from the fifteenth century has a stepwise descent in the lower voice (the tenor, or CF), while the upper voice makes a stepwise ascent to the note an octave above the goal note. If the cadence happens in first species, Zarlino calls it a "simple" cadence (Ex. a). If the upper voice contains a syncopation and dissonant suspension, it is called "diminished" (Ex. b). This latter type is preferable, the syncopation acting as a signal that a cadence is coming. In the model cadence the suspension in the upper voice is always a 7–6 suspension over the penultimate note of the lower voice.

Illustration of Proper Cadences

a.   simple

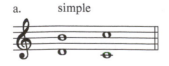

b.   diminished

The "Steps of the Cadence"

In the model proper cadence, the voice with the dissonant suspension is the upper voice, called the *cantus* or *discantus*. Ornithoparchus says, "The *Close* of the *Discantus* made with three Notes, shall always have the last upward.... The *Close* of the *Tenor*, doth also consist of three Notes, the last always descending." Thomas de Sancta Maria labels the members of the cadential suspension more precisely, calling the consonant preparation in the upper voice the "first step," the dissonance the "second step," and the resolution of the dissonance the "third step." The goal note, he says, is "after the cadence." To make a diminished cadence, the CF note two before the end (the antepenultimate note) must facilitate the consonant preparation of the suspension. That is, it must be consonant with the goal note, since that is where the resolution of the suspension is about to step back up to (Ex. 10-1a). If the third note before the end is not consonant with the final, it will be impossible to set up the suspension, as shown in Example 10-1b. In such a case, we must use a fake suspension.

Example 10-1

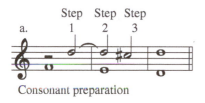

In the model cadence, the vertical interval immediately preceding the octave on the goal note is always a *major* sixth, and the melodic motion of the upper voice or the lower voice is always a semitone. The semitone occurs naturally in the upper voice when we cadence to *C* or *F*. It occurs naturally in the lower voice when we cadence to *E* or *B* (when the semitone occurs in the lower voice we call it a <u>phrygian</u> <u>cadence</u> because that is how phrygian pieces will normally end—however, the cadence to *B* is rarely used). In Example 10-2 the model cadences with natural notes are shown.

Example 10-2

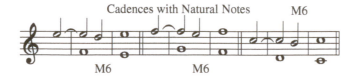

Cadential *Ficta*

If we cadence to a note other than *C* or *F*, or *B* or *E*, we must use accidentals to ensure the semitone motion in one voice. We use *C♯* to approach *D*, *F♯* to approach *G*, and *G♯* to approach *A*, as shown in Example 10-3. We can also use *B♭* to approach *A* in the lower voice if we want a transposed Phrygian cadence.

Example 10-3

In the Renaissance these accidentals were often not written, but we are sure they were performed at cadences. One meaning of the term *musica ficta* is those alterations made where none are written, including cadential semitone motions and the $B\flat$ used to avoid the tritone. Always raise the leading tone in cadences in the Dorian ($C\sharp$), Mixolydian ($F\sharp$), and Aeolian ($G\sharp$) pairs of modes.

Inverting the Model Cadence

The voice part in the model cadence gives its name to its melodic function even when it occurs in another voice. (The musicologist Bernhard Meier refers to these functions as *cantizans* and *tenorizans*.) Thus the cadential function of the *cantus* (i.e., the soprano) in the following examples occurs in the tenor, and the tenor function is taken by the *cantus*. In these cases the major sixth is replaced by the minor third or the minor tenth.

Example 10-4

"Scale Degrees"

In order to deal with evaded cadences (in which one voice doesn't go where it ought) and intermediate cadences (going to other notes than the final), it is useful to refer to the goal note as "$\hat{1}$" as if it were the "tonic scale degree" for a moment. Then we can refer to the *cantus* motion in the model cadence as $\hat{8}$–$\hat{7}$–$\hat{8}$ and the tenor motion as $\hat{2}$–$\hat{1}$. Later on we will also have use for other such "scale degrees."

The Bass Cadence

In music in three, four, or more parts, the normal bass motion is $\hat{5}$–$\hat{1}$. In two voices, however, the lower voice can sometimes have this bass function instead of the normal tenor function. Zarlino says such cadences are "used occasionally" in two parts.

In this kind of cadence the normal *cantus* motion makes a 4–3 suspension above the bass. Note that in this type of cadence, **similar motion to the octave or unison on the goal note note is now permitted.**

Example 10-5

Exercise Series C:

10-C1   In Example 10-6, Zarlino strings together a series of cadences to *E* and *F*. Label each one, identifying the goal note and the *cantizans* and *tenorizans* functions.

10-C2   Look at the ends of phrases in Exx. 1-3b, c, d, e, f, i, j, and/or k, and note which will *not* permit the use of a proper three-step cadence.

10-C3   Against the others, improvise or write the three *cantizans* notes.

10-C4   Continue the line below the given CF, making proper cadences, finding tenor motions. The goal note in the added voice may be of any duration.

Example 10-6

(Zarlino)

Exercise 10-C4

1.

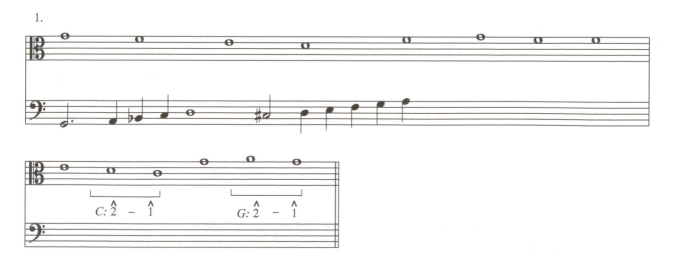

Evaded Cadences

In general, when we hear a suspension, whether a 4–3 or 7–6 above or a 2–3 below, we can imagine that the preparation note is going to be the cadential goal, and we expect to hear it in both voices, as in the proper cadences described above. While proper cadences are used to punctuate major divisions in the music, "intermediate divisions in the harmony and text" require <u>evaded</u> cadences. In evaded cadences, the expected goal note is not sounded in one or both voices. Zarlino says that instead of closing on the octave or unison, evaded cadences close on a "fifth, third, or other consonance"

1. If the voice with $\hat{7}$ goes to $\hat{8}$, the voice that properly goes $\hat{2}$–$\hat{1}$ can go $\hat{2}$–$\hat{3}$ or $\hat{2}$–$\hat{5}$ (above only), $\hat{2}$–$\hat{6}$, or (rarely) $\hat{2}$–$\hat{4}$. It may also simply go nowhere: $\hat{2}$–rest. The voice that properly goes $\hat{5}$–$\hat{1}$ can go $\hat{5}$–$\hat{4}$, $\hat{5}$–$\hat{3}$, $\hat{5}$–$\hat{6}$, or (above only) $\hat{5}$–$\hat{5}$. It may also go nowhere: $\hat{5}$–rest. Using rests to evade cadences is especially good if the next-sounding note after the rest is the beginning of a repeating or otherwise important motive.

2. If $\hat{2}$ or $\hat{5}$ goes to $\hat{1}$, then the voice with $\hat{7}$ can evade the cadence by going elsewhere than $\hat{8}$. It may continue to descend $\hat{7}$–$\hat{6}$ or skip $\hat{7}$–$\hat{3}$; It is *very rare* for $\hat{7}$ to be followed by a rest.

3. In the foregoing evasions one of the two voices went to the goal note, but it is possible for *neither* note to achieve its goal. If the voice with $\hat{7}$ doesn't go to $\hat{8}$ (e.g., $\hat{7}$–$\hat{5}$ or $\hat{7}$–$\hat{2}$), then the voice with $\hat{2}$ or $\hat{5}$ may go elsewhere as well. In these cases it is hard to tell if a cadence was even intended. Any sixth on a weak beat could be preparing a cadence, and when several steps of the CF descend, it is possible to set up a cadence with a 7–6 suspension, then to evade it by simply continuing the chain of suspensions. This raises the analytical question: When is it an evaded cadence and when just any old suspension? It is hard to tell without a text. Look back at Zarlino's fifth-species examples (Example 7-4a-d) and label all evaded cadences. As we have said, the fake suspensions in Diruta's fourth-species examples turn out to be evaded cadences (see Ex. 6-5).

Illustration of Evaded Cadences

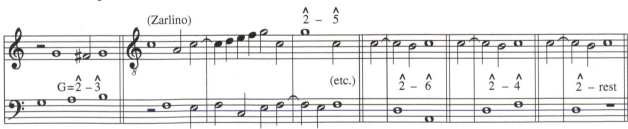

Finding Cadence Opportunities in a CF

If you are making a cadence against a CF,

1. a *descending step* in the CF can be taken as $\hat{2}$–$\hat{1}$ (proper) or $\hat{5}$–$\hat{4}$ (evaded, usable only when the CF is below) or, idiomatically, $\hat{4}$–$\hat{3}$ (usable only above, and *rare in two parts*! See Ex. 11-6 for a discussion of this idiom).
2. an *ascending step* can be $\hat{2}$–$\hat{3}$ (evaded) or $\hat{5}$–$\hat{6}$ (evaded).
3. a *descending third* can be $\hat{5}$–$\hat{3}$ (evaded).
4. an *ascending third* can be $\hat{2}$–$\hat{4}$ (evaded, and *rare in two parts*!).
5. a *descending fourth* can be $\hat{2}$–$\hat{6}$ (evaded).
6. a *descending fifth* or ascending fourth can be $\hat{5}$–$\hat{1}$ (proper) or $\hat{2}$–$\hat{5}$ (evaded and *only used above*).
7. another way to evade is to just *stay in place*: $\hat{2}$–$\hat{2}$ or $\hat{5}$–$\hat{5}$.

Illustration of Cadence Opportunities

Analysis Exercises:

10-C5   Zarlino says that cadences are used to punctuate "a significant phrase of text." A look at some examples will give you an idea of how composers use cadences to punctuate text. In Example 9-12, each of the three large sections is punctuated by a proper cadence. In Example 9-13, the first phrase of text ends with a comma and a cadence to *D*. Look at how the other phrases are punctuated musically.

10-C6   Analysis: Look for cadences in Palestrina's "Deposuit" (Ex. 15-8). Are they evaded or proper? Do they punctuate a meaningful segment of text?

10-C7   Likewise, look for cadences in Victoria's "O magnum" (Ex. 20-3a).

10-C8   Look for cadences in a Bach chorale. Label *cantus*, tenor, and bass motions.

Writing Exercises:

In Exercises 10-C9 and 10-C10, find opportunities for and realize at least five cadences. Label each with its goal note and "scale degrees," and say whether they are evaded or proper. In Exercise 10-C10, the final cadence cannot be the standard model cadence.

Exercise 10-C9

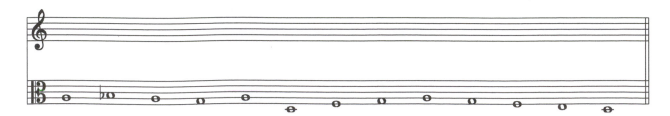

Exercise 10-C10

Cadential Goals

If you use intermediate cadences in a modeling exercise such as those suggested at the end of chapter 9, you must decide which notes to use as goals. Theorists disagree about which goal notes are appropriate for intermediate cadences in any given mode. Certainly the final and the fifth above are OK. Few authors encourage the use of the cadence to *B*, probably because the fifth above *B* is diminished. Zarlino, however, says the final, fifth, and third above the final are to be used in every mode including the Phrygian, and he gives two-voice examples for each of the twelve modes, illustrating these cadences.

Look ahead at Example 18-8 to see how three composers chose different cadence opportunities in the same CF. This is an area in which you must experiment—the results will differ according to the principal mode of the piece.

Two Parts in Mixed Values

At last we abandon the CF and write both parts in freely mixed values. The principles we use are mainly the same, but the rhythmic level by which we evaluate dissonance can change. Also, for the first time we have situations in which dissonance is not approached by oblique motion.

Hard Rules

1. When half notes occur against half notes or quarters against quarters, treat as first species. All notes that attack together must be consonant with each other.

2. When quarters occur against halves, treat as second species or diminished fourth species.
    a. Even-numbered quarters may be dissonant if passing.
    b. Rarely, a quarter under these circumstances may be a neighbor.
    c. Diminished fourth species may be used freely, although it is more common in the lighter styles. The agent is usually the weak half note. Remember that syncopated quarters are still illegal, and so the preparation will occur without the syncopation (i.e., from a dotted half note). The dot can only be dissonant if the resolution is treated as diminished fourth species.

3. Similar motion to a perfect interval is now OK in two parts as long as one of the two voices moves by step and as long as the notes immediately preceding the perfect interval form a consonance and last a half note or longer. Illustration c is wrong because the *D* in the upper voice is too short. Ill.d is wrong because the *C* is dissonant. Ill.e is wrong because the *C* is too short *and* dissonant. Ill.f and g are OK in a pinch (see soft rules on pp. 62 and 90).

4. Neither note in the perfect interval approached by similar motion may be the resolution of a dissonance, unless an anticipation is used. However, if the note of resolution is the leading tone in a cadence, it must never be doubled.

5. The note that creates the dissonance in a suspension (the agent) may skip or step to a consonance on the second half-note beat, while the patient is resolving. This does not apply to diminished fourth species, where the agent must stay put.

In order to get practice evaluating dissonance in this new situation, you may want to skip ahead to the puzzle canons before studying idioms and soft rules.

Illustration of Hard Rules

Rule 1.

Rule 2. a.

b.   c.

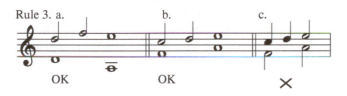

Rule 3. a.   b.   c.

OK   OK   ✕

d.   e.   f.   g.

✕   ✕   but: OK   or: OK
                                        rarely   rarely

Rule 4.

a.   b.

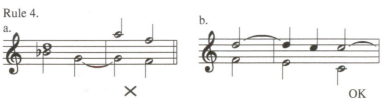

✕   OK

c.

✕

Rule 5.

OK

Repeated Notes

Hard rule relaxed: You may now use repeated quarter notes under certain conditions.

Quarters

Now we may break up a whole note into a dotted half note and a quarter (the quarter must be consonant). Angleria proposes this as a way of avoiding the clunky rhythm of a whole note followed by four quarters (Ex. 11-1).

Example 11-1 (Angleria)

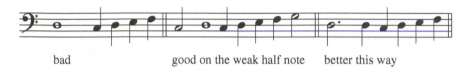

bad   good on the weak half note   better this way

Quarter-Note Anticipations

We may now also use consonant quarter-note anticipations at any time. They may occur in one voice only (Ex. 11-2a and in Diruta's Ex. 5-9, m. 6) or in both voices at the same time (Ex. 11-2b, where the patient is anticipated). The anticipation must be approached by descending step, and may be consonant or dissonant. These most often occur on the second quarter beat and are followed by a quarter and a pair of eighths. In a cadential suspension, the pair of eighths leads to the agent with an anticipation and lower neighbor figure, as in Example 11-2b at the asterisk.

Example 11-2 (Lassus)

*

Half Notes

Hard rule relaxed: You may now have a simultaneously attacked dissonance if it results from the rearticulation of a pitch. This can happen in two ways: D3q can be used against a weak half note if the two halves are understood as parts of a whole note (against which the legal D3q is allowed – Ex. 11-3a); or the agent or the patient in a suspension may be broken in two and rearticulated (Ex. 11-3b). This usually happens when the text has a new syllable, as we saw in Banchieri's Example 9-4.

Example 11-3

Rests

In chapter 8, where we used rests to precede the entrance of a motive, we said that the note before the rest could not form a dissonance with the other CF. Now, however, that rule needs to be updated: Dissonance is allowed at the moment right before the rest as long as the dissonant figure is completed. Thus a passing tone must continue to pass, a neighbor must go back to the note that preceded it, and a suspension must resolve. The basic principle is that one note still governs the behavior of the other, and you have to be clear which is which. In Example 11-4, it is the lower voice that "wins."

Example 11-4

Idioms

The following idiom is a variant of the cadential formula shown in Example 11-2. In it, the agent in the suspension is preceded by three notes in descending stepwise motion, as shown in Example 11-5a. The second of these three notes (the *F* in the example) is dissonant with the preparation of the suspension and may be considered as a legal d3q. (The first of these three notes is x-shaped because it can be either a half or a quarter preceded by another quarter.) Variations of this figure commonly found in repertoire are shown in Example b–e. In Example b, the upper voice skips to the preparation against the d3q. In Example c, the lower voice moves away in quarter notes from the sixth on the downbeat, and parallel sevenths result! This is the only situation in which you'll see that. The preparation of the suspension can also be preceded by an anticipation (Exx. d and e). The voices in this figure can be inverted, making seconds instead of sevenths, as shown in Example f (see also Ex. 12-1). The significance of this figure will become more apparent when we write in three parts, when the agent must often be approached from below.

Example 11-5

Another idiom is the 4-dim.5 "suspension." Like the preceding idiom, this one is found often in chansons, and it is probably a back formation from three-part writing: the "real" agent in the suspension is a *D* below (a lower line is shown in x-shaped notes), and the upper voice is a doubling in tenths. In two-part writing the upper voice "stands for" the real agent (Ex. 11-6). The diminished fifth must resolve to the third, as shown.

Example 11-6

Exercise Series *B*: Find the Errors

Soft Rules

1. Avoid <u>rhythmic</u> <u>unison</u> (i.e., identical rhythmic values) between the two parts for more than five halves or nine quarters maximum. Do not allow the parts to have any whole notes or eighth notes in rhythmic unison. This will ensure rhythmic independence of the parts.

2. Although syncopated half notes (tied quarters) were allowed in chapter 9 against a CF, they should be used infrequently.

Study of Treatise Examples

In Zarlino's example of ways to evade the cadence (Ex. 11-7), some of the above rules are illustrated. "Sim." indicates the newly permitted motion to a perfect interval (hard rule 3). Asterisks (*) show the agent creating the suspension, then leaving, according to hard rule 5. The dagger (†) in m. 30 shows the idiom described in Ex. 11-5. It is now possible for the agents in suspension figures to move from voice to voice as indicated in mm. 2–3.

The letter name of each suggested cadential goal has been indicated. Each cadence but the last is evaded in some way. Leading tones that would have to be altered remain natural. Some of the doubtful cadential goals (like the *A* in m. 12) are actually parts of a chain of sixths.

Example 11-7 (Zarlino)

Canons

A good way to get practice in mixed values is to reconstruct previously composed two-voice <u>canons</u> of which we are only given one voice. The original meaning of the word "canon" is "rule." In music, the rule determines how to make more than one sounding part from a written one. Zarlino shows how the two-voice piece in Example 11-8a can be written as one line with an explanatory instruction, or rule, as shown in Example 11-8b. This rule contains the two necessary bits of information: the <u>time interval</u> after which the second voice begins and the <u>pitch interval</u> (above or below) that separates the first note of the first voice from the first note of the second voice. Here the time interval is two breves and the pitch interval is an octave above.

Example 11-8a (Zarlino)

Example 11-8b Rule "Consequent at the distance of two breves an octave above."

Two singers or players could perform the piece both looking at the same single line of music. The voice starting first is called the <u>guide</u>, the second the <u>consequent</u>. They are also called, respectively, the <u>dux</u> (leader) and the <u>comes</u> (follower). The two-voice combination is called "bound" or "obligated" because every note in the consequent is determined by a corresponding note in the guide. The consequent begins when the first voice reaches a sign called the <u>presa</u>: 𝄋; the person with the consequent reads along the same line of music up to the sign called the <u>coronata</u>: ⌢ (now called a <u>fermata</u>, or stopping-place). Note that the second singer stops at the coronata, holding that note *regardless of its notated length*. The one who starts first (the guide) sings the whole line of music, while the one who starts second (the consequent) performs less music, because the two voices end together.

Example 11-9

(T = time interval; P = pitch interval)

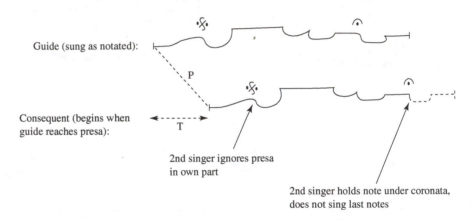

NB: the first vertical interval that is sounded when the second voice enters is not necessarily the same as the pitch interval of imitation. A "canon at the octave" can have a third as its first sounding vertical interval, which is less important than the diagonal interval between the first notes of the two voices.

Solving Puzzle Canons

Solving puzzle canons is fundamental to Renaissance musical thinking, because it entails visualizing ways to combine melodies, imagining music that is not written down. A puzzle canon is one in which you are not given the whole explanatory rule, just the original line of music (the guide), and no rule or just a hint of a rule. You must, by trial and error, find the time and pitch interval at which the second voice (the consequent) begins. You look for a consonance on which to begin, and then you start the tune at that point, looking for mistakes in counterpoint. If you come to a skip from a dissonance, or a dissonant downbeat, etc., you discard that hypothetical consequent and try another. (This exercise has "find the errors" built in!) The solution that works for more than three or four whole-note units will usually work for the whole guide. You can think of the guide as a CF and imagine sliding the consequent around on a piece of clear plastic as you did in chapter 8.

Puzzle Canon Exercise	Solve the puzzle canons below, given this partial hint: The pitch interval of imitation may be a unison, fourth, fifth, or octave above or below, and the time interval may be any *integral* number of whole notes (that is, don't imitate an odd number of half notes later). Add presa and coronata to the lines given below, and write out the complete score in two parts with bar lines. These pieces may not end with standard cadences. (Remember that the first sounding vertical interval may be any consonance.)

Puzzle Canon Exercise

Puzzle Canon Exercise	The canons below are by <u>melodic</u> <u>inversion</u>. Once the consequent has started, its melodic intervals will be the same diatonic size as those of the guide, but will proceed in the direction *opposite* to those of the guide. If you are imagining the consequent on a sheet of clear plastic, you will have to imagine it turned over top to bottom. The time interval of imitation is given by the presa; you need only determine the pitch interval between the first note of the guide and the first note of the consequent. You will find **one solution for each of the following intervals**: the unison, the third above, the fifth above, the sixth below, and the seventh above. You need try only these intervals, but beware: one of the canons has more than one solution. Do not expect conventional cadences, and note that one of the canons contains a dissonant upper neighbor, and another contains a d3q.

Puzzle Canons by Inversion

Writing a Canon from Scratch

Composing a canon is not difficult in principle. The traditional step-by-step method is shown in Example 11-10, a first-species canon. You begin by composing a short fragment as long as the time interval of imitation (a). Then you copy it into the other part, transposing it at the pitch interval of your choice (b). Then you write a counter-melody to the first fragment (c). Then you copy the countermelody into the consequent voice (d). Repeat as desired.

Example 11-10

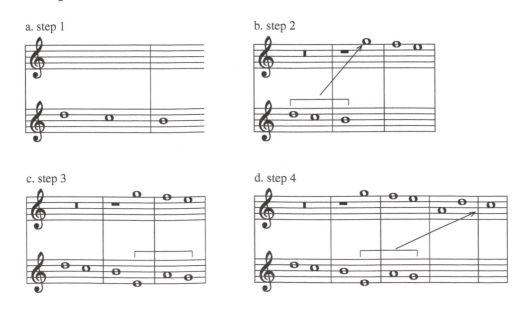

There are some problems with this method. We simply tacked the first counter-melody on to the end of the opening fragment in the leading voice. The countermelody makes a somewhat awkward continuation, even if it makes good counterpoint. You must think of your horizontal obligations as well as your contrapuntal ones.

Another problem is making a cadence. Your canon can easily go on forever; it's harder to make it stop. In order to make a cadence, one of the members of the cadence has to be present in the leading voice before the actual cadence happens. Then that member (say, the "2–1") will show up in the consequent voice later, when the leading voice has the other part of the cadential figure ("8–7–8"). If the canon is at the fourth, as here, then the bit of cadential material that occurs first in the leading voice will be at the wrong transposition level (a fourth lower) when it first occurs.

The way to compose a cadence in a canon is to write backward! Example 11-11 shows the right-to-left step-by-step method of composing a cadence. First you write the cadence (a). Then you transpose part of it ("3–2–1" here) into the leading voice (b). Then you compose a countermelody to the "2–1" fragment (c). You can keep working backward forever too. The problem is to link up the beginning and the end.

Example 11-11

a. step 1

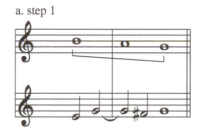

b. step 2

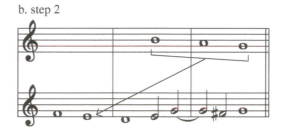

c. step 3

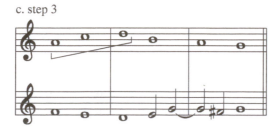

In Example 11-12, we try to connect Examples 11-10 and 11-11. What's needed is some melodic material that will fit in the two boxes in Example 11-12a. It must be the same "tune" but a fourth higher in the second box, and it has to make correct counterpoint in both boxes. (You can't use the countermelody shown in Ex. 11-11— why?) Example 11-12b shows one possible solution in x-shaped notes. Can you find others? Yes, it *is* possible that no solution exists under some circumstances; in that case, you have to set up a different "joint" between the beginning and the cadence.

Example 11-12a

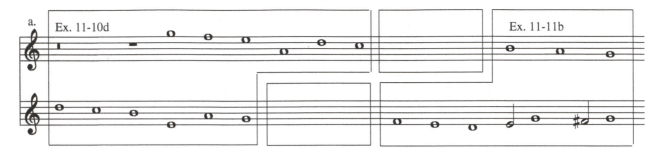

Example 11-12b

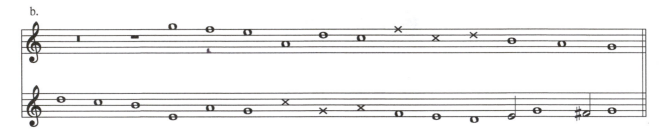

Improvising (or Writing) a Canonic Point of Imitation at the Fifth

The preceding discussion applies to any time or pitch interval. However, there is a very simple method for composing a canonic duo if you are willing to have a short (one whole note) time interval and are willing only to imitate at the fifth.

First Species

This formula for improvising or writing imitation at the fifth above or below comes from Francisco de Montanos. His formula applies to note-against-note writing with a time interval of *one measure*. He formulates his rules as prohibitions: If you plan imitation at the fifth *above*, the guide voice should sing neither a melodic second or fourth ascending nor a third or fifth descending. If you plan imitation at the fifth *below*, the guide should sing neither a second or fourth descending nor a third or fifth ascending (i.e., the opposite of the melodic intervals for imitation above). We can summarize his rules in positive terms (adding the possibility of the unison, which he seems to take for granted) as follows:

imitation at the fifth above: sing or write   1   3↑   5↑   4↓   2↓
imitation at the fifth below: sing or write   1   3↓   5↓   4↑   2↑

This method is foolproof, not only at the beginning but at every subsequent "stepping stone." If you are the leader, you have an easy task: If you're to be imitated at the fifth below, sing *any* succession of unisons, thirds or fifths down, and fourths or seconds up. Montanos' first-species examples are shown in examples on the left side of the page (Exs. 11-13a, d, f, and h). In improvisation, the singer of the consequent voice has the difficult task of hearing the melodic motion of the guide and imitating it *while singing*! And for a real challenge, you can take on both jobs: Play the guide and sing the consequent, or vice versa. You may find it hard to remember what the guide did. The only corollary we must add to these rules is that if you want to avoid similar octaves, don't follow a smaller melodic interval with a larger one in the same direction. That is, if you are imitating at the fifth below, don't follow a step up with a fourth up, or a third down with a fifth down (the latter is illegal, the former merely clumsy).

Example 11-13

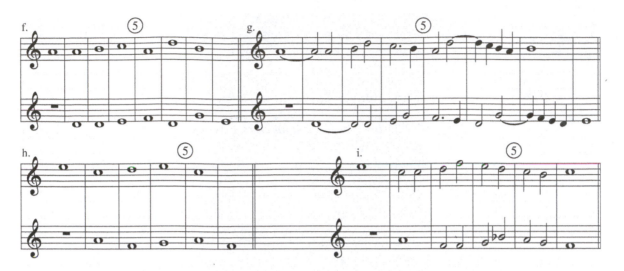

Embellishing the First-Species Structure

In the foregoing examples on the right side we find the same basic structures, but with embellishments added. In Example b we find whole notes broken into two half notes, thirds filled in by passing quarter notes, and weak lower-neighbor quarter notes. In Example c we find a dissonant upper neighbor (correctly used), a fourth filled in with passing quarters, and passing half notes. In Examples g and i we find skips to a consonance.

Note that not all embellishments will work. The skips in Examples g and i only work because you can leap from a sixth to an octave by a third up or because they fit against embellishments already added. For instance, In Example c, Montanos must have known that the passing *D* in the lower voice of m. 4 would sound good against the *B–A* of the upper voice and that the passing half notes would march together in parallel thirds. Here, too, it may be better to write out a few duos in mixed values (i.e., with embellishments) before you attempt to improvise them.

Improvising (or Writing) a Cadence

If you are improvising in first species or in mixed values, you can just stop eventually when you've had enough, but it's not difficult to cadence. Because the cadence takes two measures before the goal note (see Ex. 11-11), you cannot stay strictly canonic using Montanos' formulas, since you are imitating at the semibreve. So you have to break off imitating.

If you're improvising or writing a canon at the fifth below, the leader can take a step up, then skip up a third on the second half note, and tie. The lower singer will hear the dissonant suspension and know not to skip up the third, but to wait and go down on the next strong beat (Ex. 11-14a). If the lower singer does not hear the seventh, he/she will leap up to the *C* (Ex. 11-14b), which is illegal in two parts (but is allowed in three). Another possibility is for the upper voice to take a step up in whole notes and to make a fake suspension; the lower singer again has to move down by step instead of making the fake suspension (Ex. 11-14c). Similarly, if the upper singer is in a chain of thirds in half notes the singer can instruct the lower-voice singer to tie, moving down a step on the downbeat (Ex. 11-14d). This will take some extramusical communication between the singers (a nudge or a wink).

If you are improvising or writing a canon at the fifth above, the guide can sing a whole note, take a step down and leap up a fourth, tying into the next measure. The upper singer should hear that he/she is the agent in a suspension and just wait, not skipping up the fourth but moving down in the next measure (Ex. 11-14e). If, however, the upper singer doesn't get the idea and does skip up the fourth, the guide can step down to a whole note, becoming the agent in a different suspension (Ex. 11-14f). The upper singer can still foil the cadence, but some sign from the guide singer may produce the desired result.

Example 11-14a–f

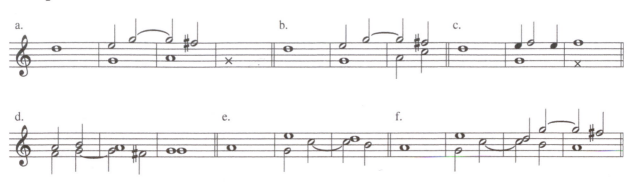

Exercise Series **D:**   Composing a Canon

In the following exercises you may want to set a text. The text will help you develop meaningful rhythmic patterns. See Appendix 1.

Exercise 11-D1   Compose or improvise a first-species canon at the fifth above after one whole note, ending with a cadence (you will use Montanos' rules).

Exercise 11-D2   Compose or improvise a first-species canon at the fifth below after one whole note, ending with a cadence (you will use Montanos' rules).

Exercise 11-D3   Compose a canon at a different time and pitch interval (you will not use Montanos' rules).

Exercise 11-D4   Take one of the canons composed or improvised in the preceding exercises and embellish it as Montanos did his examples.

Exercise 11-D5   Improvise a canon in mixed values using Montanos' rules. That is, think of the principal intervals you will sing, but break whole notes into repeated half notes, tie repeated notes together, fill in thirds and fifths with passing tones, add neighbor motions, etc. You may want to use a text to get some rhythmic ideas.

Exercise 11-D6   *Analysis* Not surprisingly, we often find composed music that uses Montanos' formula. You can see some in Examples 11-12, 12-3, 13-6, 15-4 (mm. 1–2 and 11–12), 16-12b and Exercise 19-C3. Reduce these to first-species framework. The reason we don't find it more often at the beginning of a piece is that composers like to use a longer time interval of imitation at the outset to give their pieces a more serious character, and the longer time interval gives them time to develop a more unique and individual melody. You would quickly get bored if all music followed Montanos' rules. However, inner points of imitation often have shorter time intervals. Look at mm. 32–33 of Victoria's "O magnum," where the tenor and bass follow the Montanos formula.

Exercise 11-D7   *Systematic theory* Now you can find the rules for making a canon at the fourth above or below. (For some examples of that, look at Palestrina's *Missa "ad fugam."*)

12

The Imitative Duo

The imitative duo represents a serious achievement, and goes far beyond being a mere exercise. The first publication by a young composer was often a collection of duos showing mastery of the craft of composition. Lassus was a mature and famous composer when he published his 1577 collection of duos, which were so popular they went into many printings over the next several decades. To counter the charge that two-part writing is thin sounding, Vicentino made an analogy to painting. He said, "The duo, compared to compositions in three, four, and five voices, is like the difference in painting between a nude figure and a clothed one. Any painter can make a fully clothed figure, but not everyone can make a good nude."

In the first part of this chapter you will add a line to a preexisting French chanson melody; in the second part you will write duos, first using the short themes (head motives) that are provided, then inventing your own themes. You will need to review the rules and idioms described in chapter 11.

The imitative duo consists of a series of sections or phrases, each of which begins with imitation and ends with a cadence. Each one is called a point of imitation. In between, the imitation is broken off, and free counterpoint makes the transition to the cadence. The continuity between sections is assured by the elided cadence.

Elided Cadences

One of the most important style features of Renaissance music is the overlap, or elision at internal cadences. If both voices rested at the same time, the resulting silence would seem to end the piece before it was over. When the cadence is proper, one way to achieve overlap is to have one of the goal notes sustain while the other moves on to new material. The last syllable of text sounds at the same time in both parts, but one of the parts moves away more quickly, as in m. 5 of the Morley canzonet in Example 12-1. Once both voices have sounded the goal note, either one can begin the new phrase. When the voice with the new motive has begun, then the voice that held the goal note can rest before beginning a new phrase, usually imitating. (This type of elision also works when one of the voices evades the cadence by going to a note other than the proper goal.)

A different way to elide is to use the type of evaded cadence in which one voice rests instead of sounding the goal note (review chapter 10). Then the last syllable of the phrase in that voice must be sounded on the note that precedes the goal note of the cadence, normally "2" or "5," as in m. 6 of the Lassus motet in Example 12-2. The voice that rested begins the new phrase.

Imitation

Imitation at the beginning of a phrase can be thought of as a little canon. Morley begins his consequent voice a fourth lower after one whole note, and Lassus begins his a fifth below after three whole notes. Morley breaks off imitating after six notes, using the third and fourth measures to set up the thirds that lead to the cadential 4–3 suspension. Lassus breaks off after nine notes, and uses the fifth measure to set up the sixths that lead to the cadence.

Example 12-1 (Morley)

Example 12-2 (Lassus) ("Good and faithful servant, because in a few things [you were faithful…]")

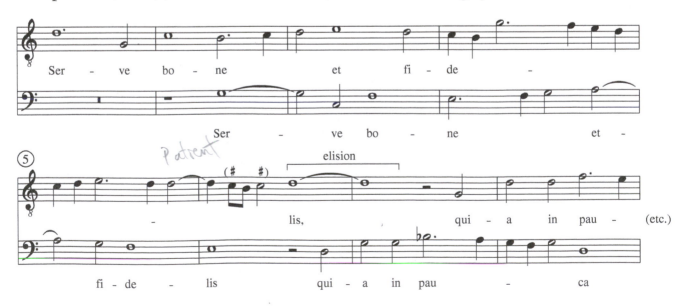

Usually the time interval and pitch interval of imitation change after the cadence, but sometimes they can change in midphrase. In the anonymous Spanish villancico excerpt shown in Example 12-3, the upper voice imitates after a whole note, but because of the addition of time in the upper voice (a longer note value and a rest in mm. 3–4), the time interval of imitation changes to a breve. In the second phrase, after the evaded cadence to *F*, the pitch interval of imitation is the unison until after the rest in m. 9, when the upper voice imitates at the fifth above. Note how the different intervals of imitation function in the context of the ranges (Dorian above, Hypodorian below). What would happen to the range of the upper part if the pitch interval of imitation *didn't* change in m. 9?

Example 12-3 (Anon.) ("How can I live when the cure I pursue has neither why nor wherefore?")

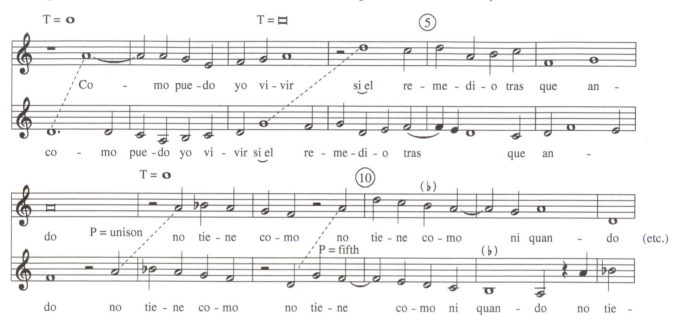

In the opening duo of Victoria's "O magnum mysterium" the pitch interval of imitation changes. Where the soprano leaps up a fourth between "mysterium" and "et," the alto stays on the same note. The subsequent imitation is at the octave, no longer the fifth. One reason might be that Victoria has to prepare the space for the long soprano descent—if the alto had leaped up a fourth, it would have bumped into the falling soprano line.

Sometimes a clause of text is repeated in a single voice, and the music repeats the short segment that sets that text. This is shown with brackets at the end of another anonymous villancico (Ex. 12-4). The consequent at mm. 24–25 breaks off imitating the guide to make the repetition. Label time and pitch intervals of imitation in Example 12-4. Note how the imitations at the octave and unison function in the context of the vocal ranges (Ionian and Hypoionian mixed in both voices).

One 4–5 suspension and two cases of diminished fourth species have been indicated with (X). Freer use of quarter notes is more common in the lighter style of secular music (e.g., Spanish villancico, French chanson, English canzonet).

Example 12-4 (Anon.) ("My eyes will always retrace the glory in which they saw themselves weeping and which they then lost. They will weep to think of the time they enjoyed it.")

Diatonic Imitation

Imitation implies that the consequent voice sounds exactly like the guide, but when the consequent is transposed, the positions of tones and semitones are often not the same. It is possible to use accidentals that make the consequent voice sound like the guide, but many awkward cross-relations will result. In most Renaissance imitation, accidentals are not used in this way, and the consequent voice stays in the same diatonic scale as the guide. <u>Diatonic</u> <u>imitation</u> can be *exact* or *inexact* as to the positions of tones and semitones, *depending on where in the diatonic arrangement the imitation falls.*

At the beginning of Example 12-3 the imitation is exact until the fifth note, because the *B* in the leading voice is answered by *F* in the consequent. In the beginning of the next phrase ("si el remedio tras") the imitation is exact. Although exact and inexact imitation are both used routinely, exact is used more. One reason is that exact imitation preserves mode-defining species. Another has to do with the pitch interval of imitation: the most commonly used intervals of imitation are the fourth, fifth, unison, and octave. Imitation at the unison or octave replicates all melodic motions, and imitation at the fourth or fifth allows for fairly long segments that imitate exactly.

The longest span that can be imitated exactly is the <u>hexachord</u> (see Appendix 3). No melody that extends beyond the range of one of the three hexachords (on *C*, *G*, or *F* with *B*♭) can imitate exactly without the use of accidentals. The hexachords are a fifth apart, and any melody that lies within a hexachord will imitate exactly at the fifth. Imitation at other intervals (the second, say, or the sixth) can only imitate for two- or three-note segments.

Imitation at the fourth or fifth above or below will introduce a pitch class other than the fifth or final. The Morley and Lassus examples have imitation at the fifth and the consequent voices introduce a note other than the fifth or final. The only way to preserve both the species and the pitch classes characteristic of the mode is to imitate at the octave or the unison, which is unusual at the beginning of a piece. Another solution is "tonal answer," discussed in chapter 19.

Counterpoint on a Pre-existing Melody in Mixed Values

Zarlino and Banchieri both recommend extracting a melody in mixed values from a previously composed polyphonic piece and treating it as a CF, adding a new voice either above or below in counterpoint to it. Zarlino takes a melody from a piece by his teacher, Willaert, and Banchieri writes against tunes by Lassus and de Rore. The basic issues are: (1) imitation opportunities; (2) cadence opportunities; and (3) rhythmic variety.

One of the richest sources of two-part music is arrangements of melodies taken from three- and four-voice French chansons. Here are the opening sections from two arrangements of the three-voice chanson "Amy, souffrez que je vous ayme" by the famous chanson composer Claudin de Sermisy. The arrangement in Example 12-5a is attributed to Constantino Festa, the one in Example 12-5b to Antonio Gardane. Sermisy's tune is the topmost line in both arrangements. The arrangers use very little of Claudin's original counterpoint, as you can see by comparing the original three-part piece, shown in Example 14-7, with these two-part arrangements.

Example 12-5 a) (Sermisy/Festa) ("Friend, allow me to love you, and don't hold me to..."); (Sermisy/Gardane)

The original was not designed to be imitative, so Festa uses <u>preview</u> <u>imitation</u> for four notes. This is a good trick: you can always "imitate" if you begin the added line *before* the given one; then you can break off just as the given voice enters. Later, after the initial imitation has been broken off, you may be able to start imitating again, as these examples show (imitations have been bracketed in both). The rhythmic alteration of the opening imitation in the Festa arrangement (the substitution of ♩ for o) is standard in Renaissance music. The two rhythms can be considered equivalent.

Note how each arranger finds a different way to imitate the octave skip in the original tune at m. 6. Gardane uses less imitation than Festa. This doesn't make his a less good piece, but in the exercises below you will be asked to use as much imitation as possible, just to explore the limits of the possibilities. Asterisks show notes in the consequent voice that are not in the same semitone arrangement as the corresponding notes in the guide voice.

Exercise Series C: Given Melodies

Step 1: Imitation

To find imitation opportunities, treat the beginning of every phrase as a puzzle canon, as in chapter 11, knowing that you will have to break off soon. Look for characteristic "theme-types" to imitate (repeated notes, slower note values, etc.) Rhythms should be imitated exactly, as if the same text were being sung, but an exception to this guideline is the optional shortening of the first note from a whole to a half. Use preview imitation only if nothing else is possible! **Imitate for as long as possible, at least four notes,** regardless of duration. **Imitate only at the fourth, fifth, unison, or octave.** Exact imitation is always preferable to inexact imitation (remember, $B\flat$ is the only accidental you are allowed). **Imitate after an integral number of whole notes.** It is worth pointing out that if you substitute a half rest and a half note for a whole note, you must include the rest in your computation of "integral number of whole notes." New points of imitation generally begin immediately after cadences.

Step 2: Cadences

Recognize whole-note motions with the scale patterns "2–1," syncopated "8–7," etc. (review chapter 10). Then decide if you want proper or evaded cadences. **You must elide the cadential goal with the following imitative theme. Label cadence types.**

Step 3: Filling In

Fill in with free material to set up the cadence. In general, strive for rhythmic variety. When both voices are in mixed values, you should **avoid having the parts march together in the same rhythmic values** for more than a few notes (reminder: the limits suggested in the soft rules in chapter 11 were no wholes, five halves, nine quarters, no eighths). Plan some thirds or sixths in this free material to lead smoothly into the cadence.

Given Melodies

Exercise 12-C1   (Locations of imitations, cadences, and filling in have been labeled in this one.)

Exercise 12-C2   Add a line <u>below</u> this line. You will need to review the idiom shown in Example 11-5.

Exercise 12-C3   Add a line <u>above</u> this line. You will need to review the idiom shown in Example 11-5.

Exercise 12-C4   Add a line <u>below</u> this line. (The *G* at * must be treated as a dissonant upper neighbor.)

Exercise 12-C5   Add a line <u>below</u> this line. (The rest suggests beginning the added voice first.)

Study of Repertoire Examples

Example 12-6 is a two-voice arrangement of a four-voice chanson by Claudin de Sermisy called "Le content est riche" (you can see the opening of the original in Example 19-26). Sermisy's original melody is in the upper voice, and an anonymous composer has added a voice below (probably for an instrument).

The piece is in four sections defined by the repetition of melodic material in the upper voice: AABA. Each A section has two phrases, defined by a half-note rest and a cadence. The lower line is different in each of the three A sections, which is why we label them A¹, A², and A³. (The A sections have been aligned for easy comparison. Note that the A3 section is shifted metrically by a whole note. To make it easy to compare it with the other A sections, m. 29 has been broken up.) Some cadence opportunities and imitation opportunities are treated differently, and in some respects, the last A section is a composite of elements from the first two. Note which cadences are evaded, which proper, which elided; note which imitations are exact diatonic transpositions, which inexact. While the mode of the lower voice is clearly authentic Dorian, the upper voice is incomplete, filling only a hexachord.

Example 12-6 (melody by Sermisy; counterpoint anon.) ("The happy man is rich in this world, and fortunate in these times. With a joyful heart and pure freedom to live at home far from worry, to be in love and not at all bashful, eyes closed to all sorrow. Stoutly do thus always, and you will live to be a hundred and more.")

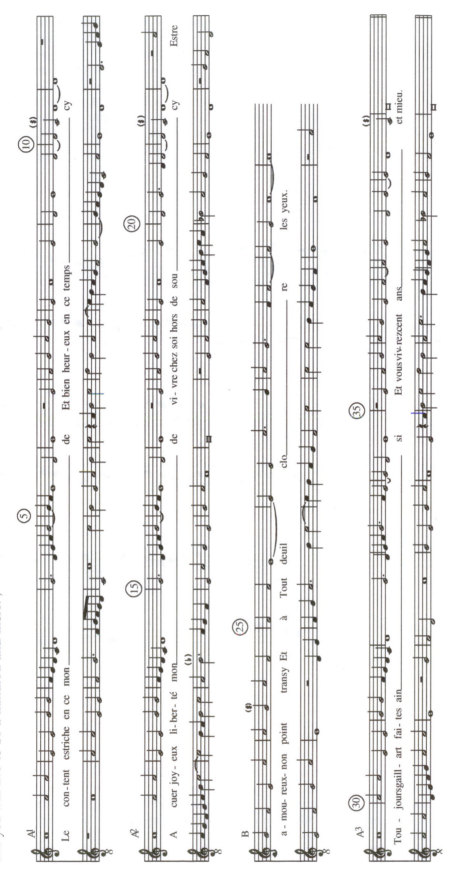

A spectacular example of a melody repeated with varied counterpoints is the two-part Italian madrigal by Willaert called "E se per gelosia" (the beginning is shown in Ex. 12-7). The soprano begins the tune again in m. 9, but with a different counterpoint. The first "accompaniment" is exact diatonic transposition at the fourth below, broken off after four and a half measures to make the cadence. Note all the differences between mm. 1–8 and mm. 9–14; note all similarities. The second counterpoint to the opening tune may in some way illustrate the obsessive quality of jealousy. (Note the skip to a diminished fifth in m. 5, not legal for us but understandable as resulting from an ornamentation of the *B*.)

Example 12-7 (Willaert) ("And if out of jealousy you are making me such company . . .")

Exercise Series *D*:   Long Given Melody

You are to add the missing voice *below* this French chanson tune, which is in the form ABAA, as labeled. Follow the procedures outlined above in Series C exercises. Make the second and third A sections different from the first—find other time and pitch intervals at which to make imitations, and change your free counterpoint as well.

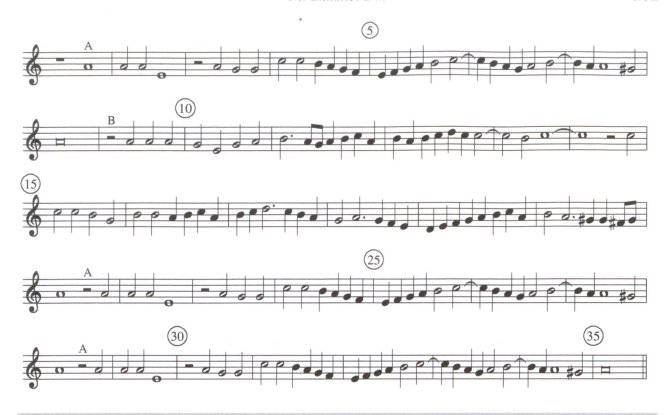

Repertoire for Further Study

Two duos appear later on because they were used as the basis for three-part writing: one is by Josquin (Ex. 15-4) and the other by Tielman Susato (Ex. 15-5). Sing both the duo and trio versions to get a good idea of where your contrapuntal studies can lead.

A duo you might want to look at from the point of view of varied counterpoints is Sermisy's two-voice arrangement of "Au pres de vous." Some French chanson tunes were used as the basis for pieces with other texts, such as masses and magnificats. For instance, Lassus took the melody of a four-voice chanson by Sermisy ("Il me suffit") and used it as the basis for a mass (the beginning of the chanson is shown in Ex. 17-2). Compare the chanson with Lassus's two-voice "Crucifixus" from that mass. Other good examples include Zarlino's duo examples for each of the twelve modes, the twenty-four Lassus duos of 1577, and Morley's two-voice canzonets.

Free Two-Part Writing

Exercise Series C: Head Motives

In the exercises that follow, you are given a head motive. **Write three solutions for each set of givens, two above and one below or vice versa. Imitate at the fourth, fifth, octave, or unison for at least two measures, and conclude with a** cadence to the given goal(s). Bracket the imitation for as long as it lasts, and indicate whether it is exact or inexact. Show when and on what note the head motive of a subsequent section might begin.

In an exercise this brief you should avoid covering more than an octave in each voice (in fact, it may not be possible to cover the whole modal octave). The given motive ends with an x-shaped note, meaning that it may be of any rhythmic value.

Review the sections on characteristic rhythm in chapter 7, cadences in chapter 10, and the idioms in chapter 11, since your work must be not only correct as to the rules of voice leading, but stylistic. You may want also to review the section "Writing a Canon from Scratch" in chapter 11, since the opening is canonic for a while.

For instance, given the following:

Example 12-8a

you could compose the following:

Example 12-8b

Note that imitation at the fourth above after one breve is not possible in the preceding example. In the second example the imitation starts at the unison but the consequent voice is below.

Example 12-8c

Exercise Series **C:**   Head Motive Exercises

Exercise 12-C1   **Exercise 12-C2**

Exercise 12-C3   Exercise 12-C4

   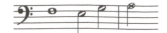

Head Motive Exercises

Exercise Series D: Composing a Soggetto   *1st Part of Assignment*

The Soggetto

Renaissance authors tell us little about what makes a good melody, probably because they were often modeling their melodies on those of pieces they already knew. An important feature of the soggetto is its characteristic rhythm. Serious pieces use longer values in the soggetto, gradually speeding up (e.g., the breve and whole notes in "O magnum"), while lighter pieces use shorter values, often in the characteristic chanson rhythm (whole-half-half). Beginning with a half rest is always an attractive option, making the second entry a little more graceful and less klunky. This will work well when the text begins with a weak syllable (e.g., "Amy souffrez").

Another feature of the soggetto is restricted melodic intervals. We have already discussed the unresolved tension in the first notes of "O magnum." Most soggetti have a fairly narrow range at the beginning, covering a fifth or less. You might want to think of the kinds of melodies you saw in Example 11-13 (Montanos' first-species canons at the fifth) as models: seconds, thirds, and fourths circling in a small space. You could also "paraphrase" a chant melody whose text you are using.

The head motives given in the Series C exercises are not complete units in themselves, they are the beginnings of longer melodies that are sometimes called soggetti (this is the precursor of the word "subject" in fugue terminology). Writing a duo from scratch means first finding or inventing a soggetto, or subject, a short opening melodic motive that is used to start each successive point of imitation, the imitative phrase that ends with a cadence.

One of the functions of the soggetto is to establish the mode of the line or of the piece as a whole. It may do this by (1) starting on the final of the mode or the fifth above, or (2) by containing a skip or outline of one of the characteristic intervals of the mode. Citations of examples of each follow:

1. "I should for grief and anguish" (Ex. 12-1) begins on the final of the mode (Ionian) and outlines the characteristic species of fifth. "Serve bone" (Ex. 12-2) begins on the fifth of the mode (Mixolydian) and outlines the characteristic species of fifth.

"Andaran siempre mis ojos" (Ex. 12-4), and "Le content est riche" (Ex. 12-6) begin on the fifth of the mode but do not outline species characteristic of the mode.

2. "O magnum mysterium" (Ex. Intro-2) outlines a characteristic first-species fifth but because that species is transposed, the first note is neither the final nor the fifth of the mode (*G*-Dorian).

For this exercise you will introduce such foreign notes only in the consequent voice, as in the Morley and Lassus examples.

The first soggetto in the piece

1. **must begin on the final or the fifth above the final.**
2. **must skip or outline a characteristic fourth or fifth of the mode.**
3. **must imitate at the fifth or fourth above or below.**
4. **must begin with long note values.** It should gradually speed up.
5. **must be imitated after one, two, or three whole notes, and the imitation must last at least three whole notes before breaking off.**

Once the first phrase has cadenced, you will introduce a new soggetto. The modal requirements for soggetti after the first are much less stringent: these tunes may begin on notes foreign to the mode, they may outline smaller intervals, and they may be imitated at the octave or unison. You may use a rest before a new soggetto, but the first note after a rest must be consonant. This means that the first note of the new soggetto must be consonant with the goal note of the previous cadence. Soggetti after the first section should begin with shorter note values.

Cadential Goals

1. **The final of the mode must be the goal of the first and last cadences of your duo.** Vicentino says this, although you will find exceptions in the repertoire (Exx. 12-1 and 12-2 both cadence to the fifth of the mode at the end of the first phrase). The first cadence may be evaded, but the last can only be proper. Intermediate cadences may be to a variety of notes. Zarlino says that the third and the fifth above are the best for intermediate cadences, but one finds cadences to every pitch class. Cadences to *B* are rarest, although Zarlino recommends them in the Phrygian and Mixolydian.

Plan your cadences in advance as a function of the mode and also in relation to the starting notes of the soggetti that follow each cadence, so that smooth overlaps may be made. One characteristic of the Renaissance duo, as we have seen, is the scarcity of moments when both voices stop and rest together.

2. **There must not be silence in both voices anywhere, and the goal note in an intermediate cadence must be at least a whole note long in one voice.** At intermediate cadences, one voice holds the goal note while the other rests and then begins the new soggetto. This means that the first note(s) of the new soggetto must be consonant with the held last note of the cadence. In "Le content est riche" (Ex. 12-6), the first phrase of the A section cadences on *E* (m. 6), allowing the lower voice to begin on *A* (as in the first and third statements) or the upper voice to begin on *E*, as in the second. You will have to plan cadential degrees partly as a function of entrance notes of later soggetti. Suppose you evade a cadence to *G* by having the lower voice go to *B♭*; then the upper voice could begin a new soggetto on *D*, but not on *A*.

Exercise Series D: Writing a Free Imitative Duo

1. Compose an imitative duo three to four phrases long, each beginning with a different point of imitation, continuing with free counterpoint, and ending with a cadence (elided with the beginning of the following phrase). You can decide with your teacher whether or not to use text; if you do, consult Appendix 1. The guide voice should not always appear in the same voice, and the time interval of imitation

should not always be the same. There is no absolute requirement for phrase length, but the whole composition should last at least forty-two whole notes.

Voice types and ranges: The two voices must be in modes that are in a collateral relationship. You must choose pairs of modes that can be accommodated by the vocal ranges for which you choose to write (thus it would not do to have the alto in the hypolydian, since the *C–C* octave is either too high or too low). In each case you may exceed the modal octave by up to two steps. Individual *phrases* do not have to fill the modal octave, though each voice's *complete* melody must. The voices may cross, but not for too long.

Structure of the duo: The first head motive has relatively strict requirements. The first voice to come in must:

- begin on the final or fifth of the mode.
- feature a characteristic modal skip or outline.
- begin with long note values and gradually speed up.

Subsequent phrases are not so restricted; requirements for each phrase are given in the following table:

	First Phrase	**Middle Phrase(s)**	**Final phrase**
Point of imitation	• Imitate at 4th or 5th • Consequent enters after 1–3 whole notes • Imitation must last at least 3 whole notes before breaking off	• Imitate at unison, 4th, 5th, or 8ve (unless imitation is by inversion, in which case any pitch interval is acceptable) • Imitate for any duration, at any time interval • Entry is elided with preceding cadence	• Imitate at unison, 4th, 5th, or 8ve (unless imitation is by inversion, in which case any pitch interval is acceptable) • Imitate for any duration, at any time interval • Entry is elided with preceding cadence
Cadence	• May be proper or evaded • Cadential goal must be the final of the mode	• May be proper or evaded • Cadential goal may be any degree of the mode (the 3rd and 5th are most common)	• Must be proper • Cadential goal must be the final of the mode

You must plan your cadential goals and starting notes of the head motives so that elision is possible. For example, the second point of imitation elides with the first cadence—which must be on the final of the mode—and so its first note must be consonant with the modal final. When you elide, the held note of the cadence must last at least a whole note and must overlap with the entrance of the new point of imitation. Remember, rests may never occur in both voices simultaneously, because the idea is to have a seamless transition between the end of one phrase and the beginning of the next.

If you choose to write four phrases rather than three, you may make one point of imitation a variation on another, for example, through invertible counterpoint, or two different imitative solutions with the same head motive, etc. As suggested in the foregoing table, you may use imitation by melodic inversion after the first phrase. You may also exchange fourths for fifths (and vice versa) in the imitation of your head motive (consult the "Tonal Answer" section of chapter 19). Your composition should feature variety in rhythm and will be more interesting if you explore the different ways of introducing dissonance. Think about using dissonant suspensions (including diminished fourth species), dissonant upper neighbors (review this idiom), a cambiata, etc. In the middle of phrases, you could try suggesting a cadence with suspensions and raised leading tones and then evading the cadence. You might also consider introducing partially imitative fragments in the midst of free counterpoint (this could be in diminution or augmentation). If you feel that breaking a soft rule is necessary in order to achieve a particular result, you may write a note to your teacher about it. You should label in the score any of these devices that you use.

Presentation: Write neatly so that your duo can be performed without problems!

- Make sure the two voices are always lined up properly.
- Use consistent spacing, roughly proportional to duration.
- Use ruler for bar lines (they don't have to extend between staves).
- Draw stems in the correct direction and of a proper length.
- Any ledger lines should be the correct distance away from the staff.
- Make noteheads big enough so that one can tell easily whether they are quarters or halves.
- Place noteheads exactly on a line or in a space.

Fitting three or four measures (at two whole notes per measure) on each system of a portrait-oriented sheet of staff paper will give good spacing results. Everything should be dark enough to photocopy easily. Make any eighth-note beams distinct from the staff lines (by angling them/making them thicker). A fine-tipped black pen is better than pencil. Group the two staves together with a brace, and leave an empty staff (or extra space) between each pair of staves. Don't let any measures start in one staff and continue in the next.

2. Write a two-part chansonlike piece according to the following scheme (similar to "Le content est riche" or the "Long Given Melody Exercise" in this chapter). Choose and label the mode you have chosen for each voice (one should be plagal, one authentic; each should stay within a tenth).

A^1 section (two phrases): imitation free cadence elide imitation free cadence elide

B section (two phrases): imitation free cadence elide imitation free cadence elide

A^2 section: same melody in upper voice as A^1 section, but different counterpoint in lower.

A^3 section: same melody in upper voice as A^1 section, but different counterpoint in lower. The final cadence is of course not elided.

Because of the repeating A tune, treatment of cadences is different in this exercise. **The first cadential goal in the A1 section may be to any degree; the second cadence must be to the final.** All cadences must be proper (sixth-to-octave or third-to-unison); however, you may evade by using a rest in one voice (the one that is about to sound the new soggetto). **The cadences in the B section must be any note(s)** *other* **than degree 1 or 5.**

You must compose different imitations against the A2 and A3 melodies. If the upper voice led in the A1 section, you should try leading with the lower voice, and vice versa; perhaps a different time or pitch interval of imitation would work. Keep this in mind when composing your own soggetto.

13

Invertible Counterpoint

Invertible counterpoint is a way of varying the presentation of a duo. It makes a new two-voice combination out of the original one by reversing the relative positions of the two voices (above becomes below and vice versa). It is economical, since you get two combinations for the price of one. For a composer, this means having some contrapuntal material to repeat in a varied form; for a student doing species exercises, the "invertible counterpoint option" means being able to reuse one of the added lines against the CF.

Invertible Counterpoint at the Octave

Invertible counterpoint at the octave (abbreviated as "ic8") means that (1) the upper voice is moved down an octave, or (2) the lower voice is raised an octave, or, more generally, (3) the sum of the intervals each voice moves when they change position is 9 (if a voice is untransposed, we write "1" meaning "at the unison").

Example 13-1

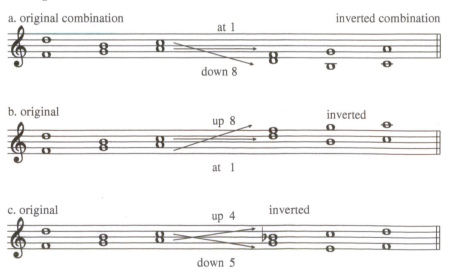

For the moment we will only use two types, which preserve the pitch classes in both voices. Note that if an interval in the original combination exceeds the interval of inversion, the parts won't cross, and you won't have invertible counterpoint. In such cases, it may be feasible to add an octave to the interval of inversion making it inverted at the fifteenth.

Example 13-2

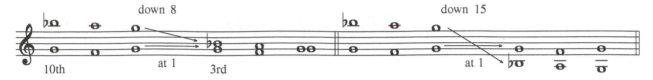

A simple way to calculate the effect of invertible counterpoint at the octave on any vertical interval in the original combination is to make a chart like this one:

interval in original duo: 1   2   3   4   5   6   7   8
interval in inverted duo: 8   7   6   5   4   3   2   1

You can see from this chart that a fifth (a perfect consonance) in the original combination becomes a fourth (a dissonance) in the inverted combination and can't be used anywhere that a consonance is required. However, if you use a fifth in the original in a position where a dissonance would do as well (say, a second-species passing tone or a third-species lower neighbor), then there is no problem.

Example 13-3

In ic8, the inverted combination sounds a lot like the original because it contains all the same pitch classes as the original, and because except for the fourth and fifth, all vertical intervals retain their qualities—perfect octaves become unisons and vice versa, imperfect intervals (sixths and thirds) become each other, and dissonances (seconds and sevenths) do too.

One hard rule: In invertible counterpoint at the octave, you can only use a fifth in the original if it occurs in a metric position and melodic situation where a dissonance would do as well.

Suspensions Inverted at the Octave

A 4–3 suspension above becomes a 5–6 consonant tie below (but beware when the dissonance in the suspension above is an *augmented* fourth—this will become a diminished fifth below, not a legal tie; see chapter 6, rule 1). A 7–6 suspension above becomes a 2–3 below, so cadential suspensions are unaffected by invertible counterpoint at the octave.

The Invertible Counterpoint Option

When you take the invertible counterpoint option for any exercise in chapters 3–8, **both your original duo and the inverted one must conform to the rules for that exercise.** Thus octaves on the downbeat in the original will invert to unisons, which are allowed. Similarly, intervals larger than an octave in the original will not invert, resulting in temporary voice crossing, which is limited or forbidden altogether, depending on the exercise. If you try to get around this by inverting at the fifteenth, your added line will probably not fit into the given range.

Invertible Counterpoint at the Twelfth

Invertible counterpoint at the twelfth (ic12) means that the sum of the intervals each voice moves when their positions are reversed is thirteen.

Example 13-4 (Rodio)

Here is the interval chart for invertible counterpoint at the twelfth:

interval in original duo:	1	2	3	4	5	6	7	8	9	10	11	12
interval in inverted duo:	12	11	10	9	8	7	6	5	4	3	2	1

You can see from this chart that a sixth (an imperfect consonance) in the original combination becomes a seventh (a dissonance) in the inverted combination.

One hard rule: In invertible counterpoint at the twelfth you must only use sixths in positions where a dissonance would do as well.

Suspensions Inverted at the Twelfth

The only kind of suspension that can be used above is the 4–3, which becomes a 9–10 below. The 7–6 becomes a 6–7, which can work as second species (it must continue passing down).

The Problem of Transposition by Fifth

For a Renaissance composer, the special appeal of invertible counterpoint at the twelfth is that all classes of vertical interval (perfect consonance, imperfect consonance, or dissonance) in the original stay the same in the inversion except for the sixth and the seventh. Unlike inversion at the octave, however, inversion at the twelfth can alter the sound of the melody. Take a melody that covers an octave; if you transpose it a fifth, the semitone positions in part of the melody change. And your skips of the mode may be seriously affected by ic12 particularly when you are doing a counterpoint in the Phrygian mode, as in Example 13-5a. The inversion shown in Example 13-5b is simply impossible. Under these circumstances, changing which voice moves a fifth might solve the problem, as it does in Example 13-5c.

Example 13-5

Exact transposition using B♭ might not always be practical because diminished fifths or augmented fourths may arise, either as vertical intervals or as melodic skips or outlines. Also, as you will see below, cross-relations arise.

Study of Treatise Examples

Example 5-4 (which we used to illustrate a cambiata) was actually Tigrini's example of invertible counterpoint at the twelfth. In the inverted combination the upper part is transposed down a fifth (starting on *D*), and Tigrini has a *B*♭ in the signature there. The danger of exact transposition, as in the Tigrini example, is that of cross-relations (*B*♭ against *B*♮). As we said in chapter 2, they are quite common in Renaissance music.

Example 13-6 (Tigrini)

We also hear a couple of cross-relations in Zarlino's example of invertible counterpoint at the twelfth:

Example 13-7 (Zarlino)

Study of Repertoire Examples

The principal compositional use of invertible counterpoint is to vary the repetition of a block of material. Here is an anonymous German organ magnificat in which each of the two CF phrases moves from the lower voice to the upper, reversing positions with the counterpoint:

Example 13-8a (Anon.) (From *An Anthology of Keyboard Compositions: Munich, Bavarian State Library MS MUS 1581. Corpus of Early Keyboard Music* vol. 40/2. Edited by Clare G. Rayner. AIM, 1976. Magnificat septimi toni, versus quartus, pp. 45–46. Hänssler-Verlag.)

Here is a diagram of the organ piece, schematizing the structure:

Example 13-8b Schema of Ex. 13-8a

A ——— CF¹ ——— B ——— CF² ———
CF¹——— A ——— CF² ——— B ———

Lassus uses the same principle in the first twenty-eight measures of the instrumental duo in Example 13-9. In this instrumental piece (called a <u>ricercar</u> or <u>fantasy</u>), Lassus moves a seven-note CF from one voice to the other; each time it goes from the lower voice to the upper, the added voice switches position with it, so in this excerpt we have four pairs of seven-note <u>periods</u> (sections of equal length). Make a diagram showing the structural repetitions of CF and added lines as we did in Example 13-8b.

Example 13-9 (Lassus)

Another example is a Benedictus by Jacquet of Mantua, whose CF, as Philip T. Jackson has shown, is based on the vowels of an acclamation to a patron:

"Ho- nor Ca- ro- lus us- que in ae- ter- num
 sol   sol   fa   sol   ut   ut   re   mi   re   re   ut.

(See Appendix 3 on solmization.)

Example 13-10 (Jacquet) ("Honor be to Charles through eternity. Blessed is he who comes in the name of the Lord.")

Exercise Series **D:** | **Complete CFs**

Using the first phrase of "Christ lag in Todesbanden," compose a setting in two parts, like Example 13-9 or 13-10, consisting of six periods. Each pair of periods is to use the same added melodic material in mixed values (labeled A, B, and C in the scheme below), but with the positions of the voices reversed, as shown below. The second combination in each pair will be the inversion of the first at either the octave or the twelfth (you must use both intervals of inversion somewhere in the piece). You may transpose the CF, the added line, or both, but explain whether your transposition maintains semitone positions, uses an important note of the mode, or fills the same space as the original. Each period must end with a cadence (to *A, C,* or *E*). See Appendix 5 for more detailed instructions on this complex exercise.

period:	1	2	3	4	5	6
upper melody:	A	CF	B	CF	C	CF
lower melody:	CF	A	CF	B	CF	C

1st pair · 2nd pair · 3rd pair

Invertible Counterpoint at the Tenth

Invertible counterpoint at the tenth (ic10) means moving one voice a tenth, or transposing the two voices so that the sum of the intervals each voice moves is 11. An extra octave may be added.

Here is the interval chart for invertible counterpoint at the tenth:

interval in original duo:	1	2	3	4	5	6	7	8	9	10
interval in inverted duo:	10	9	8	7	6	5	4	3	2	1

Ic10 is not used as much as ic8 or ic12 in Renaissance music. This may be because transposition by tenth does not preserve melodic species of interval that characterize mode, or because it transforms perfect vertical intervals into imperfect ones, or because parallel sixths and thirds are impossible, or because dissonant suspensions are impossible in two parts (later a 9–8 will be allowed). However, a cadence can be inverted at the tenth if it results in the idiom shown in Example 11-6. Ic10, used at the beginning of a piece, will cause an entry on a note foreign to the mode (see Ex. 19-2). Zarlino points out that it is often possible to perform the original and the inverted combinations together, since they will move in parallel tenths. (See chapter 14 on the importance of parallel tenths in the outer voices.) Angleria illustrates moving the lower part up a fifth and the upper part down a sixth (Ex. 13-11a and b), while Zarlino has the lower part up an octave and the lower part down a tenth (Ex. 13-12a and b).

Example 13-11 (Angleria)

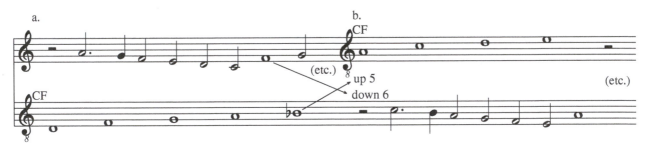

Example 13-12 (Zarlino)

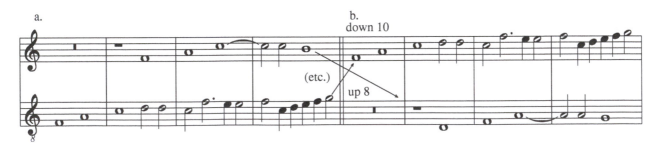

Double Counterpoint

Double counterpoint is the broad term for making a new combination out of an original. We maintain the same melodies, in the same relative temporal relationship, but we transpose one or both. Invertible counterpoint is a special case of double counterpoint in which the relative positions of the parts are reversed. Invertible counterpoint is much more common in Renaissance polyphony than double counterpoint.

You don't really need to make a chart for double counterpoint, you need only add or subtract. If you are doing invertible counterpoint at the fifth, raising the lower voice or lowering the upper voice, you just subtract 5 from each vertical interval in the original. (Double counterpoint at the fifth is like invertible counterpoint at the twelfth reinverted at the octave.)

Double counterpoint at the third is interesting because when the original is performed with its double, parallel thirds result. (The rules are the same as for invertible counterpoint at the tenth, except that no sixths are allowed at all.) The texture of two fast-moving parts in thirds above a slower-moving bass becomes extremely popular in the early 17th c., and is characteristic of the trio sonata texture of the later Baroque. Angleria's Example 13-13c, published in 1622, sounds like Monteverdi.

Example 13-13 (Angleria)

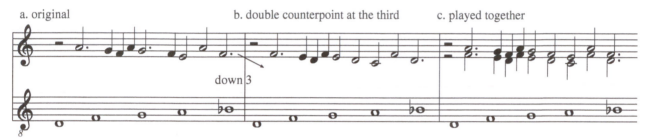

Improvising Invertible Counterpoint at the Keyboard

Many treatises refer to improvising invertible counterpoint. It's not clear how singers would have used this technique, but it's easy to see how it would be useful to a keyboard player. If you do an improvisation on a CF that is invertible, you can play it again immediately with the parts inverted, producing two sections like the one we saw in Example 13-8a. You get twice as much music for your effort. Devising something invertible is not as hard as remembering what it was you just played!

A good way to develop these chops is the start with a Series C–size CF (around five notes—it doesn't matter for now if it even ends on a characteristic note of the mode).

1. Play the CF in the left hand.
2. Play it again, adding a florid line above that contains no sixths in consonant positions so that it will invert at the twelfth.
3. Play the first CF note up an octave and the first note of the added line down a twelfth. This step is not as easy as it sounds!
4. Play the added line, starting on the new note in the left hand. You have to remember the line, and your left hand may resist the faster values.
5. Finally, play the CF in the right hand and the counterpoint in the left.

This basic training is amazingly useful for playing fugues (Bach uses invertible counterpoint often), and this will train your hands not to think of the melody always being in the right hand and the accompaniment in the left (it's easy secretly to think of the CF as an accompaniment, even though in reality it's the theme to which we write a florid accompaniment).

You might want to try inserting recognizable motives (like "la sol fa re mi") into the florid line when possible. This might make it easier to memorize the added line, especially as you move into longer CFs.

Three Parts

The material on three-part writing is divided into three chapters. In this chapter we start with first and fourth species in three parts. This allows you to compose short phrases with cadences that might later become sections of longer pieces. After that we add two parts in mixed values to a CF (if you are interested in the vastly more complicated technique of adding a canon to a CF, see Appendix 2). In chapter 15 we leave the CF behind—all three parts are now in mixed values. Finally, in chapter 16 you will find a widely used technique for making an imitative opening in three parts.

Hard Rules

The rules from chapter 11 continue to apply, except for the following.

1. In three-part first species, as in two parts, only vertical consonances are allowed. Each of the three pairs of voices must make legal two-voice counterpoint. The three pairs are the top voice with the middle voice, the middle with the lowest, and the top voice with the lowest.

2. However, a fourth may occur between the upper two parts as long as the lowest voice has a third or fifth below the middle voice. A fourth may not occur between the lowest voice and any other voice. The fourth between the upper parts is said to be "covered" by the different note in the bass. The bass may have a fifth or a third (or their compounds) below the lowest note of the fourth. You may skip to either of the notes of the fourth and you may have parallel fourths.

3. The augmented fourth and diminished fifth may be used as consonances between the two upper voices only as part of a "diminished 6/3 chord" under the following circumstances:

- a. moving by step to a 5/3 chord (the upper voice may move down by step or the lower two voices may move up by step);
- b. the two members of the augmented fourth move out by step and the third voice moves to a legal consonance,
- c. or the two members of the diminished fifth move in by step, and the third voice moves to a legal consonance (note that these are used in cadences, shown below);
- d. the diminished 6/3 occurs in a chain of 6/3 chords. The diminished 6/3 chord may be treated as a consonance.

4. At least two of the three voices must begin and end on a perfect consonance, but the third voice may make a third above the lowest note. The third in the last sonority may be a major third above the final even if the mode normally has a minor third above the final (the Dorian, Aeolian, and Phrygian modes—see Ex. 14–3).

5. In fourth species, the 9–8 (or 2–1) suspension and the 4–5 suspension may be used as long as there is some imperfect consonance at the moment of resolution. However, never double the raised leading tone at the cadence, and avoid the *minor* ninth (or minor second) suspension.

Illustration of Hard Rules

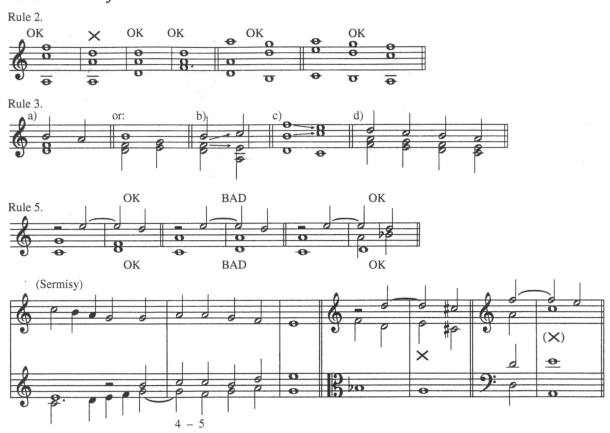

There are so many possible solutions to a CF when we add *two* other lines in note-against-note rhythm that it doesn't seem practical to memorize them all as we could when adding only one part. Consequently, instead of doing exhaustive Series A exercises, we fall back on some handy formulas that were widely used. (These formulas are also used in four-part writing, so it's a good idea to learn them now.)

Fauxbourdon

Fauxbourdon is an improvisational technique from the fifteenth century that consists primarily of parallel 6/3 chords. We find it still used in brief passages of sixteenth-century music. In fauxbourdon, the CF is sounded in the uppermost voice (*cantus*), and the other two improvisers need only look at that line. The lowest voice (*tenor*) begins and ends each phrase with an octave below the *cantus* and runs in parallel sixths with the *cantus* the rest of the time. The two challenges for the improviser of this line are (1) to calculate quickly how to get from an octave below the first note to a sixth below the second one and (2) how to get from a sixth below the penultimate note to an octave below the last note. You are already familiar with this kind of geometrical calculation: "I'm an octave below the first note; how far do I have to go to be a sixth below the second note?" Meanwhile the middle voice, the alto, sings a fourth below the *cantus* from beginning to end.

Example 14-1a shows a typical hymn tune. In Example 14-1b, we have written the hymn tune up an octave to place the lower voices in a more comfortable range. The tenor has to leap up a fourth between the first two notes; because the first phrase ends with an ascending step, the tenor can move by step down to an octave. The tenor can begin the second phrase a sixth below to avoid parallel octaves between the phrases; at the end of the second phrase, the tenor has to leap down a fourth to get to the final octave. The alto is shown in x-shaped notes, always following the melody in parallel fourths.

Example 14-1a (Hymn: Ad coenam agni providi)

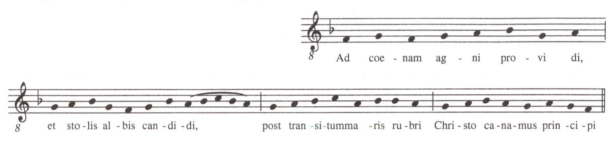

Example 14-1b and c b. the first two phrases in fauxbourdon; the last phrase with a simple cadence

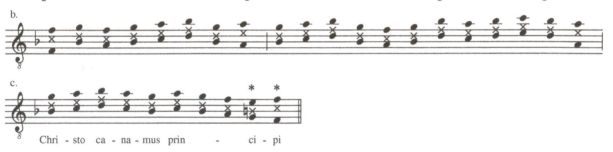

Note that because the alto follows in parallel *perfect* fourths, the cadence in Example 14-1c is the old-fashioned fifteenth-century "double-leading tone cadence". In the later sixteenth century, the same cadence would be more likely to have B♭ in the alto, the augmented fourth leading to a perfect fourth.

It is possible to improvise phrase ends with proper cadences in fauxbourdon, but this often involves altering the CF. If the CF ends with a descending step (as in the last three phrases of the same hymn), then the *cantus* singer has to overshoot the cadence, adding another goal note preceded by a lower neighbor (chromatically raised if necessary, depending on the mode). These added notes allow the tenor to descend by step to the final note of the phrase. In Example 14-1c the added notes are asterisked (compare Ex. 14-1a); the last two text syllables are moved later and now fall on the new last two notes.

If the tune is rhythmicized (i.e., with the notes arranged into a regular meter), the cadence may be embellished with a suspension. Then the antepenultimate note can be rhythmically extended, making the suspension, and the added leading tone is treated as the resolution of the suspension. The alto can either move with the tenor

(d) or move with the *cantus* (e). Note the antique "double-leading-tone" cadence in Example 14-1e; in the late sixteenth century, the alto would sing B♭.

Example 14-1d and e

You might enjoy studying Guillaume Dufay's setting of "Ad coenam" and seeing how he varied and embellished the basic note-against-note fauxbourdon structure.

The Parallel-Sixth Model

In this model the soprano and tenor run in parallel sixths, as in fauxbourdon, but the third voice is the bass, not the alto. The bass formula given in treatises alternates fifths and thirds below the tenor; either can start (in Ex. 14-2a the bass starts with a third below, in Ex. b a fifth) or, in second species, both (c and d), as shown here:

Example 14-2a–d

This pattern is found widely in four-part music; in three-part music; it is found mostly at cadences (discussed later), and in chansons in the lighter style. This may be because the spacing ends up being very wide between tenor and soprano, and the bass has to skip a lot (in four parts, the alto is added between the upper parts and it is more normal for the bass to skip). The formula given earlier for the bass is very limited; it does not apply unless the upper voices move by step. If the upper voices skip, many possible bass lines can be used. Note that in this model it is impossible to have 3-pc sonorities on every beat. We do not recommend improvising in this model, for you would have to glean these many possible bass lines from long examination of repertoire and/or by trial and error.

The Parallel-Third Model

The two upper voices in the parallel-sixth model can always be inverted with respect to each other (i.e., inverted at the octave). The widely used texture of parallel thirds above a free (and sometimes fairly distant) bass is the precursor of the trio sonata texture of the Baroque period. Example 14-3 shows Praetorius' setting of a verse of the Christmas chorale "Puer natus in Bethlehem/Ein Kind geborn zu Bethlehem" (the chorale melody is in the middle voice). Note the deviations from the otherwise-constant parallel thirds between the upper voices—why are they there? You can invert the positions of the upper voices to turn this example into the parallel-sixth model (you'll have to place many bass notes in lower octaves to accommodate the wider spacing between the upper voices).

Example 14-3 ("A child is born in Bethlehem")

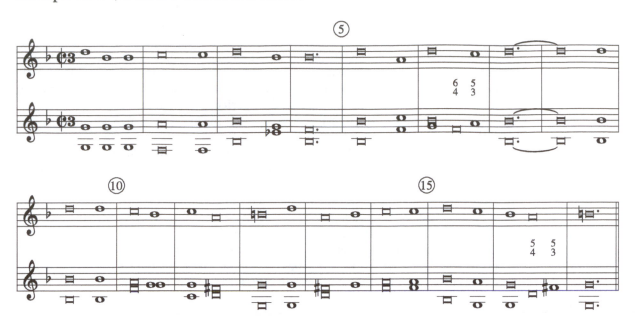

The Parallel-Tenth Model

In this model the outer voices run together in parallel tenths. Like the models shown earlier, this kind of thing is not used constantly, but it can often last many measures. This technique goes back to the fifteenth century but was still recognized as useful as late as 1609, when the famous lute-song composer John Dowland translated a treatise written almost a century before by Andreas Ornithoparchus. The author says, "The most famous manner of the Counter-point…is, if the Base goe together with the Meane, or any other Voyce, being also distant by a tenth, whilst the Tenor doth goe in Concord to both, thus:"

Example 14-4 (Ornithoparchus/Dowland)

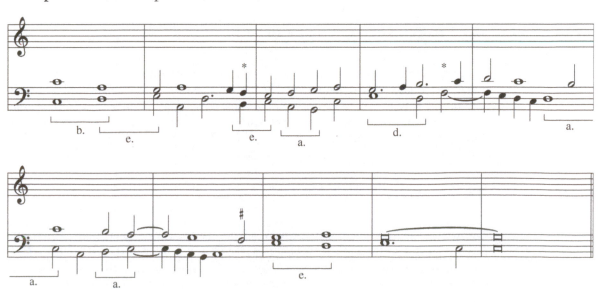

His example shows only the tenor and bass; the top voice is to be generated from the bass, sounding a tenth above each bass note. You should (a) play the two given voices and sing the soprano a tenth above the bass, (b) have another member of the class play the given voices while you sing the upper part, or (c) write out the upper part on the empty staff provided and sing the example with friends. Note the chanson idiom (Ex. 11-4) and a couple of voice-leading irregularities (marked with an asterisk) that attest to the antiquity of the example. Note that it is impossible for the first and last sonorities to contain only perfect consonance.

The difficulty in improvising or composing in this style is in knowing how the tenor can "goe in concord" with the two outer voices. It turns out that the rules for this are the same as those for making invertible counterpoint at the tenth! (See chapter 13.) Those rules are simple enough: Never have parallel sixths or thirds between the tenor and bass, and use only the 7–6 suspension. The result is exclusively contrary and oblique motion between those two voices. In Example 14-5 you will see many possible tenor solutions to outer voices moving in stepwise motion up and down in parallel tenths (the tenor solutions are shown in x-shaped notes). The occurrences of these patterns have been labeled in Example 14-4 (no labels are given when the bass skips). You could memorize these for improvisation purposes, and you will be asked to spot them in repertoire examples later.

Example 14-5a–g

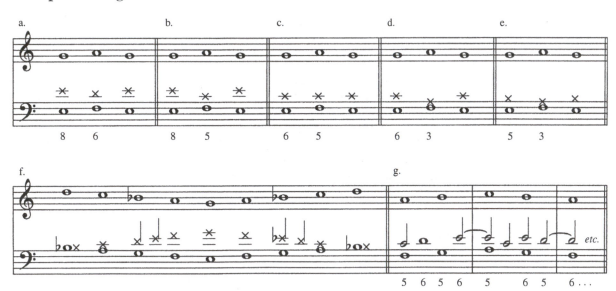

In Example 14-5f, continuous stepwise motion in the outer voices is set with a middle voice in contrary motion; over the third note one may use either the sixth or the fifth in first species (and both in second species). Note that if you are a fifth above the bass and the bass descends by step, you can't continue up stepwise; you must go up a third somehow. You can pass in second species. The only way to have similar motion is to alternate fifths and sixths in fourth species, making chains of 6–5s (Ex. 14-5g).

Final Cadences in Three Parts

You will want to review the terminology used to describe cadences in chapter 10. In Example 14-6, the model two-voice proper cadence to *G* is shown, with various possible third-voice lines added in x-shaped notes. In Example a, the *G* is suspended over two notes, both of which function as agents; the *G* is dissonant with both the *A* in the tenor and the *D* in the bass, so we call them a "double agent"! The penulti-mate chord with $\hat{5}$ in the bass provides a rich, three-pitch-class sonority that sounds like a dominant chord to us. The cadences with $\hat{5}$–$\hat{1}$ in the bass (Exx. a–c) are most likely to be used at the ends of pieces. The "octave leap" cadence, where the bass leaps from $\hat{5}$ below to $\hat{5}$ above the final is standard in the fifteenth century but used rarely in the sixteenth. The following examples are organized by which voice has the model tenor motion (i.e., the descending step, or $\hat{2}$–$\hat{1}$).

Example 14-6a–e

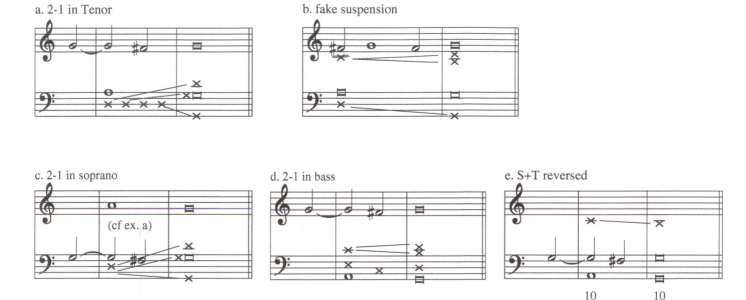

a. 2-1 in Tenor

b. fake suspension

c. 2-1 in soprano

(cf ex. a)

d. 2-1 in bass

e. S+T reversed

10   10

Final cadences always end with the goal pc in the lowest voice approached by $\hat{2}$ or $\hat{5}$, never $\hat{7}$. When the lowest voice has the model tenor motion ($\hat{2}$–$\hat{1}$) and one of the upper voices has the model *cantus* motion ($\hat{8}$–$\hat{7}$–$\hat{8}$), the third voice may sound the fifth above the final or the third above (the only imperfect consonance allowed in final cadences).

Setting up the Cadence

The essential ingredients of the cadence are the *cantus* ($\hat{8}$–$\hat{7}$–$\hat{8}$) and tenor ($\hat{2}$–$\hat{1}$) motions. These are easy to approach in the parallel-sixth model. With $\hat{2}$ in the tenor voice, we usually have $\hat{5}$ in the bass, as shown in Examples 14-6a–c; in the normal parallel-sixth model, the bass $\hat{5}$ is approached by skip (Ex. 14-7a), making legal similar motion to a perfect interval. However, by inserting a fifth into the parallel-sixth chain, we can obtain a different "pre-dominant" bass note ($\hat{4}$), approaching $\hat{5}$ by contrary motion with the tenor. This is often found preceded by $\hat{6}$ (Exx. 14-7b and c, where intervals that deviate from strict parallel sixths are shown in parentheses).

We can also approach a cadence easily from the parallel-tenth model: One of the tenths is delayed to make the typical *cantus* cadence, with an 11–10 suspension over the bass $\hat{5}$, which is preceded stepwise by $\hat{6}$. The problem with this is that the fifth above the bass (in the tenor) must be approached from below. A solu-tion is shown in Example 14-7d (the chanson idiom). The parallel-tenth model can also accommodate the cadence when the model tenor motion $\hat{2}$–$\hat{1}$ is in the bass (Ex. 14-7e—compare with Ex. 14-5a). The upper two voices in this one can be inverted back to the fauxbourdon cadence (Ex. 14-7f); in that case the *D* can go up to *E* in the middle voice.

The parallel-sixth and parallel-tenth models cannot be combined unless elements are shifted temporally, as shown in Example 14-7g; if the embellishing delays are reduced out, it would look like Example 14-7h, with parallel fifths!

The cadential suspension can be accompanied by $\hat{4}$–$\hat{5}$, making a "ii6/5" chord before the dominant chord (Ex. 14-7i). This means the fifth above the final sounds for a shorter time and may weaken the cadence.

The fake suspension is often used in final cadences, permitting the $\hat{5}$ in the bass to sound for twice as long. This can produce a "dominant-seventh" sound, as in Example 14-7j. There, the alto voice has a consonant *B* while the *F* is suspended from a previous consonance. The *F* resolves correctly while the *C* makes the "fake" suspension (a fourth) above the bass. This results in a "6/4" chord. On the next strong beat the soprano moves to the agent of a true suspension with the *C*, which resolves correctly.

Example 14-7a–j

Phrygian Cadences

Phrygian cadences are special, in that one of the essential ingredients of the cadence, $\hat{2}$, cannot be accompanied by $\hat{5}$ in the bass. This is no problem when $\hat{2}$ is in the lowest voice (Ex. 14-8a). But what bass can accompany the Phrygian suspension, resolution, and goal notes when $\hat{2}$ is in the tenor? The surprising answer is $\hat{7}$–$\hat{4}$ (Ex. 14-8b). In this way we get an especially juicy 9–8 suspension (now legal) and a perfect final sonority. This cadence is very common, but it is a source of some consternation to the modern ear to find *A* as the lowest note in a piece whose final is *E*.

Example 14-8 Phrygian cadences in three parts

a. In fauxbourdon   b. Parallel-sixth model

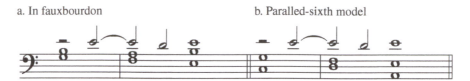

Intermediate and Overlapping Cadences

All the cadences shown earlier are "proper" (i.e., they contain a *cantus* $\hat{8}$–$\hat{7}$–$\hat{8}$ motion and a tenor $\hat{2}$–$\hat{1}$ motion, and the lowest voice always ends on a doubling of the goal note). This type of cadence is appropriate for the end of a piece or an important section. For intermediate cadences, however, we can:

1. use all the evaded types of cadence between the cantus and tenor we saw in chapter 10;
2. use the third voice (not part of the model cadence) to add an imperfect consonance (other than the third above the final) that suggests that the section is not finished (in the Renaissance there is no name for this);
3. place the *cantus* $\hat{8}$–$\hat{7}$–$\hat{8}$ cadence in the lowest voice.

Types 2 and 3 are shown in Example 14-9. In Example a, the bass has $\hat{2}$–$\hat{3}$ instead of $\hat{2}$–$\hat{1}$. Example b shows an evaded phrygian cadence. In Examples c and d, the cadence in the upper two voices is proper, but the third voice adds an imperfect consonance that would be inappropriate for a final cadence. In Example e, the *cantus* motion in the soprano is normal, but the cadence is evaded in two ways: The tenor (one of the agents in the suspension) first evades the cadence by moving to $\hat{5}$ and then to $\hat{4}$, and the bass moves to $\hat{6}$. In Example f, the *cantus* motion with a fake suspension is in the lowest voice.

Example 14-9a–f

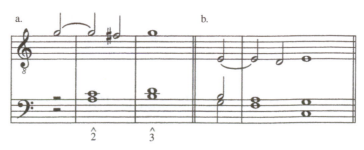

Overlapping or dovetailed cadences can be made in a wide variety of ways. In one way, one of the voices is prevented from resolving. In Example 14-10a, it is the alto that should go to *F* or *A* on the downbeat of the third measure; instead, by being suspended, it can act as the *cantus* motion in a new cadence to *G*. Example 14-10b, from a Jacquet mass, shows a cadence evaded when the soprano skips up to *C* (this a cadence discussed in chapter 11). It was forbidden in two parts but occurs often in three or four (see also Ex. 19-5 and Example Appendix 2-5). Example 14-10c shows an evaded cadence from Morley's "Joy, joy doth so arise." Analyze what you expected and say why you're surprised.

Example 14-10a–c

a.

b. (Jacquet)

c. (Morley)

| *Exercise Series* C: | Note-Against-Note Texture in Three Parts |

Although some of the foregoing examples are in mixed values, in these exercises you are to use only note-against-note rhythm, except in making cadences. The upper parts may cross, you may have repeating notes in two parts as long as the third part moves, and you may have two parts together on a unison as long as the third part has a different note (except at the beginning or end).

Exercise 14–C1 Analysis: Look at Example I-2, the opening of Victoria's "O magnum" and find brief bits of the parallel-tenth model; the parallel-sixth model; the parallel-third model; cadences.

Exercise 14–C2 Improvising or writing fauxbourdon.
  A. Choose a short CF fragment (six to nine notes—look in Ex. 1-3) that ends with a descending step, and then write it in a register high enough that the highest singer can sing it comfortably. The two lower singers, seeing only this part, improvise in fauxbourdon, beginning and ending on perfect intervals but without a cadence.
  B. Using the same fragment, the singer of the top line (the CF) announces a rhythm, including a cadential suspension, and lower parts improvise in the same rhythm, departing only to make the suspension at the cadence.

Exercise 14–C3 Writing (only!) in the parallel-sixth model.
  A. Write a short fragment so that it lies in an appropriate range for the middle voice, give it rhythm so that it ends with whole notes "2–1," and add a part above and one below. Example 1-3c (Kyrie IX) is a good example to use. Begin and end with perfect consonances in as both voices.
  B. The same as A, with rhythm and a cadential suspension.
  C. The same as A, but with the upper parts inverted at the octave (the parallel-third model).

Exercise 14–C4 Improvising or writing the parallel-tenth model.
  A. Choose a short fragment, play it in the lowest voice with parallel tenths above, and improvise or write a tenor line. Remember to look ahead: If the outer lines rise, you'll want to start your line as close to the upper one as possible so that you can go in contrary motion, and vice versa; if you get stuck at a registral extreme, skip an octave on a weak beat and start over.
  B. The same as A, sung by three people.
  C. The same as A with rhythm and a final cadence with a cadential suspension (use one of the cadences shown in Exx. 14-7e and g).
  D. (More difficult): Sing or write the CF in the tenor, and add two outer voices moving in parallel tenths.

Beginning of Sample Solution to Exercise 14–C3A

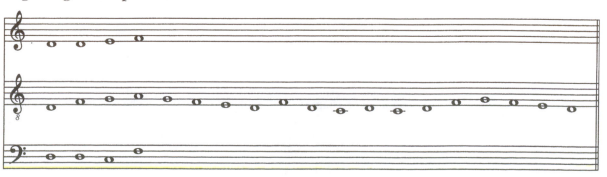

Two Parts in Mixed Values Against a CF (Hard Rules, Continued)

6. **Each line added to the CF must make legal two-voice counterpoint with the CF, as described in chapters 3–7, except for the new rule about fourths and diminished fifths between the upper parts** (see Rules 2 and 3, earlier).

7. **If two parts move together against the CF, they must be consonant with each other even when dissonant with the CF.** Occasionally we find lines running in parallel fourths.

8. **A voice may enter on a note making a dissonance if it is the agent in a suspension.** See the asterisks in the Palestrina examples immediately following. Note that the upper voices cross—be careful you are aware of which voice is on top.

Illustration of Hard Rules

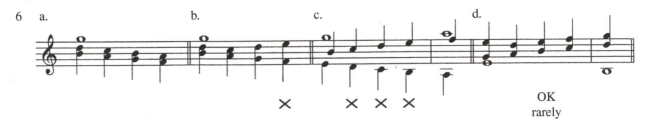

As we discussed in chapter 11, dissonant figures must be completed. In species 1–3, it is generally the shorter note that must behave itself with respect to the slower-moving note, according to the rules for its species.

Some additional ways to add a third voice to a dissonant suspension (other than in cadences) are shown as x-shaped notes in Examples 14-10a–f. A second x-shaped note is required when the resolution of the suspension would be dissonant with the first x-shaped note: In Example 14-10c and f, the resolution of the suspension would be dissonant with the x-shaped note on the downbeat, and so that note must move. In fourth species, we must never hear dissonance in another voice at the moment of resolution (Ex. g).

Example 14-10a–g

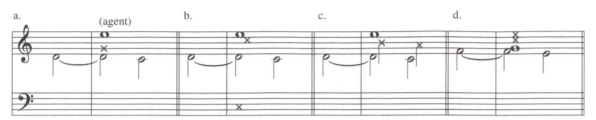

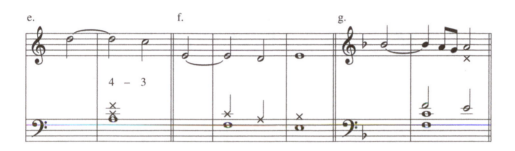

Legal d3q may now be doubled (Ex. 14-11a), and so may suspensions (Ex. 14-11b–f—we have already seen a double suspension in parallel fourths in Ex. 14-1e). We rarely find quarter-note motion against a dissonant suspension. Note that the *D* in Example 14.11d (shown with an arrow) must continue down as a dissonant passing tone or be tied as part of a fake suspension like that shown in Example 14-7j.

Example 14-11a–f

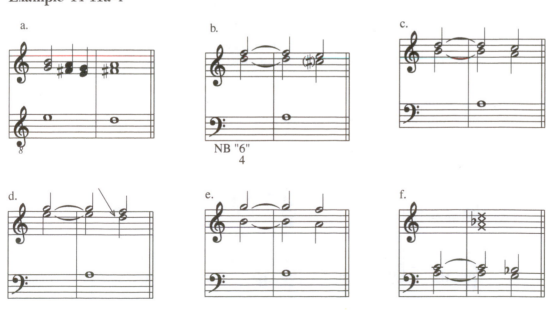

It is much harder to evaluate vertical consonance in three parts than in two. You must get used to checking each voice pair: the top voice with the middle voice, the top voice with the lowest voice, and the middle voice with the lowest voice. Here are a few examples of common errors in three-part writing; make sure you know what is wrong at each X.

Example 14-12

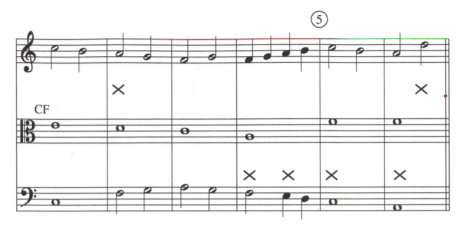

Soft Rules

1. Sonority: Try to have three different pitch classes in any vertical sonority (except at the beginning and end). When this is impossible, try to have some imperfect consonance in vertical sonorities (except at the beginning and end).

2. Rhythmic variety: You may write whole notes together in two of the three parts as long as the third part has some more interesting rhythm; avoid having all three parts moving in the same rhythm for more than two attacks. By the same token, you may move two parts in parallel motion for longer than before as long as the third part moves obliquely or contrarily.

3. You may have unisons between two parts as long as the third part has a different note (except at the end, when all parts may end on the same note).

4. The upper voice may cross. If the lower two parts cross, be careful not to have fourths. The lowest voice may not cross above the highest.

5. You may have repeated notes against repeated notes in two of three parts as long as the third voice has a different rhythm or, if you are using a text, if all the voices are involved in text declamation.

Illustration of Soft Rules

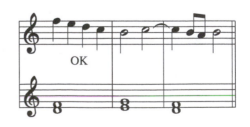

Exercise Series **B:** Find the Errors

Exercise 14-B1

Mark hard errors with X and soft errors with (X).

Exercise 14-B2

Exercise Series **C:**

These exercises are modeled on the CF fragment exercises in chapters 3–6, except that now the CF is in two voices. How would a CF get to be in two voices in the first place? Well, many composers fashioned a canon out of the given melody before adding other parts. The last movements of masses and magnificats often use this technique, and it is also found in Palestrina motets. Among the following examples you will recognize chants from elsewhere in this book, rhythmicized so as to make imitation possible. (Two of these examples, 14-C1 and 14-C4, require an added line below—for the rest you may add a line either above or below). For each one, you can:

A. play or write out the given duo and sing or write a line in first species;

B. the same as A, but in second species;

C. the same as A, but in third species;

D. the same as A, but in fourth species;

E. the same as A, but adding a line in mixed species using a rhythm of your choice from chapter 7 or a motive chosen from the exercises in chapter 8. Try to have three different pitch classes in vertical sonorities as often as possible.

Exercise 14-C1 (Morales Magnificat primi toni)

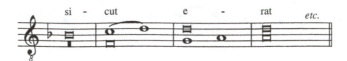

Exercise 14-C2 (Palestrina Missa "ut re mi fa sol la")

Exercise 14-C3 (chanson "Petite camusette")

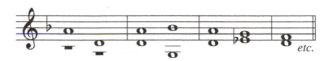

Exercise 14-C4 (Willaert "Ad coenam Agni")

Exercise 14-C5 (Morales Missa "Ave Maria")

Exercise 14-C6 (Morales Missa "Ave maris stella")

In the following exercises, add two different lines in whole notes above and two more below to each of these florid duos (to be different, the solutions above should not have two consecutive notes in common; likewise those below). Treat these as fragments. You may cross voices.

Exercise 14-C7

Exercise 14-C8

Sample solution to Exercise 14-C5 option B (second species above):

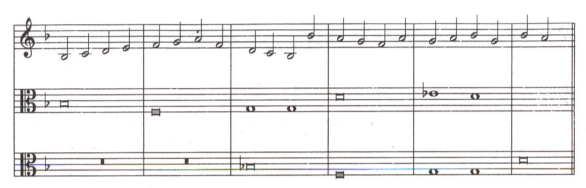

Study of Treatise Example

In this excellent example by Zarlino, seven instances of cadential $\hat{8}$–$\hat{7}$s have been indicated, among which you will find two proper cadences and five evaded cadences. Asterisks indicate fourths between the two upper *sounding* notes that are part of consonant sonorities (watch out for voice crossing). Count how many rich, three-pitch-class sonorities occur!

In this example there is a bit of motivic consistency: re-ut-fa-mi-re (labeled A), the first five notes of the CF, occurs five and a half times in the added voices, but two of these are in a free duo before the CF starts. Also, a re-la scale (labeled B) occurs five times.

Example 14-12 (Zarlino)

Study of Repertoire Example

Counterpoint With a Motive

We find good examples of this technique in the German chorale repertoire. Example 14-13 is a setting of "Vater unser" in which Praetorius uses two short rhythmic motives, labeled A and B in the beginning of the example. These motives generally maintain their rhythm and intervals, although several are incomplete. **Label other occurrences of these two motives.** Note that the transpositions maintain interval species (first-species fifth and first-species fourth) except in mm. 8–11 where the modal orientation changes, leading to a cadence on *F* in m. 13. After the final cadence to *D* in m. 16 there is a sort of coda, with the two lower parts moving against the long final note, concluding with a "plagal" cadence tacked on after the real cadence to the last syllable.

Note-Value Inflation

In early seventeenth-century music there occurred a "note-value inflation" so that the half note is the beat unit, not the whole note. Thus the half notes in the CF in Praetorius's piece should be thought of as whole notes in Renaissance style: they are the beat unit (MM 60–80). If you recopied this piece into note values twice as long, it would stylistically resemble all the other music in this book. Thus the fourth species at the end of bar 2 is not really diminished, it's just written in halved values; the syllables declaimed on quarter and eighth notes correspond to syllables declaimed on half notes and quarters; and finally, the passing notes in the last measure sound like second species, not third.

Example 14-13 (Praetorius) ("Our Father in Heaven, you who call us all to be brothers alike, and to call to you, and who will receive our prayer: let us not pray with our mouths alone, but help it come from the depths of our heart.") (From Michael Praetorius, *Gesamtausgabe der Musikaltschen Werke. Musae Sionae Teil IX (1610)*. Nr. LXV ("Vater unscr"). Karl Heinrich Möseler Verlag.)

Collateral Ranges

No particular rules were given for combining ranges in two parts, but keeping in control of the space becomes a bit harder in three and four parts. If two adjacent voices occupy the same range, they will be of the same type (authentic or plagal) and they will cross constantly (Ex. 14-14a). If they are an octave apart, they will also be of the same type, and they will never cross (14-14b). The most common arrangement in the Renaissance is a happy medium, to alternate plagal and authentic ranges between adjacent voice parts (14-14c). Zarlino refers to this arrangement as <u>collateral</u> <u>ranges</u>. It makes no difference which voices are authentic and which are plagal. This combination of ranges permits crossing for a limited segment of any voice's range, but it does not necessitate it or preclude it entirely. This arrangement also encourages nicely spaced chords. You should plan to use collateral ranges most of the time.

Example 14-14 Collateral Ranges (overlap is shaded)

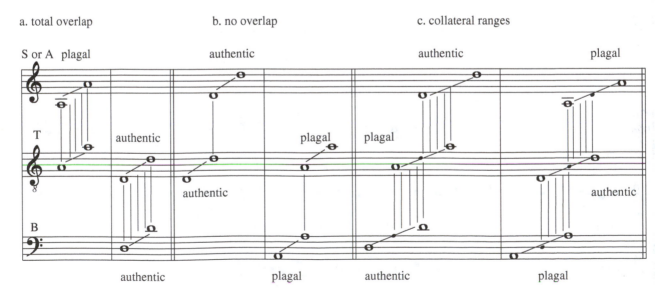

Look back at the three-voice repertoire examples in this chapter and label the ranges of the voices. To what extent do Zarlino and Praetorius use collateral ranges in those examples?

Exercise Series D: | **Counterpoint with a Motive in Three Parts**

Follow the instructions in chapter 8, taking materials from pp. 113–114. You can use the "all possibilities" exercise you did there to speed things up. Decide with your teacher whether to put the CF in breves, whether to use the inverted form of the motive, and whether to use intermediate cadences. You may want to begin with a free imitative statement of the motive in the two added voices before the CF comes in, as in Zarlino's Example 14-12. Remember to check all pairs of voices (top–middle, top–bottom, and middle–bottom) for voice-leading errors. You could also take one of the two-part exercises you wrote in chapter 8 and simply add a third voice, an exercise suggested by Zarlino and Morley. If your parts were widely spaced, you may need to add the third part in between.

As in two-voice writing, a half-note rest may be used before the repetition of a motive, as long as the notes before and after are consonant (keeping in mind the exception stated in hard rule 8 in this chapter).

In these exercises **you must use collateral ranges** as described earlier.

Real Life Exercise | In the introduction to his ricercars on "La Spagna" (two of which you saw in Exx. 9-15 and 9-16), Ortiz tells the keyboard player to improvise imitations as well as play the bass line. Suppose a friend of yours wants to play the keyboard part of one of these ricercars, and has asked you to write in some imitations. In addition to finding places to put motives in close imitation, try taking lines from anywhere in Ortiz's piece. You know that the melody of "La Spagna" contains repeated bits, so you could look at corresponding fragments and see if Ortiz's own counterpoint in one instance might fit against his counterpoint in another. This is a more liberal view of "imitation." For instance, in Example 9-15, the counterpoint in mm. 8–9 (over *C–D* in the CF) could be added to the existing counterpoints both in m. 15 and in m. 27. The reverse could be done as well (take the counterpoint from m. 27 and put it in at m. 8). When you make up your own material, try to maintain Ortiz's exact vocabulary as well: in this ricercar he uses *no* skips of a fourth, fifth, or sixth, and he never uses the rhythm ♩ ♩ ♩ on a strong beat.

15

Three Parts in Mixed Values

Without a CF, it becomes a bit harder to evaluate the voice leading in three parts. As with two parts in mixed values, we get practice by solving puzzle canons (you may want to review chapter 11). Try various possibilities, discarding solutions when a rule is broken.

Three-Voice Puzzle Canon Exercise

In these puzzles by Cerreto, the time interval (either two or three whole notes) is given, either by presas (here the presa looks like a 5 with two dots), coronatas (fermatas), or both. The two consequent voices may begin at any diatonic pitch interval, and the three voices may begin on the same note, or on two different notes, or on three different notes. The little "enigmas" in Latin or Italian are hints that are supposed to guide you to the right solution (or that you will find clever, once you have found the right solution by trial and error).

One of the difficulties with this exercise is that you don't know whether the guide is the top, middle, or bottom voice. As you sketch in possible solutions, you will need a lot of space, so it is best to put the given voice on a staff with two other staves above and below it (a note-writing computer program might make this easier). First transcribe the given tunes with bar lines to facilitate lining up the parts, and change the clef if you are uncomfortable with the given ones (tenor and soprano clefs pop up here for the first time). Other things to watch out for:

- Don't expect standard cadences—these pieces just stop.
- Expect a lot of voice crossing.
- Note that some may have more than one solution.
- The "I" in some of the hints is the given tune talking.

(**Examples 15-1a–h** from Scipione Cerreto, *Della Prattica Musica*, 1601; fac-
simile reprint, Arnaldo Forni Editore, 1969. Used by permission.)

Example 15-1a "Follow me, until I arrive at the place."

Example 15-1b "Behold your light. Two in one" (the alto and tenor clefs are a hint too).

Example 15-1c "Duo in the ratio 2:3" (i.e., the perfect fifth).

Example 15-1d "In the highest register [i.e., the notes of the gamut above a'],
harmonize two in one."

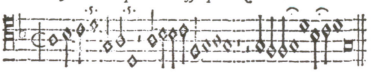

Example 15-1e "I am found below, and I go wandering / and whoever wants
me goes looking for me."

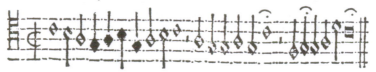

Example 15-1f "I am the guide, but whoever follows me lowers, / after a time, his uncertain path / so that he will see that what I say is a fact" (*tempo* in Italian means "time" and can also mean a breve).

Example 15-1g "I am lower than you; if to follow me / everybody rises three whole steps / what can I say, these are true signs."

Example 15-1h "If you would follow me, be humble" (i.e., lower yourself).

Hard rules relaxed: We have already seen that the preparation of a suspension can be momentarily dissonant (see Ex. 11-4), and we have seen the patient rearticulated (Ex. 11-3), both exceptions to the rule that notes that attack together must be consonant. **Now *any motion* may be used against descending stepwise D3q at *any time* (not just in cadential suspensions).**

Example 15-2

If a half rest and a half note substitute for a whole note (as often happens at the beginning of a motive), **the note entering after the rest may clash with a descending stepwise d3q,** another exception to the rule that notes entering after rests must be consonant. In this case the weak half note "wins" because it could have sounded on the downbeat, and it is d3q that is "wrong" and must resolve:

Example 15-3

Study of Treatise Examples

Zarlino recommends adding a voice to a pre-existing duo. In Example 15-4 he has added two different third voices to a duo by Josquin. First sing or play the duo. Note the repeated section in the middle. Note also how the soprano line in mm. 13–14 is echoed in the tenor in mm. 17–18; in fact, m. 18 is the inversion at the octave of m. 14. Each line leads to a cadence at the end-point of its range (*D* for the soprano, *G* for the tenor). This shows one way cadential goals and modal ranges can be associated.

Now sing the duo with Zarlino's possible added voices. Which one do you like better? Why? The commentary below on Zarlino's added voices covers melodic motions, range, cadences, imitation, repetition, rhythmic variety, and occurrences of sonorities containing three different pitch classes.

Melodic Motions

Zarlino is somewhat apologetic about the lack of stepwise motion in his added lines: "It will be noted that the added parts often have leaping movements. This is acceptable because of the great difficulty met in trying to adjust a new voice to the composition's continuous lines. For it is one thing to write three parts at one time, another to add a third to two given parts. The latter is a far more difficult task, one for a consummate musician, and deserving of high praise when carried out."

Range

The original voices of the duo are Hypomixolydian above and Mixolydian below. Zarlino adds one possible third voice *in between* the original voices—this voice is in the same range as the lower voice, functioning as a "second tenor," and it crosses a great deal. Zarlino's other possible third voice lies *below* the lower voice, and it is Hypomixolydian, resulting in a top-to-bottom arrangement of plagal/authentic/plagal (i.e., collateral) ranges.

Cadences

Another feature of this example by Zarlino is the way the third voice participates in the cadences. When the upper voices make the 2–3 or 7–6 cadential suspension, the only note Zarlino puts *below* is the $\hat{5}$ (see mm. 3, 5, and 15). When the higher of the two added possibilities is really *in between* the upper voices, then Zarlino gives that voice $\hat{4}$ (see mm. 9, 18, 21, and 27), making diminished 6/3 chords. In the last cadence the second tenor actually has $\hat{6}$–$\hat{5}$–$\hat{4}$, a possible variant.

Imitation

Considering that Josquin did not compose this duo with the idea that a third voice imitate against it, it is impressive how much imitation Zarlino manages to squeeze out of his third voices. He does this when Josquin has used figures that facilitate close imitations: the "re-fa-sol-la" motive in mm. 15 and 16, the scales in quarter notes beginning in m. 22, and the short scales beginning with a dotted half note in m. 26. These figures permit a great many imitations, and they are found in so many different pieces as to be sixteenth-century clichés.

Repetition

The little section on "re-fa-sol-la" is repeated exactly in Josquin's original duo (mm. 16–18 = mm. 19–21), but Zarlino, the enemy of direct repetition, has made his alternative added voices as different as he could, right up to the cadence, at which point he has much less flexibility.

Rhythmic Variety

Zarlino generally avoids rhythmic unison with either of the given voices for any more than three half notes (except for five half notes between bass and soprano, mm. 13–14).

Three-Pitch-Class Sonorities

The addition of a *D* under the second whole note confirms the mode and adds the third pitch class. As you would expect, the goal notes of cadences do not invite such sonorities, since the proper cadence calls for the two principal voices to close to a unison.

Example 15-4 (Josquin/Zarlino)

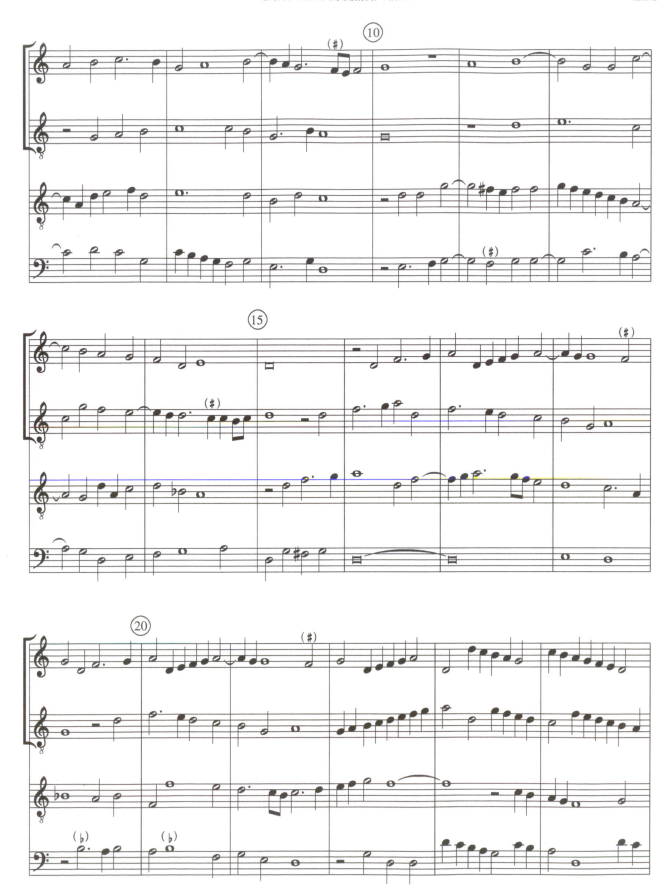

There is some dissonance treatment here that requires comment: both of Zarlino's added voices create a skip from a dissonance in m. 4. This formula, a step down to a dissonance followed by a skip of a third, is characteristic of the earlier part of the sixteenth century, and we will use it as part of the long-note cambiata, described in chapter 17. The diminished fourth species in m. 7 is allowable, but the resolution to a perfect consonance is discouraged in only two parts.

Study of Repertoire Examples

Analysis

For each of the following pieces (Exx. 15-5 through 15-8), look for the following:

- sonorities with three pitch classes (this has been begun for you in Ex. 15-5)
- use of dissonance (make sure you can "explain" each one)
- freer use of d3q as described in this chapter
- the "chanson" idiom discussed in Ex. 11-5
- imitations in which all three voices participate (even, sometimes, if the words are not the same)
- the parallel-tenth model, the parallel-sixth model, and the parallel-third model
- collateral ranges
- cadences; for each, label the *cantus* and tenor motions, describe it as proper or evaded, and say how the other voices interact with the cadence (e.g., "ii6/5," imperfect sonority in the bass".)
- text accents (and word painting, if applicable)

Comment on the use of repetition. Sometimes when a phrase is repeated, the longer setting is last (as at the end of the Banchieri motet, Ex. 9-4); sometimes the shorter setting is last, acting as a "tag" or elided with the following phrase.

The idea of a free-standing duo contained in a trio is a feature of some rep-eroitre examples, allowing them to be sung by two or three people, as available. An instructive example is a French chanson by Tielman Susato, "Ma maitresse ma bonne amye."

Example 15-5 (Susato) ("My mistress, my good friend, most humbly I beg you, keep me in mind; and I swear by my conscience that as long as I have life, loving you will be my desire.") [instruction for the duo: "Sing in two parts if you like, then all three will sing together."] [instruction for the third part: "If you want to sing, here's some advice, wait until you're needed."]

Example 15-6 is the opening of a chanson we saw arrangements of in chapter 12. Note the irregular dissonance in m. 5.

Example 15-6 (Sermisy) ("Friend, allow me to love you, and don't hold me to…")

In the opening of the Benedictus from Francisco Guerrero's Missa "De la Batalla escoutez" we hear the same combination used by Crequillon in Example 16-8. Renaissance composers routinely modeled on each other's works, and much interesting musicological investigation has been done tracking down borrowed material. Guerrero is less systematic in presenting his borrowed melodies: He uses free countermelodies that don't repeat (often running briefly in parallel motion with the principal melodies), variants of the head motives, and different time and pitch intervals of imitation.

What are his goals? In m. 5, a string of quarter notes builds up some excitement leading to the delayed entrance of the third voice. In mm. 9–10, a new section begins in which the "qui venit" motive is broken off and treated to its own point of imitation. This section cadences in m. 13, where the three "Benedictus" motives comes back and enter in close succession. In m. 17, parallel tenths in the outer voices lead to the final cadence of the first half of the movement. You may want to look at the whole movement to see if the same principles apply in the second half.

Example 15-7 (Guerrero) ("Blessed is he who comes [in the same of the Lord.]") (Guerrero, Francisco. *Opera Omnia*, vol. 4. Edited by José Llorens Cisteró. Barcelona: Consejo Superior de Investigaciones Cientificas, 1982.)

be - ne - dic - tus   qui ve -   nit   in (etc.)

nit, be - ne - dic - tus   qui ve -   nit   in no - (etc.)

nit   be - ne - dic - tus   qui ve -   nit

The following example, a complete Magnificat verse, is instructional for the way the rhythmic energy is handed off from one part to another. The strings of quarter notes overshoot their own starting place (A in the soprano) to reach a new high point (C), at which point the note values get longer and the line descends. In m. 7, the soprano and alto have ceded the floor to the bass's quarter notes. In mm. 8–9, as the bass is relaxing, the soprano and alto pick up the momentum. Mm. 10–11 are more rhythmically inactive because they mark the end of the first half of the movement and contain a cadence and the opening of the new soggetto.

Example 15-8 (Palestrina) ("He hath put down the mighty from their seat: and hath exalted the humble and meek.")

Note on Psalm and Canticle Tones

You will have noticed that Example 15-8 is somewhat peculiar, modally speaking. It begins by emphasizing third-species fourths in the head motive and then proceeds to end on *G*, which lies at the bottom of a first-species fourth, implying the Dorian or Hypodorian mode. This is because the movement is taken from a Magnificat, which is traditionally chanted monophonically on a *tone*. Psalm and Canticle tones (the Magnificat is technically a poem called a canticle) consist primarily of a single note called a *reciting tone* on which the bulk of the text is intoned. However, this main note is introduced by a little melodic formula, and the middle and the end of the line are punctuated by other little melodic motions. There are eight such tones, and they bear little resemblance to the modes you have studied. Example 15-8 shows the seventh verse (the one Palestrina set). Look for occurrences of the various melodic formulas in the Palestrina.

Example 15-9 (Magnificat tone 2 transposed)

Exercise Series C: Fill in the missing portions of these pieces, looking for opportunities to imitate, cadence, and use the three-voice models introduced in chapter 14.

Exercise 15-C1 ("Let's go gaily, my cutie, you and me...")

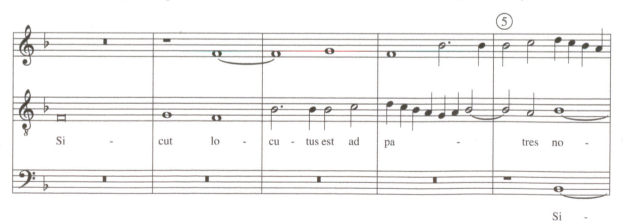

Exercise 15-C2 ("As he promised to our forefathers, Abraham and his seed, for ever.")

Free Three-Part Writing

A free trio is like a free duo: It consists of a point of imitation that breaks off to make a cadence, then a cadence, then a new point (or a varied repetition of the old point), leading to another cadence, etc. Since the cadence in two voices consists of two obligatory motions, (the tenor and the *cantus*), the elision only takes place at the goal note (or what Sancta Maria calls "after the cadence"). In the excerpts from chansons by Susato, Sermisy, and Palestrina (Exx. 15-5, 15-6, and 15-8), the new phrases are elided as in two-part music, with the new soggetto beginning after the goal note has been reached.

Elided Cadences in Three Parts

However, in three parts, the elision at the cadence offers new possibilities. The soggetto of the new point of imitation can begin *while* the other two voices are cadencing; that is, it may enter at the resolution of the cadential suspension (step 3) or during the dissonance (step 2), during the preparation (step 1), or even earlier ("before the cadence").

In the Guerrero example (15-7), look at the cadence to *G* in mm. 8–9. The tenor has the *cantus* function, the bass has the tenor function, and the soprano enters at the moment of preparation. (This is the cadence discussed above in Example 14-10b) If you look ahead at Ex. 16-2a by Palestrina, you'll see an example where the new soggetto enters on the third step of the cadence (mm. 6 and 8). And a really long overlap can be seen in Example 16-14 by Palestrina, where the soprano enters long before we even think a cadence is coming (mm. 64–66)! Finally, look at Victoria's "O magnum:" At which step of the cadence does the tenor enter in m. 8? Identify the other cadences in that piece, and discuss the degree of overlap with each new soggetto.

If you want to take advantage of this new opportunity, you can do these short preparatory exercises.

Exercise Series **C:**

Exercise 15-C3 Add a soggetto *above* the given cadence that begins (a) before the cadence; (b) on step 1; (c) on step 2; (d) on step 3. In order to give these new soggetti a little élan, it will be helpful to imagine a bit of text (an intermediate phrase like "in nomine Domini").

Exercise 15-C4 Add a soggetto *below* the given cadence that begins (a) before the cadence; (b) on step 1; (c) on step 2; (d) on step 3. Think about text as in Exercise 15-C3.

Exercise 15-C5 Add a soggetto *in between* the voices of the given cadence that begins (a) before the cadence; (b) on step 1; (c) on step 2; (d) on step 3. Think about text as in Exercise 15-C3.

Given cadence:

Exercise 15-C6 Add the two normal cadential motions (tenor and *cantus*) to the soggetti provided here, making the soggetto enter (a) before the cadence or (b) on the second step of the cadence. The two voices may fit above, below, or on either side of the given soggetto, and there may be several possibilities for each.

Exercise 15-C7 Add the two normal cadential motions (tenor and *cantus*) to the soggetti provided here, making the soggetto enter (a) before the cadence or (b) on the first step of the cadence. The two voices may fit above, below, or on either side of the given soggetto, and there may be several possibilities for each.

Ex. 15-C6   **Ex. 15-C7**

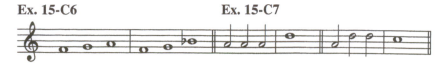

Exercise Series **D:**   Free Three-Part Composition

Exercise 15-D1   Use melodies in chapter 12 to make three-part settings.

Exercise 15-D2   Add a voice in a collateral mode below one of the duos you wrote in chapter 12.

Exercise 15-D3   Compose a canon at the unison in three voices. Try to have a standard cadence.

Exercise 15-D4   Compose a canon in which the second and third voices both enter a fifth above the guide. Try to have a standard cadence.

16

The Three-Voice Invertible Canon

One of the most common patterns of imitation in a three-voice texture is the invertible canon. In it, the time interval between the first two entries is the same as that between the second and third entries. (If the time intervals were different, we would call it "free" imitation.) It is also characterized by the order of vocal entries: if the second voice enters below the first, then the third will enter above the second; if the second voice enters above the first, the third will enter below the second. This order of entries is why we call it invertible: the first two entries make between them a duo, or two-voice combination, or module (we use these terms interchangeably) that is repeated in invertible counterpoint between the second and third entries.

The Two-Voice Combination, or Module

It is in the nature of imitation that the beginning of the melody both precedes its end and accompanies it. We can label the beginning A and the end B, as shown in Example 16-1. In a three-voice invertible canon, the module called "A below B" recurs as "A above B." The original module and the inverted module (bracketed) are of course the same length, because the time intervals of imitation are the same, and the lengths of A and B are the same. The modules begin when the next voice enters. The melodic continuation represented by "etc." does not concern us now.

Example 16-1

In the above example, the second voice enters below the first and the third enters above the second. The module "A above B" is the the inversion at the octave of "A below B." If you inspect the vertical intervals, you can see that the fifth on the downbeat of m. 4 becomes a fourth in m. 6. (In "Row, Row, Row Your Boat" this dissonance doesn't matter, but in Renaissance polyphony it matters a lot.) We will not use invertible counterpoint at the octave here because we want the variety and complexity that come from imitation at the fifth.

Study of Repertoire Examples

The Benedictus movement of Palestrina's Missa "Gia fu" (Ex. 16-2a) is a three-voice invertible canon from beginning to end. In this piece, the tenor-bass combination in any two-breve period generates the alto-bass combination in the next two-breve period through invertible counterpoint at the twelfth. You can see that the bass of mm. 3–4 has been moved up an octave to become the alto in mm. 5–6, and the tenor in mm. 3–4 has been moved down a fifth to become the bass in mm. 5–6. Ignore the tenor in mm. 5–6 to focus on the modular duo, which has been schematized in Example 16-2b as "B above A" followed by "A above B."

The vertical intervals in the first modular duo and its repetition have been labeled; all corresponding intervals add up to 13 (as in the chart in chapter 13). While sixths in consonant positions never occur between these pairs of voices (T-B or A-B), they *can* occur between the tenor and alto (as at m. 7). Since the tenor-alto combination never has to be inverted, the tenor line is always free with respect to the alto.

Note how Palestrina is able to make cadences, and what happens to them when they are inverted at the twelfth. The evaded cadence in m. 4 becomes a proper cadence in m. 6 because $\hat{5}$–$\hat{4}$ in the bass becomes $\hat{2}$–$\hat{1}$ in the soprano. In the proper cadence in m. 6, the middle voice has $\hat{2}$–$\hat{3}$ which becomes $\hat{5}$–$\hat{6}$ in m. 8. Look at the complete score to see the final cadence. This movement ends on *D*, and the ranges of the voices in the excerpt are clearly collateral: from top to bottom, authentic/plagal/authentic.

Example 16-2a (Palestrina) ("Blessed is he who comes [in the name of the Lord.]")

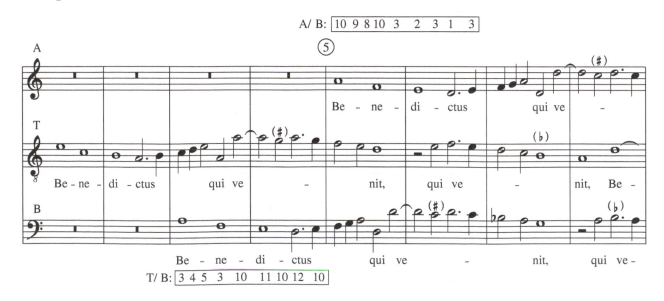

Example 16-2b

			A - 5 + 8
A	B		C
	A - 5		B - 5

Seamlessness

It may seem counterintuitive to slice through the tenor line just at the moment the bass enters, and to say that a structural unit (the module) begins here, but that is precisely the reason that Renaissance music is characterized as <u>seamless</u>. Palestrina makes it seem as though the bass is interrupting the tenor. He does this by using melodic elements of greatest continuity in the guide melody just at the point where the module begins. Two of these are generic, featureless patterns: regular note values (quarters) and scalewise motion. Furthermore, sense of continuity is heightened by the increased speed of the tenor just before the bass enters. Compare this with the relatively clunky, <u>periodic</u> phrasing of the four-part folk round "Have You Seen the Ghost of John," where the last note of each phrase but the second is long, stopping the phrase dead. The phrases mostly line up, starting and ending together, and don't overlap at all (the only true elision is between the second phrase and the third):

Example 16-3

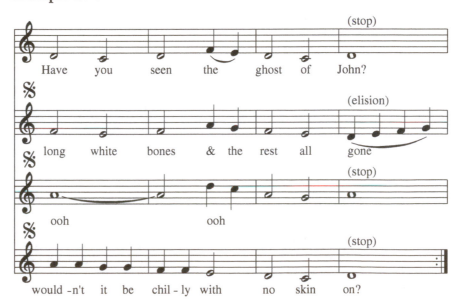

Another way to give the impression of seamlessness is to make sure the time interval of imitation is not the same as (or an integral multiple of) the metric unit (the breve). In the following example the duple meter is at odds with the three-whole-note periods of the module. The melodic element of continuity that blurs the edge of the module is the sustained note on the syllable "-fi-":

Example 16-4 (Palestrina) ("He was crucified also for us...")

Text is another factor that can blur the borders of the structural duo. In the following diagram of Example 16-5, the module is two breves long, so the metric periods and the modular periods coincide, but the the words are placed so that their beginnings and ends never coincide with the module. The words have been presented schematically in the boxes that represent the duos.

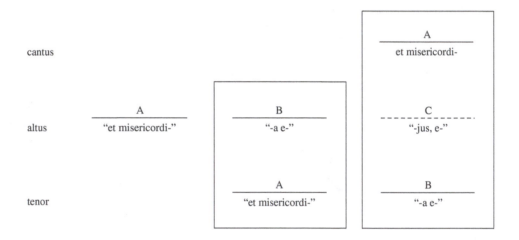

The Invertible Canon Opening

Invertible canon is most often used to build a shorter section of a piece, often the beginning of a phrase. An example is the beginning of the "Et misericordia" section of Victoria's "Magnificat tertii toni" (Ex. 16-5). Note where imitation breaks off to prepare the cadence.

Example 16-5 (Victoria) ("And His mercy [is from generation to generation.]")

Sometimes invertible canon is used in the middle of a phrase. Look back at the Susato chanson "Ma maitresse" (Ex. 15-5). A couple of the imitations that involve all three parts are in fact invertible canons (m. 11 and mm. 37–38). Look back also at the puzzle canons at the beginning of chapter 15; which ones had more than one solution? Why?

Exercise Series C: Short Invertible Canon Opening

Compose an invertible canon modeled on the preceding Victoria example, using Example 16-6 as a guide. Step 1: Write melody A first, transposing it down a fifth in the second voice. Step 2: Add B after the first A (it must be invertible at the twelfth), copy it down a fifth after the second A and copy A into the third voice an octave above the second A. Step 3: Fill in C (free material) between A and B. Step 4: Lead to a cadence on the final. To ensure continuity, avoid changing note values between A and B, and if you are using a text, avoid changing words or syllables across the boundary of the modular duo.

Example 16-6

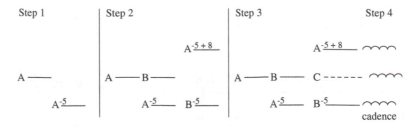

Vocal Ranges, Interval of Imitation, and Order of Entries

There are four ways to order the entries of a high voice, a middle voice, and a low voice in an invertible canon: MHL, MLH, HLM, and LHM. The Victoria was MLH; the following examples illustrate the remaining types. The As and Bs have been labeled and the vertical intervals in the modular duo labeled.

Example 16-7 (from Missa "En espoir" by Clemens non Papa)

Example 16-8 (from Missa "Mort m'a privé" by Thomas Crequillon)

Example 16-9 From Orlando di Lasso, Missa "Puisque j'ay perdu," in Siegfried Hermelink, ed., *Messen 10-17; Messen des Druckes Paris 1577. Sämtliche Werke Neue Reihe,* Bärenreiter, 1964. Used by permission.

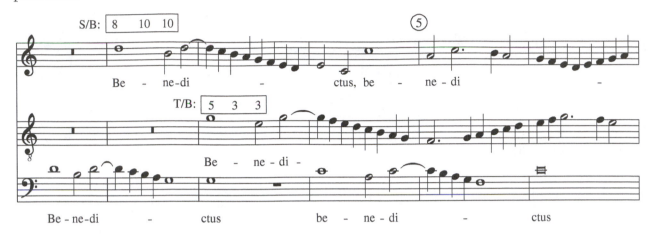

Label A's and B's in Example 16-9. Examples 16-5 and 16-7 to 16-9 have been schematized in Example 16-10. The first line, after the composer's name, summarizes the order of entries, the intervals of imitation, and the vocal ranges from top to bottom. In each schema, the ranges are sketched in terms of the important notes of the mode each is in.

In this formula, all voices must start on the modally important notes (final and fifth), and imitation must be at the fifth or the octave (imitation at the fourth is impossible). Thus the middle voice always starts either a fifth above the lowest voice or a fifth below the highest voice. Ranges are collateral (except when a voice is excessive or incomplete). In the Lassus example each voice starts at the high extreme of its range, but in all the others the first note of each voice is in the middle of its range.

Example 16-10

a. (Ex. 16-5, Victoria) MLH; -5 +8; plagal/incomplete/plagal

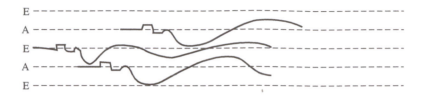

b. (Ex. 16-7, Clemens) HLM; -8 +5; plagal/authentic/mixed

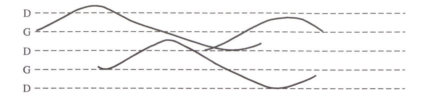

c. (Ex. 16-8, Crequillon) MHL; +5 -8; authentic/plagal (and later mixed)/authentic

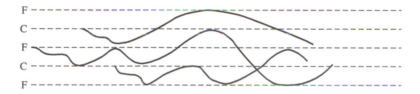

d. (Ex. 16-9, Lassus) LHM; +8 -5; plagal/authentic/plagal

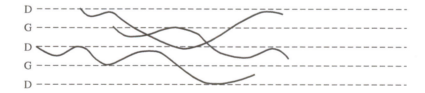

Exercise Series *C:* Invertible Canon Openings on Given Motives

The following motives (or *soggetti*) have been taken from Renaissance pieces that use invertible canon openings. You are to assume that each melody contains an A and a B. To find where A and B divide means finding when the imitating voice enters. Treat each one as a puzzle canon, looking for a time and pitch interval that will create a combination invertible at the twelfth (i.e., a combination that contains no sixths). If you can imitate at the fifth *above* you can model on Ex. 16-10 c; if you can imitate at the fifth *below* you can model on Ex. 16-10a or d. Then compose a complete invertible canon opening, adding free material (C) and leading to a cadence on the final of the mode. Label the mode of each voice, box the modules, and label the vertical intervals in the original combination and the inverted combination.

Given Motives for Invertible Canon Openings

Exercise 16-C1

Exercise 16-C2

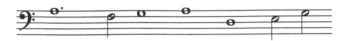

Exercise 16-C3

Exercise 16-C4

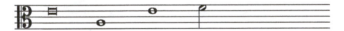

Exercise 16-C5

Exercise Series **D:**   Benedictus Project

First, read the "Rules for Text Setting" in Appendix 1. You can do Part 1 alone or both parts.

Part 1: Use one of the given head motives for the word "Benedictus." Invent the continuation (for "qui venit"), being sure that the duo is invertible at the twelfth. Plan your scheme of collateral voice ranges, order of entries, and time and pitch intervals of imitation. Don't worry about crossing voices—as you know, this is almost inevitable when you use collateral ranges. After the third A melody is in, you need not continue the B melody exactly in that voice; simply lead to a cadence. You may repeat the word "Benedictus" and the phrase "qui venit" together or each part separately. The cadence must be to the final of the mode on "ve-nit" unless you are also writing the second part, in which case it should be to the fifth of the mode.

Part 2: After the cadence on "-nit," begin a new point of imitation using one of the given head motives for the phrase "in nomine." You may repeat the words "in nomine" and "Domini" separately or together, cadencing to the final of the mode on "-mi-ni."

Head Motives

Exercise 16-D

Triple Counterpoint

In triple counterpoint, the relative positions of all three melodies can be changed. In the three-voice module below, lines A, B, and C can be moved with respect to each other. A and B can be reversed, A and C can be reversed, and C and B can be reversed. However, in this particular combination, A can never be the lowest voice (why?). This means that of the six possible permutations of A, B, and C, only the four shown in Example 16-11 are usable.

Example 16-11

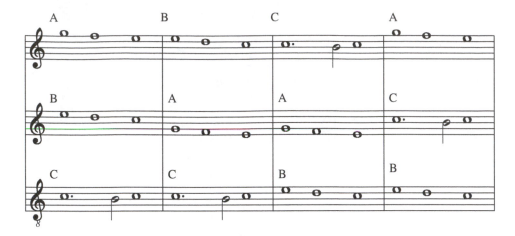

In the permutations shown above the transpositions are always by octave. This means that the restrictions on which possible permutations can be used depend on the rules for invertible counterpoint at the octave. The reason A can never be the lowest voice is that in the original its first note makes a fifth with the first note of C; if A were to appear below C, an illegal fourth would result.

We will not discuss triple counterpoint invertible at the octave here for the reasons cited earlier: we want to explore the complexity and variety afforded by invertible counterpoint at the twelfth.

In the following examples from Zarlino, two melodies move down an octave and one moves up a fifth. In both, the soprano and tenor are moved down an octave to become the tenor and bass, and the bass is moved up a fifth to become the soprano. This means that the relationship between soprano and tenor is unchanged, but the bass must be invertible at the twelfth with *both* soprano and tenor.

Example 16-12a (Zarlino)

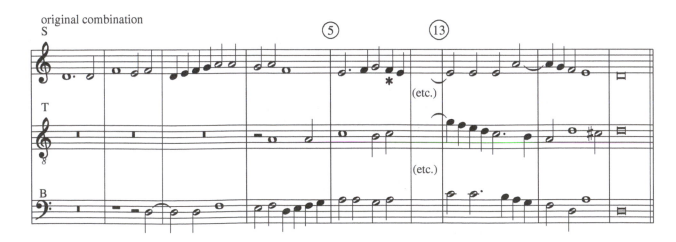

inverted combination

Note how the standard cadence in the original is transformed in the inverted combination. Also, be sure you know what's happening in m. 5 at the asterisk. An interesting feature of this technique is its effect on vocal ranges: the bass voice in the original is authentic Dorian, but it becomes plagal in the inverted combination. How does this affect the principle of collateral ranges?

The special requirements of Zarlino's example is that **in the original:**

1. No sixths can occur in consonant positions between the bass and either the middle voice or the top voice. This is because the bass is inverted at the twelfth with respect to both the original middle voice and the original top voice;

2. No fourths can occur between the middle voice and the top voice. This is because the original middle voice is now the bass line and fourths are illegal with the bass.

Another interesting feature of this technique is the effect of invertible counterpoint at the twelfth on the number of different pitch classes in the vertical sonorities. In Example 16-12b the asterisks show sonorities of only two pitch classes in the original that acquire a third in the inverted combination. The daggers indicate sonorities of three pitch classes in the original combination that are reduced to two in the inversion.

Example 16-12b (Zarlino)

number of pitch classes:

number of pitch classes: 3   3   2   2 3   2   3

Example 16-13

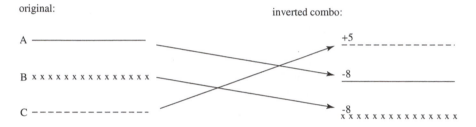

original: inverted combo:

A ————————————————   +5
                                                                            - - - - - - - - - -

B x x x x x x x x x x x x x x x   -8
                                                                            ————————————————

C - - - - - - - - - - - - - -   -8
                                                                            x x x x x x x x x x x x x x x

---

Exercise Series C: **Exercise 16-C1**   Go back to the series C exercises in chapter 14 (the two-voice CFs), and compose a bass line in whole notes that can be transposed up a twelfth as in Zarlino's Example 16-12b (schematized in Ex. 16-13).

Exercise 16-C2   Go back to the series C exercises in chapter 14 (the two-voice CFs), and compose a bass line in mixed values with a motive that can be transposed up a twelfth as in Zarlino's Example 16-12b (schematized in Ex. 16-13).

Repertoire Example for Analysis

The purpose of triple counterpoint is to allow varied repetitions, which can be used to build larger sections. Sing Example 16-14, an excerpt from the Crucifixus section of Palestrina's Missa "Repleatur os meum laude." In the example, five combinations have been boxed. How do the repetitions contribute to the overall structure of this section?

    1. In each box, label the melodic material that is reused. Use letters A, B, C, D, etc. Disregard transposition. In some voices only a small portion of the material in the box is repeated elsewhere. Note that the words are not always associated with the same melodic fragments.

    2. Show which boxes contain the same three melodies. (E.g., "The first box has the same three melodies as the third box.")

    3. Explain how one boxed set of melodies is a transformation of another. (E.g., "A and B are moved up a sixth and C is moved down a seventh.")

Example 16-14 (Palestrina) (". . . and His reign shall have no end.")

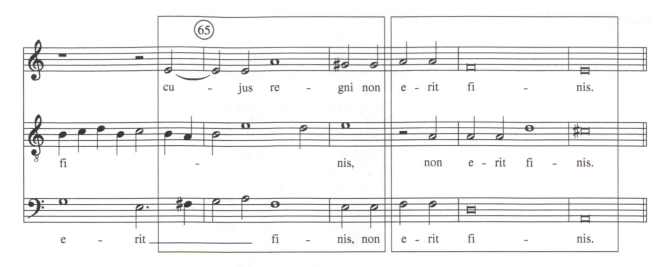

More Repertoire for Analysis

There are so many examples of the invertible canon in the repertoire that a good exercise for you would be to open any volume of Palestrina masses and scan the openings. For more triple-counterpoint-spotting fun, try William Byrd's motet "Tristitia et anxietas," from his 1589 collection, at mm. 20–35; or the Osanna movement of Victoria's Missa "O magnum mysterium"; or the Benedictus from Palestrina's Missa "O admirabile commercium."

Four-Part Writing

Hard Rules for Note-Against-Note Four-Part Writing

1. Never use 6/3 chords at the beginning or end. You may begin and end with perfect sonorities exclusively (unisons, octaves, and fifths in any combination), or you may include thirds. In the final sonority of a mode whose third above the final is normally minor, the third may be altered to become major (cf. Praetorius' Ex. 17-8c).

2. Never use diminished triads in root position. They may be used in first inversion as described in the rules for three-part writing in chapter 14.

3. Use 6/3 chords less than a quarter of the time. Use diminished 6/3 chords as described in chapter 14.

4. Never have more than an octave between soprano and alto, or alto and tenor. The only exception is when crossed voices keep adjacent *sounding* notes an octave or less apart. The bass may be up to a twelfth from the tenor. It is best to plan adjacent voices in collateral (alternating plagal and authentic) ranges.

5. Augmented fourth species may be used to create 6/4, 5/4, and 6/5 chords. The most common use of these is approaching cadences (as "II6/5") but others are possible.

6. You must use three different pitch-classes in each vertical sonority (easier to accomplish in four parts than three) except the first and the last.

7. Use standard cadences.

Before moving on to exercises, we will look at several strategies for composing four-part note-against-note music. It may look like a chord succession to us, but in the Renaissance it was more often described in terms of interval successions between the voices. In one model the tenor and soprano move predominantly in parallel sixths; in another, the outer voices move in parallel tenths; in another, the outer voices alternate vertical intervals sequentially; and finally, there is free writing. After you have studied these models, the exercises will be easier. The soft rules are on p. 257, and the exercises follow.

Illustration of Hard Rules

1.

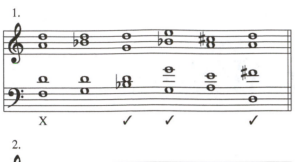

2.

3.

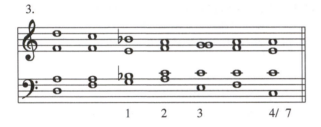

4.

5.

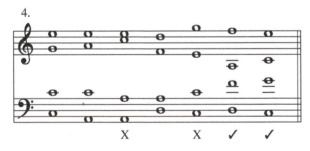

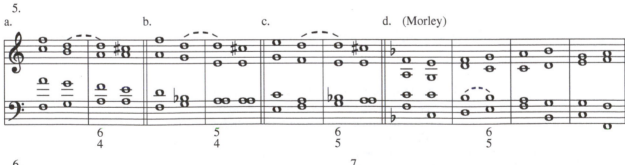

6.

7.

The Parallel-Sixth Model

French chanson melodies were often set in note-against-note counterpoint, the added voices following the given melody in rhythmic unison. Such popular music from the early 1500s is often built on a framework consisting of a duo in which the tenor and soprano move mostly in parallel sixths. The bass is added to this duo, and the alto is added last. In the parallel-sixth model, the bass tends to skip a lot, while the alto does not. At the ends of phrases, normally the tenor and soprano move to an octave at the cadence, the tenor having $\hat{2}$–$\hat{1}$ and the soprano making $\hat{8}$–$\hat{7}$–$\hat{8}$. The soprano delay that makes the syncopated 7–6 suspension is the only deviation from the note-against-note texture (at m. 3 in Ex. 17-1).

Example 17-1 (Sermisy) ("It is day, says the lark...")

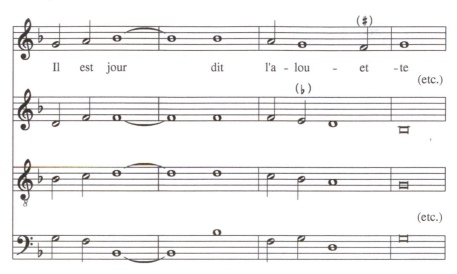

The homorhythmic climax of the opening section of Victoria's "O magnum mysterium" is an example of the parallel-sixth model. From the end of m. 16 to the middle of m. 19 the tenor and soprano move in parallel sixths with only small exceptions. The skips between *F* and *B♭* in the bass, in the context of a phrase centered on *G*, is a characteristic sound in a great deal of Renaissance music and is one consequence of the parallel-sixth model.

The Parallel-Tenth Model

We have already studied moving the outer voices in parallel tenths (chapter 14). Example 17-2 is the beginning of Sermisy's "Il me suffit," whose melody is in the soprano. The first four chords fit the parallel-tenth model, then the parallel-sixth model takes over (note the fifths in mm. 5 and 6 that result from rhythmic anticipations in the soprano). In general, we can say that the parallel-tenth model permits the bass to move more smoothly; it also permits the sixth-to-octave motion to be made by alto and bass instead of tenor and soprano.

Example 17-2 (Sermisy) ("My pains are enough for me, since they have brought me to death.")

Il me suf - fit de tous mes maulx Puis qu'ilz m'ont li - vré a la mort.

Ad Hoc Sequential Patterns

Pietro Cerone suggests ways to fill in a four-part texture based on melodic motions in the soprano and successions of vertical intervals between the outer voices (including, but not limited to, parallel tenths; note that he never uses sixths between the outer voices). Example 17-3 shows a few of the patterns, which he intends beginners to copy wholesale. Some are presented both simple and embellished. Note the bits of close imitation in the embellished versions.

Example 17-3 (Cerone)

a. soprano rising by step, making 10ths and 8ves with the bass

b. skips of a third down, making 15ths and 12ths with the bass

c. skips of a third up, making 10ths with the bass

d. skips of a fourth down, making 17ths and 12ths with the bass

e. skips of a fifth up, making 12ths and 17ths with the bass

Ad Hoc Free Writing

Thomas Morley gives an extended lesson in four-part note-against-note writing, beginning with outer voices and concentrating on doubling as a basic principle (Ex. 17-4). Because Morley's style is to unfold slowly and dramatically, you will find the main points summarized on p. 252. The master begins by giving the student the outer voices and asking him to fill in the inner parts:

Example 17-4a (Morley)

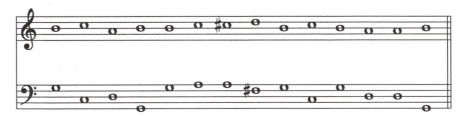

He says the student is to include notes a fifth, an octave, and a tenth above the bass (i.e., in our modern terms, to have complete root-position triads with the root doubled). Morley adds that a sixth is possible above the bass, in which case it substitutes for the fifth. (The fifth and sixth together are possible under certain circumstances, making a 6/5 chord.) The student hands in the following:

Example 17-4b (Morley)

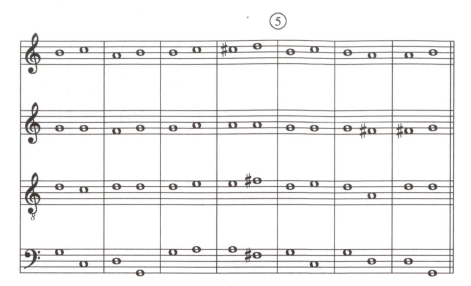

The master responds that the pupil has parallel octaves between the tenor and bass that result from the omission of the tenth (*E*) in the second chord. The *C* in the tenor is unnecessary since there is already one in the given soprano. He also criticizes the parallel fifths between the tenor and bass at the fifth and sixth notes, the doubled *F♮* at the eighth note, and finally the parallel fifths between the tenor and bass at the eleventh and twelfth notes. The master then proposes the following correction: "In this example you may see al your oversights mended." The 5/4 chord at the asterisk results from an augmented fourth-species supension in the alto:

Example 17-4c (Morley)

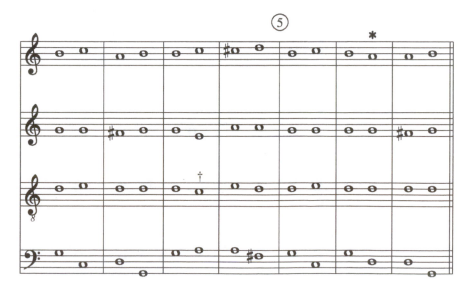

The student objects that strict adherence to the rule prescribing a fifth, octave, and tenth above every bass note will produce illegal parallels when the outer voices move in tenths, as in the sixth note of Example 17-4c, which does not contain an octave above the bass (at †, where the bass and soprano are in parallel tenths). The master replies: "Then for avoiding of that faulte, take this for a generall rule, that when the base and treble ascend in tenthes, then must the tenor bee the eight to the treble in the second note as for the example [bracketed Ex. 17-5a]: but by the contrary, if the base and treble descend in tenthes then must the tenor bee the eight to the treble in the first of them [bracketed in Ex. 17-5b]." Morley conceives these chords in pairs as shown by brackets. In the higher of the two chords in each pair the tenor doubles the soprano on the third of the chord, allowing the tenor and alto to move in contrary motion to the bass.

Example 17-5a and b (Morley)

a.

b.

The pupil asks, "May you carrie your tenor part higher then your counter as you have don in your example of tenths ascending?" (at the fourth note of Ex. 17-5a). The master answers, "You may. The parts may go one through another" (i.e., they may cross). The pupil wonders why the crossing was necessary; that is, why the *D* was not given to the alto and the *A* to the tenor. The master responds that then he would have had parallel fifths between the soprano and alto, and parallel octaves between the soprano and tenor.

The master goes on to allow a diminished fifth at the fourth note because it is approached obliquely and resolved correctly, moving by contrary motion to a third. The chord is a "dominant 6/5" resulting from a supension in augmented fourth species between alto and tenor (Ex. 17-5c).

Example 17-5c

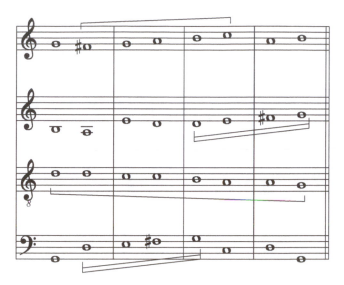

Then the pupil praises several features of the finished product: "This example I like very wel for these reasons, for...if you marke the artifice of the composition you shall see that as the treble ascendeth five notes, so the tenor descendeth five notes likewise...Last of all the counter in the last foure notes doth answere the base in fuge from the second note to the fifth." (These features have been bracketed.)

The pupil tries to write his own example from scratch:

Example 17-6a (Morley)

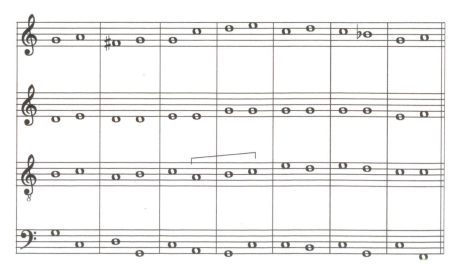

The master points out the parallel octaves in the fifth and sixth notes, and questions the spacing of the voices, asking why the sixth, seventh, and eighth tenor notes are not an octave higher and in the alto. The pupil responds that he was concerned about the ranges of the voices. The master says: "I like you well for that reason, but if you hadde liked the other waie so well you might have altered your cliffes thus:

Example 17-6b (Morley)

"whereby you should both have had scope enough to bring up your partes, and caused them to come closer together, which woulde so much the more have graced your example: for the closer the partes goe the better is the hermony, and when they stande farre asunder the harmonie vanisheth." The previous examples had all been in soprano, alto, tenor, and bass clefs—the master now moves the alto and tenor part into higher clefs: treble, mezzo-soprano, alto, and baritone, and puts the tenor A–B–C an octave higher into the alto and has the tenor take E–G–G of the alto.

The master finally criticizes this example for cadencing out of the mode: "You have in the closing gone out of your key, which is one of the grosest faults which may be committed…the leaving of that key wherein you did begin, and ending in another."

To sum up, the foregoing discussion illustrates:

* the principle that notes should be placed a fifth, an octave, and a tenth above the bass (except that a sixth can be substituted for a fifth)
* the possibility of 6/5 chords at the whole-note level resulting from augmented fourth species
* the importance of parallel tenths in the outer voices
* the exception, when the outer voices move in parallel tenths, to the principle of doubling the bass note in 5/3 chords—in that case the higher chord doubles the third, which is in the soprano (this exception is unnecessary when one of the chords is a 6/3)
* the rule that a raised tone (the F♯ in Ex. 17-4b) should not be doubled
* that illegal parallels may be avoided by crossing inner voices
* that little bits of imitation are desirable (just as in Zarlino's two-part first-species Example 3-5)
* that the voices should maintain their proper ranges as defined by clefs

- that tight spacing among the upper three parts is desirable
- that pieces should end where they began.

Study of Repertoire Examples

Falsobordoni

A common use of note-against-note counterpoint in liturgical repertoire is to set melodies called <u>psalm tones</u> (refer to discussion in chapter 15). Such settings are sometimes called *falsobordoni*. Morley gives one example for each of the eight psalm tones. Below are his settings of tones 2, 3, and 7, with the psalm tone melody in the tenor. By tradition, some psalm tones end on a note other than the starting one, so they can't end where they began. Note how few 6/3 chords Morley uses, how much more the bass skips than the other voices, and how closely the upper three parts are spaced. What do you think are the principles behind these harmonizations?

Example 17-7 (Morley)

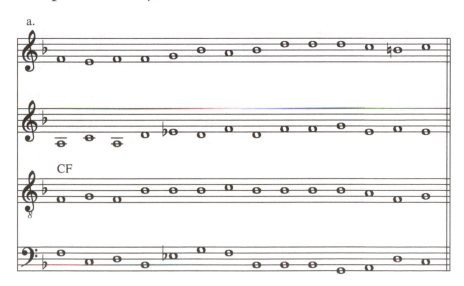

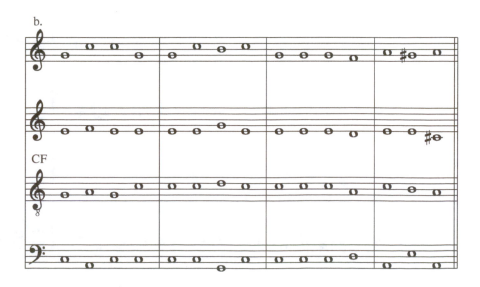

c.

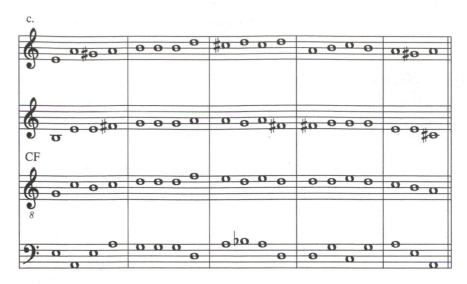

Lutheran Chorales

Another common use of note-against-note counterpoint is to set Lutheran chorales. Praetorius made hundreds of such settings. In the examples below, note how these pieces differ from those of Morley as regards doubling and spacing. Look for 6/3 chords, diminished 6/3 chords, 6/5 chords, and voice crossing in the inner parts used to avoid illegal parallels. Praetorius seems to favor contrary motion between the bass and soprano.

Disregard figuration in short values in "Christ lag" for the moment. In "Da Jesus," a Phrygian melody, note how the 2̂–1̂ is treated. A second setting is given in Example 17-8c, showing a standard way to deal with the Phrygian cadence: the final *E* in the soprano sounds as the fifth above an *A* sonority, with the lower voices moving to the *E* sonority afterward, giving the effect of a <u>plagal</u> <u>cadence</u>. Only the first two phrases are shown in Example 17-9.

Example 17-8 (Praetorius) (From Michael Praetorius, *Gesamtausgabe der Musikaltschen Werke. Musae Sionae Teil VI (1609). Nr. CVII; Nr. CIX; Nr. CXXXI. Karl Heinrich Möseler Verlag.)*

a. ("Christ lay in Death's bonds, given for our sin; He is risen again and has brought us Life. Let us be joyful, praise God and be thankful, and sing Alleluia.")

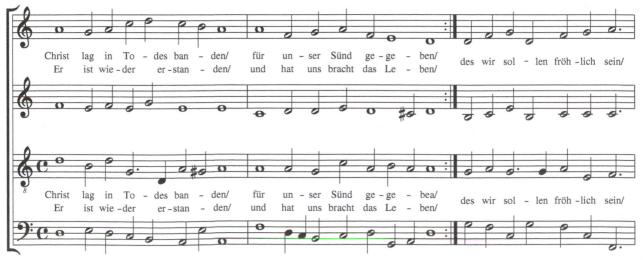

Gott lo-ben und dank -bar sein/ und sin-gen Al -le -lu – ja/ Al – le -lu – ja.

b. ("As Jesus was on the cross and His body was wounded, with bitter sorrow the seven words that Jesus spoke, ponder in your heart")

Da Je - sus an dem Kreu -se stund/ und ihm sein Leich -nam war ver -wundt/ so gar mit

bit -tern Schmer – zen/ die sie -ben Wort/ die Je -sus sprach/ be -tracht in dei -neim Her – zen.

c.

Cadences in Four Parts

Cadences in four parts, like all cadences, are clichés, formulas that you are encouraged to memorize and borrow. Several are shown in Example 17-9, which are taken from Banchieri's list of one hundred and from assorted repertoire. Many of these are the same as three-voice cadences, with an alto added (often making degrees $\hat{5}$–$\hat{5}$). All of these cadence types can be transposed to any mode *except* the Phrygian. In the Dorian mode we often find the sixth degree flatted. (Note in the second of these examples that a seventh above the bass has been tied over from a preceding consonance.)

Example 17-9a Cadences with a breve in the bass and a fake suspension

Example 17-9b Cadences with normally prepared suspensions

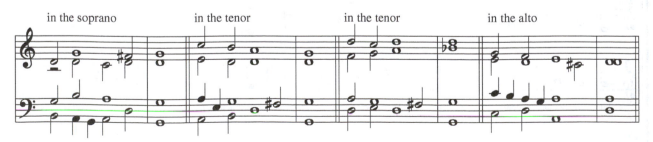

Example 17-9c Cadences with the chanson idiom in the tenor

Example 17-9d Phrygian Cadences

Phrygian Cadences

The Phrygian cadence, as explained in the section on three-part cadences, cannot be made in the same way as the others, and examples of it are shown in Example 17-9d. If $\hat{2}$–$\hat{1}$ is not in the bass, then there are few possibilities for the bass. It can have $\hat{2}$–$\hat{6}$, $\hat{7}$–$\hat{6}$, or (most often) $\hat{7}$–$\hat{4}$. In the last case, the goal of the cadence is *E* even though the lowest note of the sonority is *A*. Such a cadence often has a so-called "plagal" ending tacked on so that the final chord is *E* (as in Ex. 17-8c). Overlapping and evading cadences can be done in four parts just as they were in three.

Soft Rules

Lead the upper voices smoothly, but let the bass skip a lot. Avoid skips of a sixth in the bass. Cross inner voices to achieve parallel triads without voice-leading illegalities. Try to imitate the CF in the other voices (label your effort).

Just as there are six "clinks" when four people toast, there are six ways to pair the lines in a four-part texture: SA, ST, SB, AT, AB, TB. Each one of these pairs must be inspected for voice-leading errors. Remember to judge which species is in operation at any given moment, and which voice has the agent in a suspension.

Exercise Series **A:** Writing Against Parallel Sixths

Find a bass line for each of these successions of parallel sixths (including a few other intervals created by anticipations or delays). Then fill in an alto part for each one.

1.

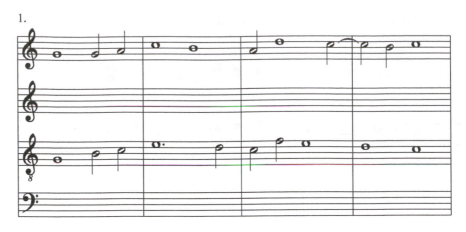

2.

Exercise Series **A:**   **Filling In Outer Voices**

Fill in the inner voices following the principles outlined by Morley and summarized on p. 252.

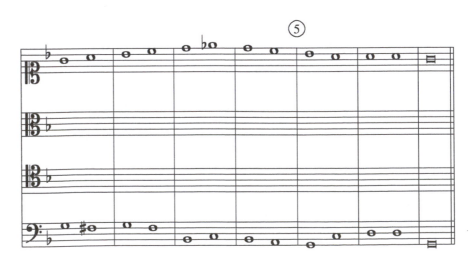

Exercise Series *B*:   Find the Errors

Mark hard mistakes with X and soft ones with (X),

Exercise 17-B1

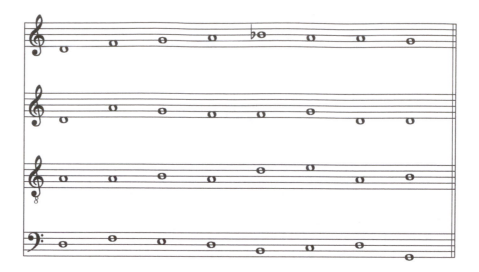

Exercise 17-B2

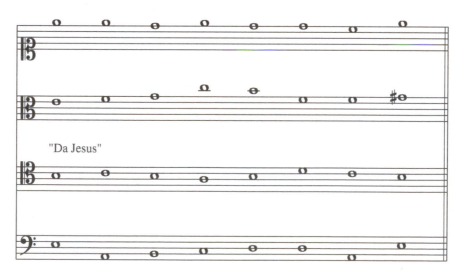

"Da Jesus"

Exercise Series *D*:   Four-Part French Chanson

Using one of the given tunes (or a short segment) in the specified voice, begin by constructing a duo out of sixths. You may begin with an octave, and if there is a $\hat{2}$–$\hat{1}$ cadence in the soprano, or an $\hat{8}$–$\hat{7}$–$\hat{8}$ cadence in the tenor, you must break out of the parallel-sixth model to cadence. Once the duo is completed, add a bass line. The bass is considered to enrich the interval succession. It adds harmonic support, generally by making root-position sonorities. First-inversion chords should occur on weak beats and for shorter durations. The bass may skip a lot more than the upper voices. Finally, add the alto. Once you see where your bass and alto are headed, you may want to rewrite your duo to deviate from the parallel-sixth model, occasionally introducing fifths and 7–6 suspensions as the result of anticipations or delays in one of the voices.

Exercise 17-D1

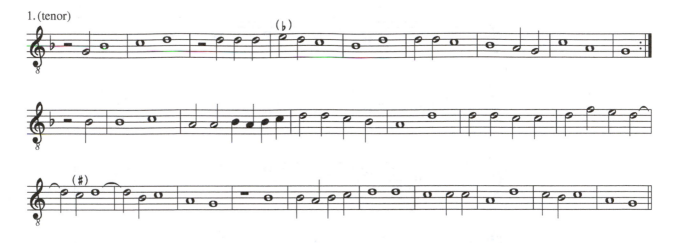

Exercise 17-D2

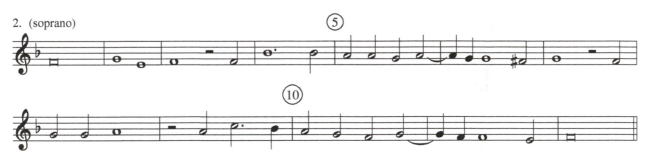

Exercise Series D: Free Four-Voice CF Settings

1. Set a Lutheran chorale tune (e.g., "Vater unser," Ex. 1-3g) as the soprano in a note-against-note texture.

2. Set a short cantus firmus from chapter 1 as the tenor in a note-against-note texture. Any fragment that ends on the final will do (e.g., the last thirteen notes of "La Spagna").

18

Adding Three Parts in Mixed Values to a CF

The rules for the addition of three parts to a CF are the same as those for adding two parts. Voices that move together must be consonant with each other, even if they are both dissonant with the CF note. The principles for writing suspensions are the same as in three parts.

Hard rule relaxed: In four parts you may move to a perfect interval by similar motion even if both voices skip. If the soprano is one of the two voices involved, it is preferable if its skip is not more than a third. See Example 18-3 at the asterisks.

Idiom: The Long-Note Cambiata

In this form of the cambiata the dissonance is still a quarter, but the first note can be a dotted half and the following notes can be half notes. The figure may now consist of four or even just three notes. See another example in Example 18-4 in m. 23.

Example 18-1a

Example 18-1b (from Guerrero's Ex. 16-15)

A new chord type, to be added to the 6/5 chords covered earlier, is the seventh chord. Zarlino, who did not have that terminology, calls it "four parts in thirds with one another, with no octave sounding among them, as in this manner":

Example 18-2 (Zarlino)

The seventh chord is shown at the asterisk. The seventh (*E*) is prepared and resolved correctly down to a sixth (*D*) above the bass; the voice that had the fifth (*C*) above the bass must move so as not to conflict with the *D*, which it does by passing down to *A*.

Four-Part Counterpoint with a Motive

Here is one of Zarlino's examples of counterpoint with a motive against a CF (Ex. 18-3). It begins with preview imitation, like his three-part example (Ex. 14-12). Later, a scalar motive consisting of five quarter notes recurs often, both ascending and descending (sometimes the first note is a dotted half, sometimes a quarter). Note intermediate cadences to *F* and to *E* (evaded). There is no cadence to the final *G* of the CF (m. 22) because the CF ascends from $\hat{7}$ to $\hat{8}$ so Zarlino tacks on a "plagal" cadence. Asterisks indicate similar motion to a perfect interval with both voices skipping.

Example 18-3 (Zarlino)

Study of Repertoire Examples

Palestrina's Missa "Ecce sacerdos magnus" is built on the same version of this chant that Banchieri used to make his little motet (Ex. 9-4). Each of the three sections of the Kyrie uses the CF in breves in a different voice: it's in the soprano for the Kyrie, the alto for the Christe (the CF is transposed down a fifth), and the tenor for the Kyrie. The other voices repeat various motives within these sections. The motives are for the most part repeated exactly for four notes at least, but their continuations are varied. Label motives and cadences in the section shown in Example 18-4.

Example 18-4 (Palestrina) ("Lord have mercy; Christ have mercy; Lord have mercy.")

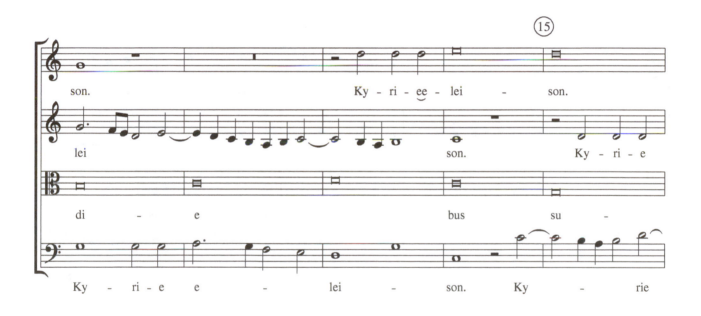

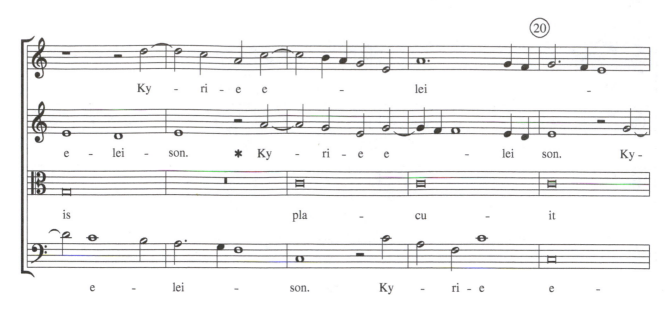

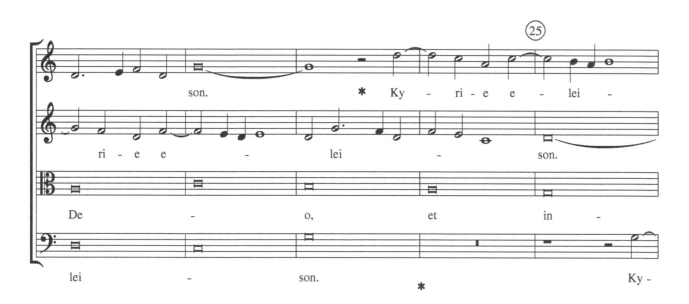

Another fruitful source of examples of this technique is the English In Nomine, a kind of cantus firmus composition usually for consort of viols or keyboard. Examples 18-5–18-7 show the first twenty breves of consort In Nomines by Tallis, Taverner, and Byrd. Label occurrences of each motive in the examples. Do the cadences coincide with the introduction of new motives?

In the three examples, asterisks are placed where voice-leading anomalies occur. These include a lower neighbor in half notes, a couple of dissonant upper neighbors in quarter notes and dissonant accented passing half notes, a half-note echappée, and an irregular use of dotted half and quarter against two half notes. We will take these as English mannerisms, and we will not model on them.

Example 18-5 (Tallis)

Example 18-6 (Taverner)

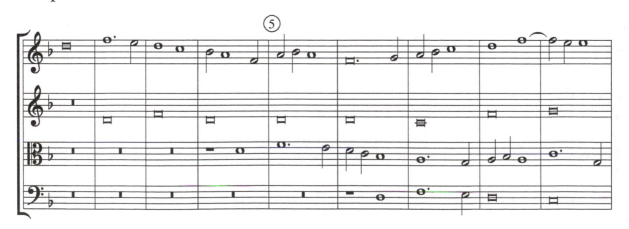

Example 18-7 (Byrd)

Example 18-8 shows the first twenty notes of the CF and the places cadences occur in each of the three examples. Most of the cadences are to *D*, the final, but they are made in a variety of places. Tallis has the fewest cadences—what is the effect of this? Taverner's cadences to *F* and *C* come immediately before cadences to *D*, making for a special intensity as the cadence to the "wrong" note is righted (how might you perform these cadences?). Byrd's two cadences in quick succession reflect imitation at the breve between the soprano and tenor. This example demonstrates the freedom composers have in choosing where to make cadences against a CF.

Example 18-8

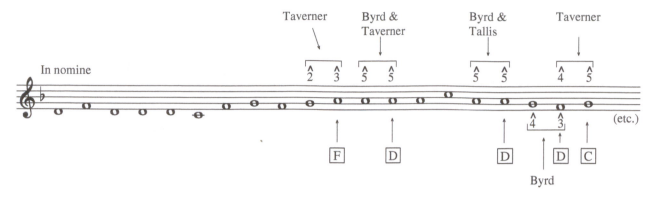

Surely the silliest example of this technique is Banchieri's "Contraponto bestiale alla mente" (counterpoint improvised by animals). The basses sing the CF while a dog, a cat, an owl, and a cuckoo repeat motives representing their respective noises. Try improvising on a different CF using the same motives.

Example 18-9 (Banchieri) ("There is no trustworthiness in a hunchback, likewise one who limps. . .")

Exercise Series A: All Possible Motive Placements

Find all possible placements of a given motive against a given CF, as you did in chapter 9. If you are using the materials (short motive and CF) from an old two- or three-voice assignment, then you have already done this step. If you are going to use the same materials but are now adapting them for an exercise in breves, you will have to do this step afresh, since the short motive can fit more often against breves.

Exercise Series *D:*   Four-Part Counterpoint with a Motive

Once you have found all possible placements of the motive, you have to inspect them to see if any work well *overlapping with each other*. If so, you will be able to have them in close imitation; if not, you will always be writing free material in two voices against the *soggetto* in one. It is a good idea to precede occurrences of the motive with rests.

1. CF in whole notes. Using the materials given at the end of chapter 9 (CFs and mixed-value motives), compose four-voice settings around a CF in the tenor. Make each voice enter with the fast-moving motive in preview imitation before the CF enters. Make at least one intermediate cadence for every ten CF notes. Use only a total of one whole rest per part per eight measures maximum (may be apportioned in half rests).

2. CF in breves. You actually have more freedom in longer CF notes. Do the exercise as above, but you may use more rests: one whole note worth of rests per part per four measures.

Other Repertoire for Study

There is so much Renaissance music based on this principle that only a few outstanding pieces are mentioned here: Missa "L'homme armé" by Morales; Frescobaldi's Fiori Musicali, and the Benedictus movement from Palestrina's Missa "Ad coenam Agni providi."

19

Four Parts in Mixed Values

This chapter contains no rules, only possibilities. It begins by describing three standard types of structure: the pair of nonimitative duos, the pair of imitative duos, and the canon. In these structures a two-voice combination is repeated exactly, a very economical and consistent method of composing. These three types account for a large proportion (probably over half) of Renaissance polyphonic music.

The theorist who provides us with the most information on the three repetition types is the encyclopedic Pietro Cerone, from whose treatise the short examples below are taken. He calls them *entradas* or openings, but adds that they may be found anywhere in a piece.

The Pair of Nonimitative Duos

In this structure two voices begin, usually more or less at the same time and with more or less the same rhythm, and are answered by the other two voices. Cerone is particularly fond of this structure because, since the duo is homorhythmic, the words are easier to understand than they are in an imitative texture. Given the preference for alternating plagal and authentic ranges, the duos are most often arranged so that the tenor and soprano can correspond as to range, and likewise the alto and the bass. One of the most frequent deployments of the duos is to have a soprano-alto duo imitated an octave lower by the tenor and bass, or vice versa. Another deployment is to have a bass-alto duo answered by the tenor and soprano; in this case the second pair will be a fourth or fifth from the first. In Example 19-1 the module is one breve long, and it is imitated a fourth above.

Example 19-1 (Cerone)

The second section of Victoria's "O magnum mysterium" begins with a repeated nonimitative module on the words "ut animalia." In this case the module consists entirely of parallel thirds, which is quite common. To the repetition an octave higher in the soprano and alto, Victoria adds a third line in the tenor.

In addition to simple transposition within the module, the relative positions of the voices can be inverted in the second pair, as shown in Example 19-2. The invertible counterpoint can be at the tenth, as here, or, more commonly, at the octave or twelfth (see Marenzio's Ex. 19-23 and Merulo's Ex. 19-24).

Example 19-2 (Cerone)

Exercise Series A: Answering a Nonimitative Module

In each of the following short exercises, you are given the opening duo and you are to supply the answering duo, puzzle-canon style. Look for cadence opportunities in the duo.

Exercise 19-A1

1.

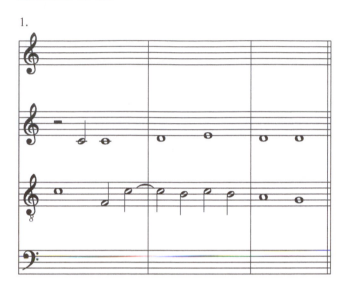

Exercise 19-A2

2.

Exercise 19-A3

The Pair of Imitative Duos

This structure is like the foregoing in that a duo is answered by another duo, except that here the duos are imitative. Cerone calls the leading part before the second voice comes in the *passo* and the rest, from the moment of the second voice's entry, the "accompaniment." His term *passo* corresponds to our term "head motive." If you chop off the head motive of the leading part, you have a two-voice module, just as in the nonimitative duos described above.

Given the preference for collateral ranges, if the imitation is at the fourth or fifth, then the first duo will most often be in adjacent voices (S-A or T-B, less often A-T) and the second duo will be transposed an octave (as in Ex. 19-3 and Victoria's "O magnum mysterium"). Likewise, if the imitation is at the octave, then the first duo will most often be in nonadjacent voices (S-T or A-B) and the module will be transposed a fourth or fifth, as in Example 19-4. The second duo may also be varied by invertible counterpoint, as in Example 19-5.

Example 19-3 (Cerone)

Example 19-4 (Cerone)

Example 19-5 (Cerone)

An important feature of this type is the time interval of imitation. Usually the time interval between the two voices that form the duo (t1) is shorter than the time interval between the entrance of the second voice and the entrance of the third (t2). Obviously, if the original contrapuntal combination is to be maintained, the time interval between the voices of the answering duo will be the same as that in the opening duo (t3 = t1). In Example 19-3, t1 = o, t2 = ⧢, and t3 = o. (Label the time intervals in Victoria's "O magnum mysterium.")

If t1 t3, then the vertical intervals of the second combination will be different from those of the first, and the contrapuntal combination will not be repeated. In that case we are dealing with free counterpoint. Occasionally t2 is shorter than t1. If all three time intervals between the four entrances are the same, then we are dealing with a canon, which will be discussed later.

The Elided Cadence in Four Voices

When the duo is imitative, it often happens that the standard two-voice cadence in the opening duo is elided with the first notes of the soggetto in the third voice. We practiced such elisions in chapter 14; review the "Steps of the cadence." Given the duo in an upper-voice pair, one of the most common means of elision is for the soggetto to begin with $\hat{5}$ under the cadential $\hat{2}$ and $\hat{8}$–$\hat{7}$. Thus the soggetto begins on an important note of the mode and it begins with a member of a cadence. The $\hat{5}$ may be a breve or semibreve; if a semibreve, the suspension will be normal fourth species; if a breve, the suspension will be in augmented values. It is possible for the $\hat{5}$ to move to the goal note (as it does in Victoria's "O magnum mysterium") or to some other note ($\hat{5}$–$\hat{6}$ in Willaert's motet "Benedicta es," Ex. 19-6), or to be sustained while the lower voice, imitating at the fifth below, sounds the goal note, as in Marenzio's motet "Magnum haereditatis mysterium" (Ex. 19-7, written for the same occasion as the Victoria). In this last case, the first note in the tenor provides the cadential $\hat{5}$ and the bass provides the $\hat{1}$.

Example 19-6 (Willaert) ("Blessed art Thou, Queen of Heaven...")

Be - ne - dic - ta   es ...

(etc.)

Example 19-7 (Marenzio) ("Great mystery of birth...")

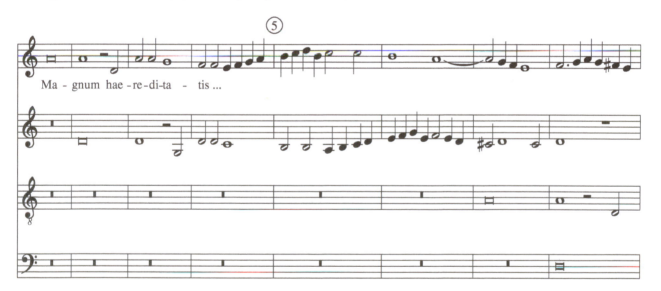

Ma - gnum hae - re -di-ta - tis ...

Exercise Series A: Writing Elided Cadences in Four Voices

4. Supply the missing parts of the cadence in mm. 1–3
5. Add entries on *G* and *C* in whole notes
6. Add entries on *G* and *C* in whole notes
7. Add entries on *F* and *C* in whole notes

Exercise 19-A4

Exercise 19-A5

Exercise 19-A6

Exercise 19-A7

Exercise Series C: Answering an Imitative Duo

Answering Duos

Exercises 19-C1–19-C3. Given these two voices, supply the answering duo in the other two voices. Write in these parts, continuing until you must break off imitating and write free material. Remember to maintain rhythmic variety and sonorities with three pitch-classes. Imitate for as long as possible.

Exercise 19-C1

(etc.)

Exercise 19-C2

(etc.)

Exercise 19-C3

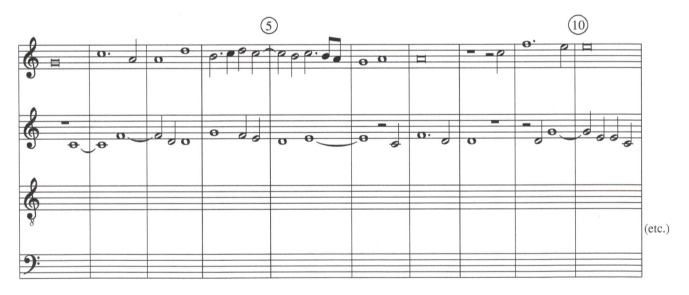

(etc.)

Completing a Four-Voice Texture

Exercises 19-C4–19-C5. These exercises give you more freedom, which makes them more difficult. Add the missing two voices, making sure to repeat material occurring in the given voices. The total duration of rests in the parts you add should not exceed sixteen whole notes in both parts combined, distributed as you like. In 19-C5, three melodic fragments have been labeled; they must be recombined in triple counterpoint. Start filling empty measures right away.

Exercise 19-C4

(etc.)

Exercise 19-C5

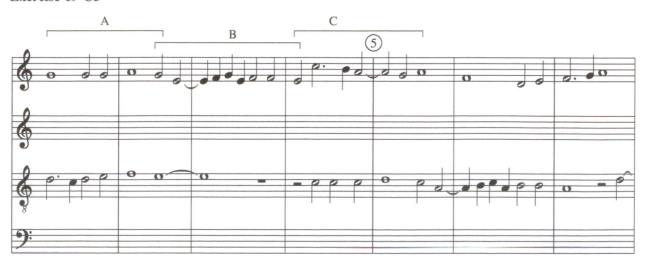

Composing a Pair of Imitative Duos

Joachim Burmeister, writing in 1606, describes in detail the process of composing a four-part imitative opening. He calls the four voices the leader, the first follower, the second follower, and the third follower. He lays them out on four lines like this:

Example 19-8a (Burmeister) (From Joachim Burmeister, *Musical Poetics*, trans. Benito V. Rivera, ed. Claude V. Palisca. Copyright 1993 Yale University Press.)

He does not comment that the overlap between the leader and the first follower is duplicated between the third and fourth followers but not between the second and third followers. We can recognize, however, that he is sketching a pair of imitative duos. Burmeister continues: "The remaining vacant places will be filled with apt and fitting concords...so that the setting will achieve a natural and effortless growth."

Example 19-8b (Burmeister) (From Joachim Burmeister, *Musical Poetics*, trans. Benito V. Rivera, ed. Claude V. Palisca. Copyright 1993 Yale University Press.)

Example 19-8a represents only an approximate layout—when Burmeister actually adds the other parts he alters the time interval between the second and third followers (he shortens t2), and he eliminates the cadence to *G*, preferring to use the subject's falling *C-F* fifth as $\hat{5}$–$\hat{1}$ of an evaded cadence to *F*. Note the rhythmic augmentation of the fourth and fifth bass notes that slow down the ending of the first phrase, and the parallel fifths between the tenor and soprano in mm. 6–7 (a misprint or a careless error!).

The Canon

There are two types of four-voice canon. One is the invertible canon you studied in chapter 16. Now, however, it has a fourth voice in the same relationship to the third voice that the first was to the second, as shown in these examples from Cerone. One advantage of this type is that it maintains voices in their proper (collateral) ranges.

Example 19-9

a. (Cerone)

b. (Cerone)

The other type we call the <u>transposed</u> <u>canon</u>. In this type, the successive intervals between the voices are the same, so the whole duo is merely transposed up or down. This type has fewer requirements because the duo is never inverted. This type of opening is rarely found at the very beginning of a piece, because it causes the introduction of pitch classes and species foreign to the mode. It is not immediately obvious what mode the example by Willaert (Ex. 19-10) will end in. For other examples, see Rhau's collection listed in the bibliography, which contains transposed canons by Verdelot (#116), Mouton (#117), and Fevin (#118); see also Marenzio's madrigal "Spuntavan" at the words "tra lor scherzando," and Palestrina's famous motet "Sicut cervus" at the words "ita desiderat."

Example 19-10 (Willaert) ("If I don't see my girlfriend [I'll die of suffering].")

Si   je   ne voy m'a - mi ...

Exercise Series *D:*   Four-Voice Openings

In these exercises you are given a short head motive and you are to build various imitative and non-imitative openings. You must leave the motive in the voice in which it is presented and you must compose the other voices within the given ranges. Sample step-by-step workings-out are shown below. Sing each one.

Given this motive:

Example 19-11a

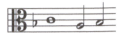

we compose two sample nonimitative openings:

Example 19-11b

In the first sample (Ex. 19-11b), (1) we make a nonimitative duo in the soprano and alto (we enliven the rhythm by substituting a half rest and a half note for the whole in one of the voices); (2) we repeat the duo in the tenor and bass; (3) we continue the soprano and alto as accompaniment to the second duo, and add a cadence.

Example 19-11c

In the second sample (Ex. 19-11c), (1) we compose a nonimitative duo that is invertible at the twelfth; (2) observing that the second duo contains a cadence opportunity ($\hat{5}$–$\hat{6}$ in the bass) we plan to repeat the duo *later* in the tenor and bass so we can set up a suspension in the upper voices; (3) we write the continuation of the soprano and alto containing the suspension, and add a cadence.

And we compose two sample imitative openings:

Example 19-11d

In the third sample (Ex. 19-11d), (1) we look for a place to imitate at the fourth or fifth (since no imitation at the fourth or fifth is possible after one whole note, we start on *G* after two whole notes); (2) we place the answering duo an octave lower, leaving an extra beat so that t2 is longer (we do this so as to avoid making a canon); (3) we complete the lower duo and add accompaniment above.

Example 19-11e

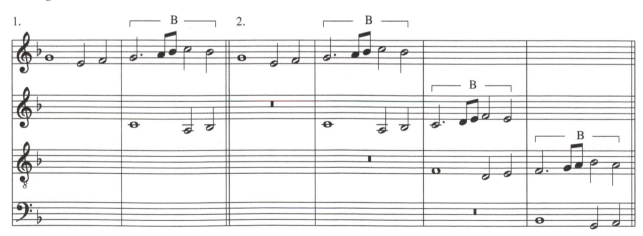

3.

In the final sample (Ex. 19-11e), (1) we begin a fifth higher, bringing in the given tune second, and compose an accompaniment (B); 2) keeping the same time interval, we introduce the tenor and bass at successive fifths, making a transposed canon and retaining the accompaniment (B) at the appropriate transposition; (3) we fill in the missing material in the soprano and alto.

Exercise Series D: Writing Four-Voice Openings

Using the given motives, compose various imitative and nonimitative openings as illustrated above. In addition, you can pick from the longer soggetti, which are guaranteed to provide imitations that are invertible. You or your teacher may pick from:

1. Nonimitative modular openings
- with the module in the soprano and alto, imitated at the octave below by tenor and bass;
- with the module in the tenor and bass, imitated at the octave above by soprano and alto;
- with the module in the soprano and tenor, imitated at the fourth or fifth below in the alto and bass;
- with the module in the alto and bass, imitated at the fourth or fifth above by the soprano and tenor;

2. Imitative openings
- with the module in the soprano and alto (either may begin), imitated at the octave below by tenor and bass;
- with the module in the tenor and bass (either may begin), imitated at the octave above by soprano and alto;
- with the module in the soprano and tenor (either may begin), imitated at the fourth or fifth in the alto and bass;
- with the module in the alto and bass (either may begin), imitated at the fourth or fifth by the soprano and tenor;

For all of the above structures, instead of simply transposing the first duo, you may vary the second duo through invertible counterpoint at either the octave or twelfth (as in Merulo's Ex. 19-23).

3. Canonic openings
- Invertible
- Transposed

Head Motives

Imitate after a breve or more, as in the samples above.

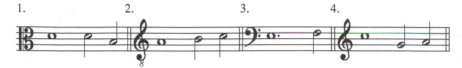

Complete Soggetti

These contain both head motives and continuations, and are to be treated as puzzle canons, imitating after one, two, three, or four whole notes. They are guaranteed to contain the possibility of imitations that are invertible at the twelfth.

Miscellaneous Techniques and Free Counterpoint

Techniques Combined

The above techniques are often combined to make longer, less symmetrical and predictable structures. The most common are shown in the schemas in Example 19-12.

Example 19-12

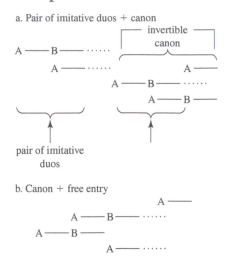

a. Pair of imitative duos + canon

b. Canon + free entry

Tonal Answer

A <u>tonal</u> <u>answer</u> is an alteration in the consequent voice in an imitation. For example, a fifth in the guide might be answered by a fourth in the consequent, or vice versa. This enables both voices to outline the characteristic notes of the mode and permits imitation at the fourth or fifth without introducing pitches other than the fifth or the final of the mode. As we saw in Victoria's "O magnum mysterium," if two melodic fifths are imitated a fifth apart, three different pitch classes are sounded, one foreign to the mode. If the tonal answer affects only the first melodic interval, before the consequent comes in, then the rest of the duo can be in exact imitation (Ex. 19-13a). Look for tonal answers in later points of Victoria's "O magnum."

Example 19-13a (Cerone)

If the tonal answer affects notes after the consequent has come in, the consequent can be altered as well, preserving the different intervals of the mode *and* maintaining the vertical intervals of the combination. In Example 19-13b, the countermelody *C-B-A-G* in the soprano (m. 2) is "answered" by countermelody *F-F-E-D* in the alto (m. 3), maintaining the vertical intervals of the module.

Example 19-13b (Cerone)

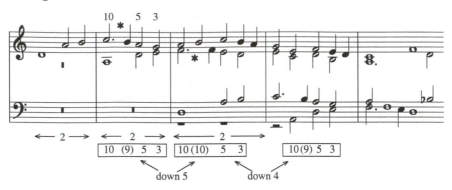

In the beginning of the second half of "Now Is the Gentle Season" by Morley (Ex. 19-14), the consequent differs from the guide in *two* places (marked with brackets), causing both the ascending and descending modal outlines to be maintained. We would classify this opening as a pair of imitative duos even though the imitation is not exact.

Note how the two versions of the head motive contribute to the evaded cadence in mm. 7–8: the rising fifth of the tenor supports the cadential suspension $\hat{8}$–$\hat{7}$, and the rising fourth of the bass makes the $\hat{5}$–$\hat{1}$ resolution supporting the $\hat{7}$–$\hat{8}$. The two versions of the motive stated successively in the soprano end up outlining the whole modal octave with its characteristic skips.

Example 19-14 (Morley)

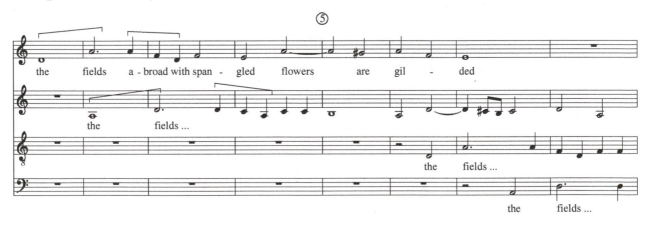

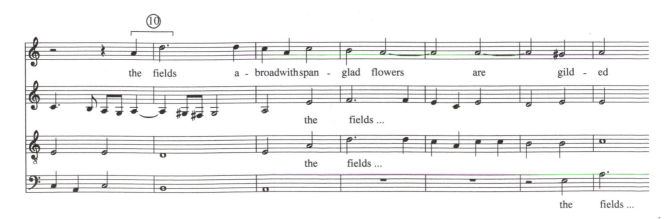

Tonal answer permits successive adjacent voices to enter on succssively alternating fourths and fifths (outlining the mode) *at the same time intervals* (i.e., in canon). This is in contrast to transposed canon, where successive adjacent voices entered on successive same intervals, and invertible canon, where imitation at the fourth was impossible. If you tried to start adjacent voices on alternating fourths and fifths without tonal answer, the resulting vertical intervals would be hard to work with (e.g., fifths become fourths in Ex. 19-15). For another example of entries at alternating fourths and fifths after the same time interval see Brumel's (#124) in Rhau's collection listed in the bibliography.

Example 19-15 (Cerone)

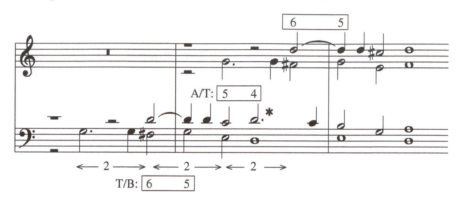

Changing Time Intervals

Sometimes we find the same melodies recombined at a different time interval, producing a new combination of vertical intervals. The second time interval is often shorter than the first, creating an intensification called <u>stretto</u> ("squeezed" or "packed close" in Italian, because the entries are closer together). In Lassus's motet "Gressus meos" $t1 = 4$ and $t2 = 12$, and in the second combination, $t1 = 1$ and $t2 = 5$.

Example 19-16 (Lassus) ("My footsteps [you will guide...]")

Tinkering with the time intervals of imitation is another way to solve the problem of successive entries at the fourth and fifth. The pair of imitative duos makes imitation at the fourth possible because t1 t2, but shorter, subtler changes in time intervals are possible. Example 19-17 is the beginning of a section of Palestrina's Missa "Te Deum laudamus." In it, the first three voices enter on *F*, *C*, and *F*, successively lower. The first tenor enters after two breves and makes a third below the *E* on "ter" of the alto. Suppose the second tenor had entered at the corresponding time: its *F* would have made an augmented fourth with *B* on "ter-" of the first tenor. Palestrina could have started the third voice on *G*, making a transposed canon, but that would spoil the symmetry of the mode. If you want entries on alternating fifth and final of the mode in the same direction (imitation at the fourth below and fifth below), and you want to maintain the duo, you can use a little bit of free counterpoint to connect them.

Palestrina puts the third entrance off one beat and writes a free continuation in the first tenor, consisting of just the *A* on "ra." Now the first tenor line is one step lower than the corresponding place in the alto ("-ra" of the first tenor corresponds to "ter-" of the alto), and the duo can be restated between the lowest voices a fifth lower than mm. 3–4. Thus a fourth after two breves is answered by a fifth after two and a half breves, with a small adjustment in the syllable placement.

Example 19-17 (Palestrina) ("The heavens and earth are full of [Thy glory.]")

In the above example, it is the second combination (mm. 5–7) that is reused, against which Palestrina writes free counterpoint. This second combination is sounded five times in all, the last time (mm. 14-15) with a stretto between the first and second tenor parts. It is common in stretto for one or more of the soggetti to be incomplete, and here the first tenor only has the first five notes of the soggetto. This stretto is the first extended bit of four-part writing in the movement, and climaxes the section.

All of the melodic material that is not labeled in this example is free counterpoint. It consists of close imitations of the five-note scale that is part of the countermelody B, running in parallel thirds and making lively contrast to the static repeated notes of principal soggetto A.

The above example shows how more time accommodates more pitch space. The extra time needed to accommodate the different pitch interval of the third entry can be built into a canon, as in this example from Palestrina's Missa "Ad fugam" (Ex. 19-18).

Imitation at a fourth after a whole note is followed by imitation at a fifth after two whole notes.

Example 19-18 (Palestrina) ("The heavens and earth are full of [Thy glory.]")

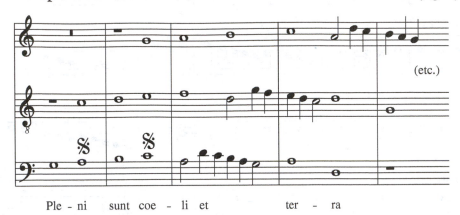

Ple - ni sunt coe - li et   ter - ra

Another example of stretto can be found in Morley's "Now Is the Gentle Season," in the second part, at the words "The nightingale her bower hath gaily builded."

Melodic Inversion

We mentioned in chapter 9 that there were several kinds of melodic inversion. These are all used in imitative music in four and more parts. At the opening of his five-voice motet "Jubilate Deo," Palestrina begins an imitation by inversion on the same note, and does not maintain semitone position.

Example 19-19 (Palestrina) ("Rejoice in the Lord.")

Ju - bi - la - te De - o

Inversion that maintains semitone position is used in this opening of an instrumental ricercar (Ex. 19-20). After the soggetto has been presented, imitations by inversion recur intermittently.

Example 19-20 (attributed to Giaches Brumel)

(etc.)

Mirror Inversion

<u>Mirror</u> <u>inversion</u> combines melodic inversion with reversal of the relative positions of the parts (invertible counterpoint), and results in an exact replication of the vertical interval succession. It can be used in both nonimitative and imitative contexts. In a nonimitative example, Lassus uses mirror inversion to vary one of the counterpoints against the CF (see Ex. 13-9, mm. 22–28). The melodic inversion maintains semitone positions in both voices (including the accidentals). The only restriction in this kind of counterpoint is that dissonant suspensions won't work.

Marenzio uses mirror inversion to vary the presentation of an imitative duo in the motet "Quem dicunt homines" (Ex. 19-21). To see how he buried these combinations in a continuous four-voice texture, look at the complete score.

Example 19-21 (Marenzio) ("Quem dicunt homines…" ["Whom do men say [that I, the Son of man, am?]"])

The composer of the anonymous organ piece in Example 19-22 has used imitation by inversion starting on the same note and not maintaining semitone positions. The piece ends with an elaborate cadence.

Example 19-22 (Anon.) (From *An Anthology of Keyboard Compositions: Munich, Bavarian State Library MS MUS 1581. Corpus of Early Keyboard Music* vol. 40/1. Edited by Clare G. Rayner AIM, 1976. Alia fuga, p. 94. Hänsler-Verlag.

Study and Analysis of Repertoire Examples

One of Marenzio's favorite devices is the close linking of nonimitative modules. In the excerpt from "Spuntavan gia" (1581) shown here (Ex. 19-23), the module consists of two voices, A and B, that have been bracketed. The first time it is heard, in the soprano and bass, the module is elided with material from the preceding phrase. When the module repeats in the alto and second soprano (called "Quinto," or fifth voice), we see that the last two notes of the module (on "-torno") can harmonize its first three notes. When the soprano and bass repeat once again, they have exchanged material, inverting it at the twelfth. The repetitions continue until the cadence (although the inner voices must be altered since they make combinations not invertible at the twelfth). The tenor has free counterpoint, filling out a trio texture with the soprano and bass, each repetition slightly different. The passage is emphatically periodic.

Example 19-23 (Marenzio) ("[The flowers brightened up the earth] and the hills all around.")

This movement from an organ mass by Claudio Merulo (Ex. 19-24) is based on a Kyrie that you have used, and that you have seen used by several theorists (CF notes are marked with "x"). The opening duo is a nonimitative module consisting of the CF in the alto and a counterpoint in the soprano. In m. 8 the tenor begins the CF at the same pitch level as the alto, and the bass has the same line the soprano had, transposed down a twelfth. The tenor-bass combination in mm. 8–10 is the inversion at the twelfth of the soprano-alto combination in mm. 1–3. Against the continuation of the CF, Merulo repeats a short motive. Note that because the CF ends *C–D*, there is no cadence, and the last long *D* is embellished with a plagal cadence. The ornaments are idiomatic to the keyboard, and help to obscure the simple structure of the movement.

Example 19-24 (Merulo) (From Claudio Merulo, *Messe d' intavolatura d'organo 1568. Corpus of Early Keyboard Music*, V. 47, V. Ed. by Robert Judd. AIM, 1991. Kyrie, p. 20. Hänssler-Verlag.)

You now have enough information to begin analyzing any Renaissance piece. For each "point," or section, you may choose from the following structures:

1. *Full-textured.* This means four voices in homorhythm as described in chapter 17. Note whether either the parallel-sixth or the parallel-tenth models operate.

2. *Pair of nonimitative duos.* Note how the second duo differs from the first (transposition, ic12, etc.).

3. *Pair of imitative duos.* Label the time and pitch intervals of imitation, and note tonal answer. Note how the second duo differs from the first (transposition, ic12, etc.).

4. *Canon.* Specify how many voices participate in the canon and whether it is an invertible canon, a transposed canon, or one that uses a tonal answer.

5. *Free counterpoint.* If no combination repeats, you are looking at free counterpoint. This is not to say that no *melodic* material repeats, but that no pair of melodies repeats in the same vertical relationship.

In addition, label all cadences and note how they correspond to the introduction of new material, new sections, etc. Here are two samples for you to practice on, with leading questions to guide you:

Example 19-25 (Lassus) ("Christ rising from the dead...")

What is the principle of the opening of Lassus's motet "Christus resurgens"?
How are the motives transposed? How do these transpositions affect the soprano
line? What does the soprano line have to do with the text?

Example 19-26 (Sermisy) ("Rich is the happy man...")

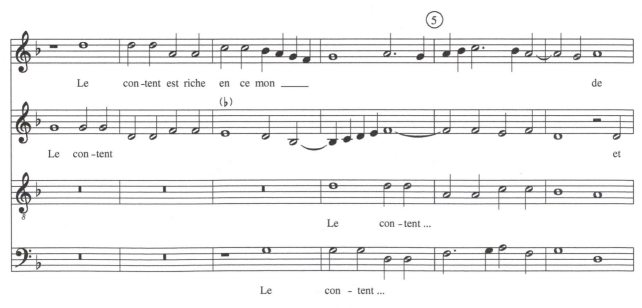

We saw a two-voice arrangement of the melody of this Sermisy chanson in chapter 12. Note how the opening imitation here differs from that one; what is the principle behind it? Some soggetti, like this one, are so flexible as to allow several time- and pitch-intervals of imitation. What is the principle behind the second point, at "et bienheureux"?

20

Composing a Whole Piece

You now have all the technique you need to compose and connect sections convincingly. But then what? Do you just stick one point after another? How many entries should you have? How many internal cadences? To which notes? When do you use homorhythmic texture? Is there any relation between the various melodies that form the basis for the different sections of a piece? We know very little about how Renaissance composers thought about whole pieces. Did they have a sense of wholeness or coherence or unity? We will now briefly look at what we know about overall form.

Text

Mode and Affect

Some present-day musicologists think that the sole aim of Renaissance music was to "express" the text. Zarlino says the soggetto should suit the words, so some notion of changing melodies to suit the different phrases of text seems reasonable. Furthermore, many Renaissance theorists say the mode should suit the text, and that modes may be changed in the course of a piece. So a soggetto might emphasize different outlines and skips as the emotional color, or affect, of a text changed.

Cadences

Cadences are normally made to the final and the fifth above the final. Zarlino suggests making intermediate cadences to the third above the final as well, but this seems much less common in practice. Regarding the foreign skips and outlines introduced to reflect the text affect, some authors say that cadences to the appropriate mode (signified by the skips) may be made. In this way the text can help determine both melodic material and cadence notes.

Rhythm

The rules for text setting in Appendix 1 sum up the relation between syllable length and rhythm. We also know that Renaissance authors thought that longer notes should be used at the beginning of a piece, and that soggetti in general should start relatively slow and speed up.

Madrigalisms

These are metaphorical associations, as when the word "slow" is set to a long note, or "quick" is set to many short notes, or rests are inserted between syllables of the word "sigh" (*so-*ⵣ*-spir* in Italian). Words about painful emotions can be set with chromatic motions or unexpected dissonance, while the word "breeze" is likely to be set as a long scalewise melisma.

Texture

Text can determine texture to some extent. We often find solemn statements, or acclamations to a saint or member of the Holy Trinity, made in full homorhythmic texture (see "O beata Virgo" in Victoria's "O magnum mysterium"). The word "joking," on the other hand, is more likely to be set to short phrases in an imitative texture.

Text and Form

Usually each new line of text gets a new soggetto. In this way the text can determine how many tunes you hear, although there are forms in the Renaissance in which new lines of text are sung to previously heard music (e.g., Palestrina spritual madrigals, French chansons).

Other Ways to Derive Soggetti

One of the questions we asked above had to do with relationships between the different soggetti in a piece. We have already discussed using a soggetto and its inversion in the same piece, and varying a combination by presenting a soggetto and its countermelody in mirror inversion. Below are some other ways to derive a new soggetto from old ones.

Countersubject as Soggetto

Zarlino suggests that a composer can use a countermelody from a previous section as the principal soggetto of a subsequent section.

Example 20-1 (Zarlino)

(etc.)

Inganno

Another way to derive a soggetto from a previous one is to maintain the solmization syllables of the original and change the hexachords from which they are drawn, creating new contours. The first theorist who describes this technique is Zarlino; later theorists call it *fuga d'inganno* (deceptive imitation) or *fuga di nome* (imitation of names). Inganno is a close relative of change-of-pitch interval of imitation in midtheme (chapter 12) and tonal answer (chapter 19).

Example 20-2

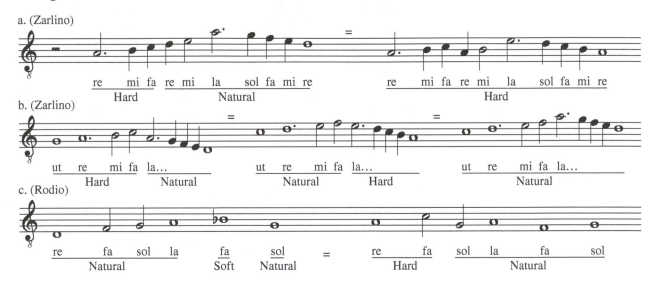

This technique is used to create varied motives to put against a CF and also new soggetti for new points of imitation. It is found in instrumental as well as vocal music.

The techniques described in this section give a kind of consistency to the material, but do not contribute to the overall organization of a piece. We have yet to find what causes the parts to hold together (cohere) or to form a single unified entity.

Large-Scale Structures

Apart from the text, what could determine the overall form of a piece? By form we mean the layout of the sections through time: their lengths, their order of presentation, and the abstract patterns they make.

Beginning, Middle, and End

We already know that beginnings are characterized by slow note values and intervals that clearly delineate the mode; as we will see, longer time intervals of imitation are also appropriate for beginnings. Middles are characterized by more modal ambiguity, faster note values, and shorter time intervals of imitation. Ends of sections or pieces are characterized by some kind of increased tension leading to a cadence. The tension can result from rhythmic unison, density of rhythm (attacks per whole note), thickening of texture, or approach to registral extremes (usually high, but sometimes, especially in the bass, low).

The end of a piece is special according to Pontio, who makes it an exception to Zarlino's rule prohibiting direct repetition of the entire contrapuntal combination: "The composer and the contrapuntist should avoid as much as possible repeating inventions using the same vertical intervals and melodic motions, because they give no variety at all, except if it is the repetition of an ending, as Cipriano de Rore did in the second part of his canzone "Alla dolce ombra."

Contrapuntal Types

Cerone said explicitly that his commonplaces were suitable not only for beginnings but middles of pieces. Since he says no more than this, we must conclude that no particular commonplace was more suitable for the beginning than for the middle, and that a piece would indeed be assembled from a variety of such structures. In an important article, Christopher Reynolds finds a symmetrical layout of contrapuntal structures in a chanson by Josquin. However, no one has yet established how widespread this practice was.

Durational Structures

Other authors have discovered that the various sections of certain pieces are related through their lengths. One of the most interesting ways to relate lengths is to have sections whose proportions correspond to the <u>Golden</u> <u>Mean</u>. This is a way of dividing a span into a larger part and a smaller part, such that the larger is to the whole as the smaller is to the larger: 1 : .618 :: .618: .382.

"O Magnum Mysterium" Revisited

At last we can give names to the various parts of the whole motet. Summing up a lot of notes in a single name is kind of like standing back and squinting at a painting: we can get an idea of its overall shape. The shape, schematized in Example 20-3b, is a function of many elements: the text, the melodic material, the texture, the contrapuntal structures, the abstract layout of the parts, and the cadences.

Cadences are indicated by the name of the goal note beneath the schema. Usually cadences concide with the end of a segment of text and punctuate the joints between points of imitation; such cadences are shown boxed. However, sometimes cadences fall *within* sections as determined by text repetition or prevalent melodic material; these are circled.

The contrapuntal types discussed in chapters 17 and 19 are labeled with numbers; each "point" gets an identifying number in parentheses and a superscript number that identifies how many times it has been heard. Melodic material that repeats is shown with straight lines, free counterpoint (melodies that are never repeated) with wavy lines. Some melodic material is labeled with lower-case letters to clarify discussion.

Example 20-3a "O magnum mysterium"

runt por-ta-re Do — mi-num Ie — sum Chri — stum. Al-le-lu-
runt por-ta-re Do — mi-num Ie — sum Chri-stum. Al-le-lu-
runt por-ta-re Do — mi — num Ie — sum Chri-stum. Al-le-lu-
Ie — sum Chri — stum.

ia, al — le-lu — ia, al-le-lu-ia, al-le-lu — ia, alia, al — le-lu — ia, al-le-lu-ia, al-le-lu — ia, al-le-lu-
ia, al — le-lu — ia, al-le-lu-ia, al — le-lu — ia, al-le-lu-
al-le-lu-ia, al-le-lu — ia, al-le-lu-

le — lu — ia, al-le-lu — ia, al — le
la, al-le-lu — ia, al — le-lu — ia, al-le — lu-
la, al-le — lu-ia, al-le-lu — ia, al-le — lu-
la, al-le — lu-ia, al — le-lu — ia, al-le —

lu — ia.
ia, al-le — lu — ia.
ia, al-le — lu — ia.
lu — ia, al-le — lu-ia.

Example 20-3b Schema of "O magnum mysterium"

1. Oh great mystery and wondrous sacrament
2. that creatures should see the birth of the Lord
3. Lying in a manger.
4. Oh blessed virgin whose womb was worthy to carry the Lord Jesus Christ.
5. Alleluia!

Section 1

From the schema it is easy to see why mm. 16–19 can be considered a climax: in addition to the change of texture using the parallel-sixth model (2) and the progressively more frequent repetitions of melodic fragment *a*, the cadences, too, get packed together more closely. From the beginning of the piece to the first cadence is 8.5 breves; to the next cadence is four breves, then three to the third and three to the fourth. The first time we heard fragment *a* it might not have occurred to us that it would eventually be part of a cadence; it is the $\hat{5}$–$\hat{5}$, the most featureless part of a cadence. The melodic fragment labeled *x*, on the other hand, is the most obvious part of the cadence, as it contains the $\hat{8}$–$\hat{7}$–$\hat{8}$ suspension figure. The first time it occurs, *x* sets "mysterium" in the soprano; the second time it sets "sacramentum" in the alto, and the combination *a* + *x* is inverted at the octave (m. 15).

Section 2

Section 2 begins with a nonimitative two-voice module (3^1) consisting of parallel thirds. When the module is repeated up an octave (3^2), a third line is added in rhythmic unison, making a periodic effect. This section continues with a homorhythmic phrase (4^1) on "viderent Dominum natum," again with no overlap between any of the voices.

So far section 2 is like section 1 compressed: in the same way that the repetitions of "et admirabile" (the adjective) created tension leading to the completion of the phrase on "sacramentum" (the noun), here the repetitions of "animalia" (the subject) lead to "viderent Dominum natum" (the predicate). The difference is that in section 2 there is no long point of imitation preceding the repetitions; it is as if Victoria plunges us into the middle of the process to maintain a strong momentum. Imagine the effect of beginning another point at a long time interval of imitation.

The thickening of texture through "ut animalia" supports the intensification toward the four-part "viderent Dominum" phrase, suggesting that in spite of the periodic homorhythmic declamation, performers should not breathe between (3^2) and (4^1). It is the lower three voices of (4^1) that are repeated transposed up in (4^2), so those three voices are what we call the module (the soprano in mm. 23–24 is a bit of free counterpoint). While (4^1) cadences to *D* on "natum," the cadence of (4^2) is extended, so that "natum" in the tenor ends on *D* as $\hat{5}$ of a cadence to *G*.

The extended cadence with its longer melisma, the reduction in the number of voices, and the return to *G* serve to decrease intensity toward the end of section 2. The bass $\hat{5}$ of the cadence to *G* is taken by the first note of the new soggetto on "jacentem."

Section 3

Like section 1, this section is made of imitative duos. However, the treatment of the duos is different in almost every possible way: here the time interval of imitation (t1) is much shorter, the time between duos (t2) is shorter, the first two duos, (5^1) and (5^2), are characterized by tonal answer, and the second duo (5^2) is the inversion at the octave of (5^1). Furthermore, the tenors and basses reiterate their duo (5^3); this repetition affords the section substantial overall length in spite of the shorter time intervals that help maintain momentum.

The melodic fragment labeled *w* is a nonimitative accompaniment to the imitative duo in the lower voices; the first time it sets "-centem," the second, "-sepio."

The fourth occurrence of "jacentem" (6) is not a repetition of the other duos, but rather free counterpoint in which both voices use the ascending-fourth version of the head motive at a distance of a fourth. The plausible climax of this section could be the downbeat of m. 37: the top three parts have high points, and all four parts are in rhythmic unison.

Section 4

The silence in all voices before the acclamation to the Virgin is striking, but not surprising in Renaissance music. Victoria sets this second occurrence of the ejaculation "O" as differently as possible, contrasting the opening soprano solo with full-textured homorhythm. All of section 4, from m. 40 to m. 52 (7) is free counterpoint (i.e., no combination repeats). One of the most exciting things about this piece is the extended preparations for the cadences. Look at mm. 37, 49, and 62.

Section 5

The "alleluia" section begins in triple meter, and consists of a three-voice homorhythmic phrase (8^1). The three parts of this nonimitative module repeat immediately with the bass an octave lower and the top two voices inverted at the octave; the alto in (8^2) is free counterpoint. This pair of phrases is like the "viderent Dominum" pair but in reverse: here the texture expands. Perhaps to break up the regularity of the four-beat phrases, Victoria adds a two-beat free phrase before the alto, tenor, and bass take up the module again (the tenor and bass are slightly altered). Melody *n* is almost unnoticeable in its new context with the free soprano line.

Finally the alleluias turn duple, and the piece concludes with the most rhythmic density, in terms of quarter notes per measure, of the whole piece. There is a pair of imitative duos (9) in this section. The final cadence is to the downbeat of m. 64, and a plagal ending is tacked on. The coda under the pedal (the sustained final *G*) in the soprano contains the last "alleluia" soggetto (*p*); this tune had to be crafted in such a way that it could be sounded, in imitation at the fifth, against the long *G* in the soprano that allows the piece to slow down after the cadential finish line.

Form

What patterns can we discern in the schema? If we take the silence before "O beata" as a principal divider, we can imagine two shorter pieces that both begin with the exclamation "O." Both halves contain elements that speed up, so the silence is an opportunity to rest before starting over.

The first part is a little mirror (or palindrome) consisting of two imitative points flanking a pair of nonimitative modules. Likewise, on a larger scale, the outer sections form a palindrome around sections 3 and 4, with the silence in the middle. However, the symmetry of the palindromes is at odds with the increasing tension that operates within each section and between several sections.

One thing we should try to account for is the exact placement of the silence before m. 40. If we divide 39 (the number of measures before the chord on "O beata") by 63 (the number of measures before the cadential arrival before the coda) we get .619, very close to the golden mean. This computation does not, however, take into account, among other things, the four-measure coda.

Variety Revisited

What we learn from the analysis of the Victoria is how uniformity and variety operate together. Repetition provides uniformity, but Victoria constantly varies the presentation of his basic materials (soggetti, duos, three-voice modules) in such a way as to drive the piece forward.

Since it is difficult to maintain momentum for the entire duration of a piece, it is necessary to fall back and regroup from time to time. The major resting place is m. 39, but the cadences at the ends of sections provide opportunities to relax before building to a new climax. You could imagine a hierarchy of resting places and climaxes that would help plan a performance of the piece. Knowing the shape will help you find the things you like to bring out in a piece, from juicy dissonances to textural climaxes, and it may also help you memorize the piece, so that you always know what's coming up next.

Finally, you might want to try modeling a piece on "O magnum mysterium." Write a piece that corresponds to the schema in Example 20-3b with sections the same lengths. Filling in these blanks, these empty durations, is a game we know Renaissance composers played, and you are now equipped to play it with them.

Appendix 1: Text Setting

Word Stresses and Phrasing

In the sixteenth century the music often reflected the syllable stresses, especially at the beginnings of text phrases, where they would give clear rhythmic definition to a thematic idea. The reason to choose a Latin liturgical text is that we have so many excellent models. But we can also find compositions that set short poems in French, English, German, Italian, or Spanish. For student compositions, short texts are recommended.

In Latin, accents in words of two syllables fall on the first syllable; other stresses are shown with accent marks. The Text of the "Benedictus" section of the Sanctus movement of the Ordinary of the Mass is given here:

> Benedíctus qui venit in nómine Dómini.
> (Blessed is he who comes in the name of the Lord)

This text is often set to a smaller number of voices than the rest of the Mass (if the Mass is in four voices, the Benedictus might be in three; if the Mass is in six, the Benedictus might be in four). It is often broken into two phrases punctuated by a cadence. Even though the first phrase has only three words, it can be spun out nicely into twenty breves of music (see Ex. 15-7 by Guerrero).

An assortment of different rhythms for this first phrase, all taken from repertoire, is shown in Example Appendix 1-1.

Example Appendix 1-1

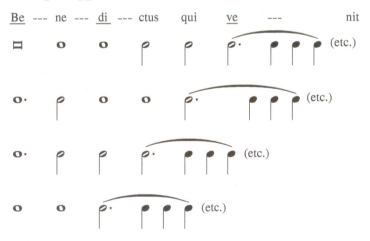

Word accents are often emphasized musically by <u>agogic</u> <u>accent</u> (a relatively long note among shorter ones) as well as by <u>metric</u> <u>accent</u> (strong position in the measure). Sometimes, when these long notes occur on weak parts of the measure, they suggest a different meter, as shown in the introduction (Example I-5). This is a good way to give lines independence. Often an unaccented syllable falls on a strong beat, as in Morley's "the fields abroad with spangled flowers" (Ex. 19-14), where "-gled" falls on a strong beat.

Kyrie eleison ("Lord have mercy on us") is an especially useful text phrase to use, because it has the unusual quality of containing anywhere from four to seven syllables, depending on elision of vowels.

Ky-riee-lei-son	(4 syllables)
Ky-ri-ee-lei-son	(5 syllables)
Ky-ri-e e-lei-son	(6 syllables)
Ky-ri-e e-le-i-son	(7 syllables)

Another good source of short texts is the Magnificat, of which we find many excellent examples as well. Each verse is usually divided into two parts, like the Benedictus text (See Ex. 15-8 for a setting of verse 7; a setting of verse 10 is used as Exercise 15-C2; and a setting of verse 5 is shown in Ex. 16-5.) Some verses are divided into more than two phrases, each with its own point of imitation, like verse 6.

1. Magníficat ánima mea Dóminum.
2. Et exultávit spíritus meus in Deo salutári meo.
3. Quia respéxit humilitátem ancíllæ suæ: ecce enim ex hoc beátam me dicent omnes generatiónes.
4. Quia fecit mihi magna qui potens est, et sanctum nomen eius.
5. Et misericórdia eius a progénie in progénies timéntibus eum.
6. Fecit poténtiam in bráchio suo, dispérsit supérbos mente cordis sui.
7. Depósuit poténtes de sede et exaltávit húmiles.
8. Esuriéntes implévit bonis et dívites dimísit inánes,
9. Suscépit Israel púerum suum recordátus misericórdiæ suæ,
10. Sicut locútus est ad pátres nostros, Abraham et sémini eius in saécula.
11. Glória Pátri, et Fílio, et Spirítui Sáncto:
12. Sicut erat in princípio, et nunc, et semper, et in saécula saeculórum. Amen.

1. My soul doth magnify the Lord: and my spirit hath rejoiced in God my Saviour.
2. For he hath regarded: the lowliness of his handmaiden.
3. For behold, from henceforth: all generations shall call me blessed.
4. For he that is mighty hath magnified me: and holy is his Name.
5. And his mercy is on them that fear him: throughout all generations.
6. He hath showed strength with his arm: he hath scattered the proud in the imagination of their hearts.
7. He hath put down the mighty from their seat: and hath exalted the humble and meek.
8. He hath filled the hungry with good things: and the rich he hath sent empty away.
9. He remembering his mercy hath holpen his servant Israel:
10. As he promised to our forefathers, Abraham and his seed, for ever.
11. Glory be to the Father, and to the Son, and to the Holy Ghost;
12. As it was in the beginning, is now, and ever shall be, world without end. Amen.

Text Underlay

The exact alignment of text syllables with notes is rarely clear in Renaissance music. Often a fragment is printed under the first note, often one set of words is meant to apply to a whole movement, and often a symbol like ditto marks indicates repetition of a text phrase. In the later sixteenth century, musical motives and text phrases are more consistently paired than earlier, but in all cases the singer or editor has many decisions to make on coordinating notes and syllables—decisions on text underlay.

For an example of difficulty in aligning syllables and text, look at the Bene- dictus by Jacquet in chapter 9 (Ex. 9-12). Beginning in m. 18, I have associated motive C with "in nomine" and z′ with "Do-." The end of "Domini" in mm. 20–21 is accommodated nicely by the two nonmotivic notes *B* and *A*. The next statement of z′, however, is not followed by these notes—another C follows immediately. In order to make "Domini" fit into z′, the syllables "mi-ni" would have to be changed awkwardly on quarter notes, breaking one of Zarlino's rules (see below). The alter- native is to make z′ a melismatic continuation of "in nomine" even though "-ne" is not a long syllable, breaking a different rule of Zarlino's. Neither solution is perfect. You will see other compromises elsewhere in the underlay decisions I have made. For another solution, see Philip T. Jackson's transcription, upon which this one is based.

Zarlino's Rules for Text Setting

If you want to set text, you will find these rules helpful. They are based on Zarlino's famous ten rules.

1. Long notes should carry long syllables (underlined in the example below), and short notes, short syllables.

2. Rarely place a syllable on a quarter or shorter value, or on a note imme- diately following a quarter. However, when a syllable is placed on the quarter fol- lowing a dotted half, another must be placed on the following note. See Morley's Example 12-1.

3. It is OK to repeat "some part of a text of which the sense is complete" if "it is done in order to emphasize words that bear a serious message worthy of consid- eration." As we see in many examples, however, sometimes much smaller fragments of text, even single words, are repeated.

4. If the penultimate syllable is long, it may have a melisma.

5. The last note (of a phrase, before a rest) must carry the last syllable.

Note that accented syllables need not fall on the strong part of the breve or whole note. Text declamation in the Renaissance often seems syncopated or poly- metric because the word accents create groups of threes and twos independent of the beat. It is good to keep in mind the possibility of setting the long syllables with long or high notes (giving them agogic or tonic accents) when they do not fall on the strong part of a metric unit (see Ex. I-5).

You may want to set text in your exercises. This is appropriate beginning in the exercises in chapter 8, where you can add a short bit of text to the given motives in series D exercises, applying syllables to the given rhythmic values with one or two syllables left over to end the phrase with (a few possibilities are suggested below in Ex. App. 1-2). You may repeat half notes if each bears a new syllable. Each time the motive reappears, repeat the whole text segment. Because the whole exercise will have so few words, you'll have to think of these as fragments of some longer setting.

Example Appendix 1-2

For a more ambitious exercise, you could compose a complete mass movement or motet, modeling on examples by Jacquet (Ex. 9-12) or Banchieri (Ex. 9-4), in which each section of a longer text is characterized by its own motive. For instance "Benedictus," "qui venit," and "in nomine Domini" could each be set to different motives against a long CF or three repetitions of a shorter one.

Appendix 2: Canon Against a CF

Improvising or writing a canon against a CF was practiced widely in the Renaissance. It seems to me the hardest thing to improvise because it requires the most memorization. Vicente Lusitano, in his 1553 "Most Easy Introduction" (*Introduttione facilissima*), gives patterned CFs and verbal rules for making two-voice canons at different time and pitch intervals. For instance, for Example Appendix 2-1a he says, "sing a fifth above, then a third above, then a third above, then a unison." If you wanted to create a canon at the fourth after one minim, you could simply memorize these thirteen patterns. Zarlino, a few years later, gives similar rules. This seems like a lot of work to us today, but you can amaze your friends by asking them to give you a CF and then improvising a canon. Of course you'll have to connect these bits to each other, and you'll have to teach your line to someone else so that they can follow you a fourth higher. (Note that only one uses a suspended dissonance, and that many include three-pitch-class sonorities.)

Example Appendix 2-1 Lusitano's canons at the fourth above after one minim, relized from verbal descriptions ($\sqcap$ = length of pattern, ✓ = 3 pcs, * = dissonance)

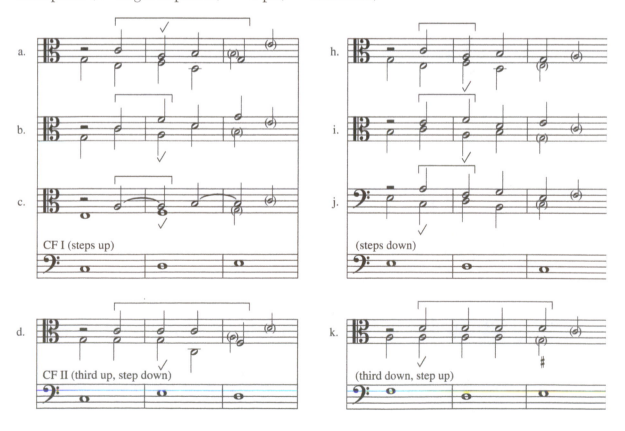

319

Study of Treatise Examples

Two-Voice Canon Against a CF

This difficult challenge was clearly a routine exercise, and examples are found in many treatises (but rarely in repertoire).* Example Appendix 2-2 is from a series of canons written against the first notes of Kyrie IX by Cerreto. His complete set of canons runs through every possible pitch interval of imitation, but only selections are shown here. He also composed a set in which the canonic voices are below the CF.

Note that sometimes he uses the standard three-voice cadence, and sometimes he writes other kinds. Compare numbers 4 and 6. They show that a standard cadence is possible even when writing canons at different pitch intervals. How is this possible? (Think about which notes in the consequent correspond to which notes of the guide.) Why do you think Cerreto waits a full whole note to start the guide voice in canon 2?

Example Appendix 2-2 (Cerreto)

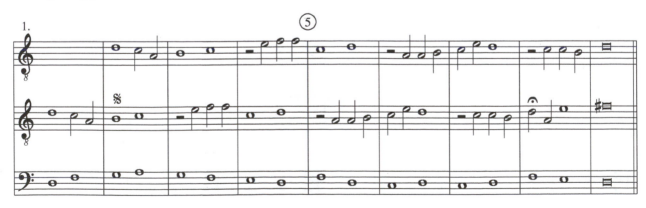

*For examples by Zarlino, see the article by Denis Collins listed under "Other Items of Interest" in the bibliography.

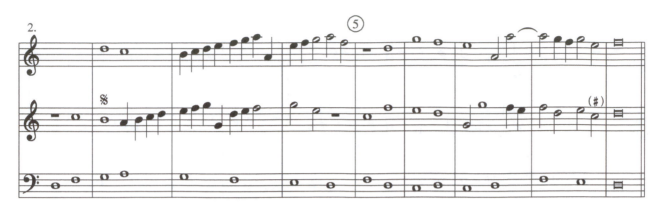

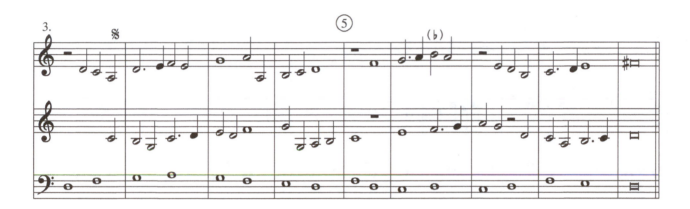

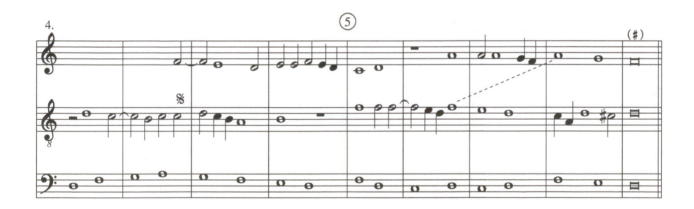

5.

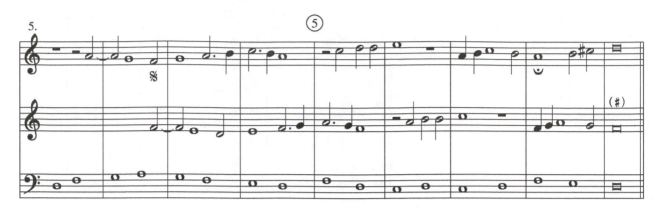

6.

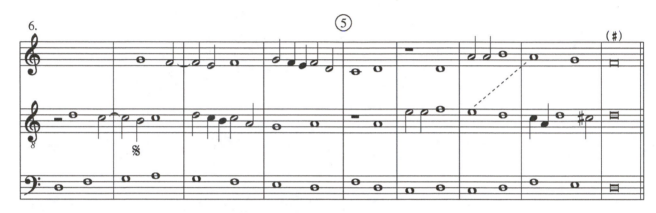

7.

Thomas Morley demonstrates a very effective method for writing a canon against a CF: first **compose a first-species framework, then divide it;** he embellishes the whole notes by breaking them (dividing them) into figures of shorter note values (<u>diminutions</u>). We have discussed how second, third, and fourth species can be considered diminutions of first; Morley's technique for canon calls upon our ability to do those diminutions. His first-species framework is shown in Example Appendix 2-3a, and the divided version in Appendix 2-3b. This example uses several second-species diminutions (consonant skips, accented consonant 6–5 passing tones, and just plain repeated notes), third-species diminutions, and diminished fourth-species fake suspensions, but no fourth species. His embellishments have an obvious quality; they do not really transform the line much (compare Montanos Ex. 11-13).

Example Appendix 2-3a ("thus plaine")

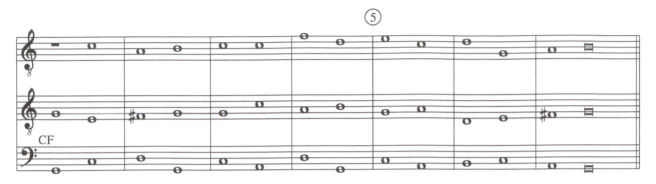

Example Appendix 2-3b ("thus divided")

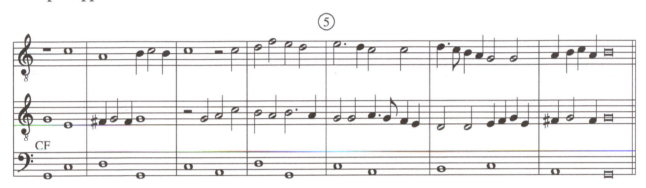

Morley's dialogue continues:

PUPIL: "I praie you . . . that you will let me trie what I could doe to make two parts in one in the fift in counterpoint." ("Two parts in one" means a canon; "in the fift" means at the fifth; and "in counterpoint" means in first species.)

MASTER: "I am contented, for by making of that, you shall prepare the waie for your selfe to the better making of the rest."

PUPIL: "Here is then a waie, I pray peruse it."

Example Appendix 2-4a (Morley)

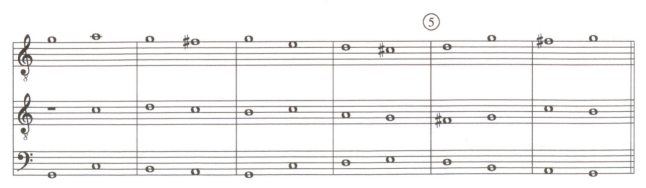

MASTER: "Seeing you have done this so wel plain, let me see how you can divide it."

PUPIL: "Thus, and I praie you peruse it, that I may here your opinion of it."

Example Appendix 2-4b (Morley)

MASTER: "This is wel broken." The pupil's example uses second-species repeated notes and a great deal of fourth species. Look back at his first species; you can see that there are many descending steps, the essential melodic element in dissonant fourth species. Note the frequency of diminished 6/3 chords.

The student finally tries a canon at the fourth above on the same CF: "Here it is in descant wise [mixed values] without counterpoint [first species], for I thought it too much trouble, first to make it plaine and then breake it."

Example Appendix 2-5 (Morley)

The master then shows examples of canons on the same CF at various pitch intervals, including this one at the tenth:

Example Appendix 2-6 (Morley)

Exercise Series A: Warmups

You should review canonic writing in two voices in chapter 11; however, the CF presents special difficulties. For the first step, the making of the "plaine" whole-note version, Morley warns that if you are writing a canon at the fourth above after one note, the leading voice should not go up a third or down a fourth. Of course not, as this would create a dissonance with the entrance of the consequent voice! We can make a more general statement about writing the first-species canon in terms of the CF:

If you are writing at pitch interval X, for each note you write, ask yourself, "What legal note can I write here that, when transposed X, will be consonant with the next note(s) of the CF?"

Let's say we are given the first notes of Cerreto's CF, and the assignment of composing a canon at the second above ($X = +2$) after one whole note. First, we look for a whole note to put against the first CF note that will answer the question above. Because it's the beginning of a piece, we must start with a perfect consonance, so we try D first (Ex. Appendix 2-7a). D, transposed up a second, gives E, not consonant with the second note (F) of the CF (Ex. Appendix 2-7b). Then we try A (Ex. Appendix 2-7c); A transposed up a second gives B, also not consonant with the F (Ex. Appendix 2-7d).

Example Appendix 2-7

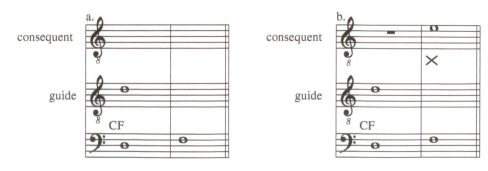

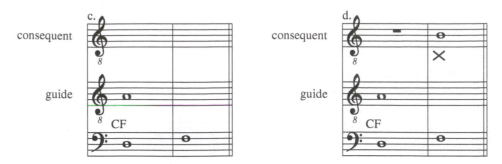

We wondered why Cerreto waited a full whole note to start his guide voice in canon 2—it is because *there is no note* that makes a perfect consonance with the D that, transposed up a step, will make a consonance against the second CF note!

If we change the time interval from one whole note to two, there is no problem: both *D* and *A* work, as shown here:

Example Appendix 2-8

Similarly, if we change the pitch interval of imitation, there will be no problem. What we learn from this is that adjustments in either pitch interval or time interval can make anything possible.

In the Warmup Exercises below, you are given two CF notes, and you are to find **all possible** ways to start a canon at the unison, fourth, or fifth above, one whole note later. Write two whole notes in the leading voice, and a whole rest and one whole note in the other. **Assume this is the beginning of an exercise and begin at the usual perfect consonances above or below the first note; do not cross voices.**

Example Appendix 2-9

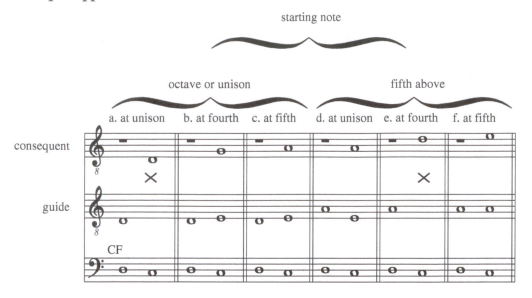

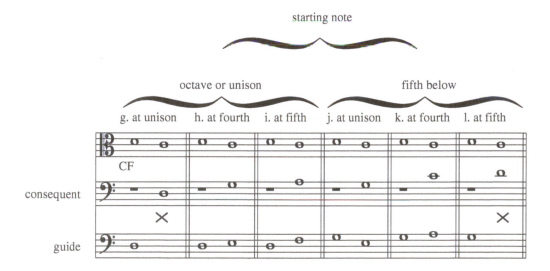

As in all Series A exercises, you need hand in only the correct solutions (in Ex. Appendix 2-9b, c, d, f, h, i, j, and k). Note that solution h is the same as solution b, but inverted at the octave. Also, solution k is the same as solution b, but inverted at the twelfth.

Warmup Exercises

Exercise Appendix 2-A1   **Exercise Appendix 2-A2**   **Exercise Appendix 2-A3**   **Exercise Appendix 2-A4**

Exercise Appendix 2-A5   **Exercise Appendix 2-A6**   **Exercise Appendix 2-A7**   **Exercise Appendix 2-A8**

Exercise Series C: CF Fragments

When you ask yourself the question "What legal note can I write here that, when transposed *X*, will be consonant with the next note(s) of the CF?" you need to bear in mind that you are more concerned with finding a consonance to put in the second measure than with how you will approach that consonance. *Do not reject a solution because of parallel perfect intervals—these can often be broken up in the diminution stage.*

Example Appendix 2-10

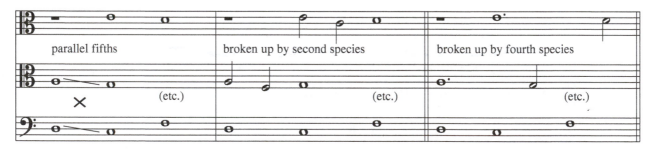

CF Fragment Exercises

Compose beginnings of canons in mixed value against the following CF fragments (above or below). You can start with "plaine" first species and then divide, or you can jump right in with smaller note values. You need not end with a standard cadence. If you begin with first species, remember to look fo opportunities to tie so that the embellishments are not so obvious.

Exercise Appendix 2-C1

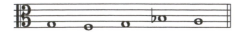

Exercise Appendix 2-C2

Exercise Appendix 2-C3

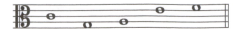

| Exercise Series *D:* | Complete CFs |

We wondered earlier how Cerreto was able to make the same cadence in two canons at different pitch intervals. The answer is that the time intervals are not the same: in number 4, the note that corresponds to the *A* in the upper voice on the downbeat of the next-to-the-last measure is the *F* three whole notes earlier; in number 6 the note that corresponds to that same *A* is the *E* two whole notes earlier.

The following examples show how the same cadence can be made in four different canons (dotted lines connect the *C* in the upper voice with the notes that correspond to it). The message here is the same one we keep coming back to: *Imagine relationships between lines by sliding one tune up and down and back and forth against the other.*

Example Appendix 2-11

a. 8ve above after 2

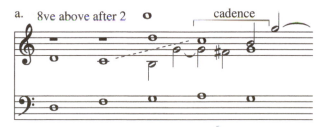

b. 5th above after 2

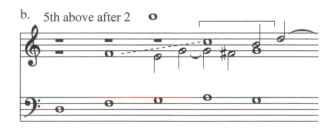

c. 4th below after 1

d. 3rd below after 2

1. Complete this canon at the fourth above. Some students have found it easier to begin at the end and work backwards!

Exercise Appendix 2-D1

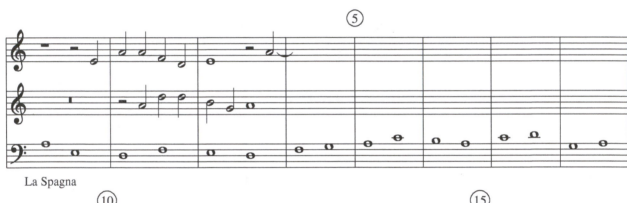

La Spagna

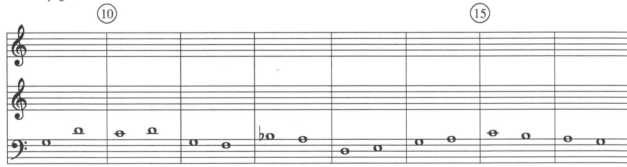

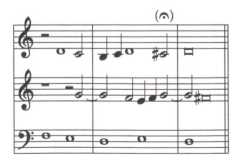

2. Complete this canon at the sixth below.

Exercise Appendix 2-D2

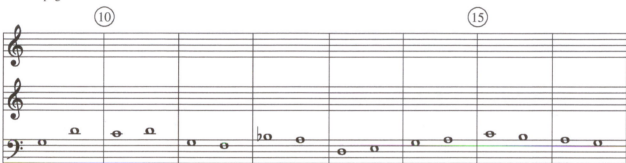

La Spagna

3. Complete this canon at the seventh below. You may follow the composer's lead in using whole rests, necessary for this difficult exercise. Remember that the notes before and after rests must be consonant.

Exercise Appendix 2-D3

La Spagna

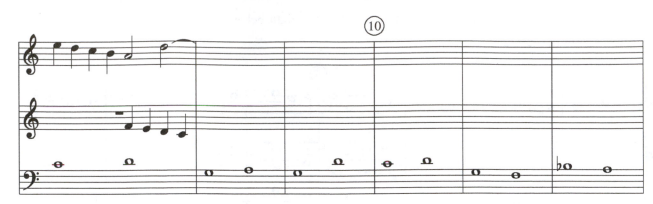

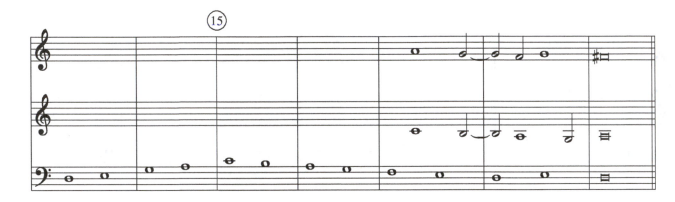

4. Complete this canon at the seventh below.

Exercise Appendix 2-D4

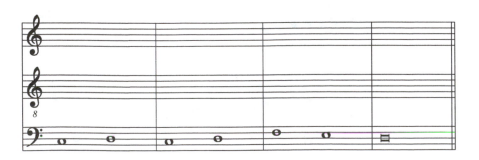

5. Compose a canon against the CF of your choice, at the unison, fourth, fifth, or octave, at the time interval of one or two whole notes. You must decide with your teacher whether or not standard cadences are required. They make the job a lot harder, as we have seen, but they are not impossible to come up with, as Example App. 2-11 shows.

6. Compose a canon against the CF of your choice in which the CF may be placed both above *and* below the two added lines, transposed either an octave (or double octave) or a twelfth. This means both lines of the canon must be invertible with respect to the CF. You need not write a standard cadence.

Appendix 3: Solmization

In the Renaissance, musicians used a different solmization system from the ones we use now (fixed or movable "do"). They used a six-note scale pattern called the <u>hexachord</u> that contains only one semitone, in the middle: TTSTT. The lowest note in the pattern is called ut and the notes that follow in ascending order are named re, mi, fa, sol, and la. The semitone occurs between mi and fa. If you are sight-reading within the span of a hexachord, all you need to remember is the position of the semitone—all the rest of the intervals are whole tones. This makes clef reading a piece of cake!

Example Appendix 3-1

The medieval pitch system, which Renaissance musicians inherited, contained all the natural notes plus B♭. In this eight-note world, the diatonic hexachord can be found in three locations: starting on *C*, starting on *F*, and starting on *G*. The names mi and fa, then, can refer to *E-F* (in the natural hexachord), *A-B♭* (in the soft hexachord), and *B♮-C* (in the hard hexachord).

Example Appendix 3-2

	H	N	S	H	N	S	H
E							la
D						la	sol
C						sol	fa
B							mi
B♭						fa	
A					la	mi	re
G					sol	re	ut
F					fa	ut	
E				la	mi		
D			la	sol	re		
middle C			sol	fa	ut		
B♮				mi			
B♭			fa				
A		la	mi	re			
G		sol	re	ut			
F		fa	ut				
E	la	mi					
D	sol	re					
C	fa	ut					
B	mi						
A	re						
G	ut						

H = Hard, N = Natural, S = Soft

Renaissance solmization is like movable do with incomplete scales. You can pretend that ut in the natural hexachord (on *C*) is the first degree of an incomplete *C*-major scale, while ut in the soft hexachord (on *F*) is the first degree of an incomplete *F*-major scale. Since each of these "scales" is only six notes long, you have to change hexachords when you exceed the six notes. For instance, if you want to sing a scale from *C* up an octave to *C*, you start on "*C* ut" and when you get to "*A* la" you change its name to "*A* re" and continue on up in the hard hexachord:

Example Appendix 3-3

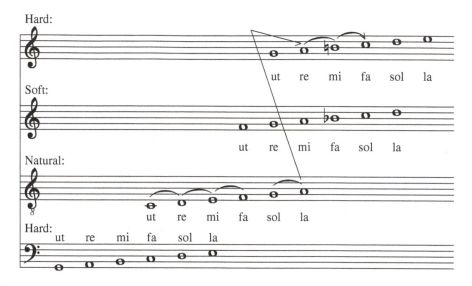

The importance of this solmization system is that the note names reflect exact diatonic transposition. For any pattern or melody that is transposed exactly, the solmization names will be the same in both versions, but the notes will be different. For example, the famous Renaissance tune "la sol fa re mi," can be found as *AGFDE* (natural) or *EDCAB* (hard) or *DCB♭GA* (soft).

As you can see from Example App. 3-2, *G*s, *A*s, *C*s and *D*s in the middle register can have three solmization names; *F* and *E* can have two, and *B*♭ and *B*♮ can each have only one. Likewise, any solmization name can apply to one, two, or three letter-named notes. Inganno, described briefly in chapter 20, is a game composers played in which they took advantage of these multiple associations to create new melodies as variants of old ones. They switched hexachords in the middle of a tune, as in this excerpt from a Lassus instrumental duo based on "la sol fa re mi," but in which different melodic contours are created by drawing syllables from the natural and soft hexachords.

Example Appendix 3-4

The fact that the solmization syllables sound like parts of Latin or Italian words (they were originally syllables of a chant in Latin) led to various kinds of puns being made. Orlando di Lasso symbolized himself in music with the syllables "la sol." Josquin Desprez paid homage to a patron by carving a tune out of the Duke's name and title: Hercules Dux Ferrariae (Hercules the Duke of Ferrara) becomes, in music, re ut re ut re fa mi re (see chapter 9). The lowest note of the medieval pitch space was called *gamma* (Greek for *G*), and its solmization syllable was ut; this note, *gamma-ut*, gave its name to the entire space, the gamut, and by extension, to any complete span.

The expression "*una nota super la semper est canendum fa*" (a note above la is to be sung fa) describes the use of *B*♭ above *A* when there is an *F* in the melody below (see the Introduction). If the *B*♭ weren't used, a mi contra fa would result (the mi is the *B*, the fa the *F*). The expression "mi contra fa" found in Shakespeare, to mean something wrong, comes from this musical injunction.

Appendix 4:
Sample Motive Placements

All Possible Placements of re fa sol la Against "Ave Maris Stella" (first twenty notes only)

Appendix 5:
The Invertible Duo

The exercise on p. 185 involves constructing a continuous two-voice piece in which a CF "migrates" from one part to the other. Skeletons of this type of piece are shown in Examples Appendix 5-1 and Appendix 5-2. A good preparatory exercise is to fill in the missing measures. This will give you a feel for what it will take to write one from scratch, which is a real challenge in terms of overall structure, or architecture. It is extremely difficult because you must make several choices that are interrelated:

1. Because the CF line and the counterpoint are constantly switching back and forth, you have to connect them smoothly in each voice. You can't just stop, rest, and start the inversion. You must make some kind of elision. In Example Appendix 5-1, in m. 8, the goal note of the cadence in the upper voice is the first note of the CF in the second period. The last note of the CF in the lower voice is shortened to allow counterpoint A^2 to begin in the same measure. Because a measure is "missing," the first period is only fifteen measures long, even though each statement of the CF contains eight notes. In measure 15, we find a different kind of elision: the last note of the CF in effect occupies the whole measure, and the new CF begins in the lower voice a measure later (m. 16). Still, an effect of overlapping is achieved by having the upper voice begin the counterpoint before the new CF starts.

2. Because each period must end with a cadence, you have to be sure your cadence is invertible. If you are inverting at the octave, you have no problem: the 7–6–8 interval succession inverts to 2–3–1, and vice versa. However, inversion at the twelfth is more problematic: the $\hat{2}$–$\hat{1}$ of the normal CF motion inverts to $\hat{5}$–$\hat{4}$; it is an evaded cadence (see chapter 10) that ends on the vertical interval of the fifth (see Ex. Appendix 5-1, mm. 22–23). This cadence, which contains interval succession 11–10–12, inverts nicely at the twelfth to become 9–10–8 in mm. 30–31. For the exercise you should use this type of cadence, although other evaded cadences (especially $\hat{5}$–$\hat{6}$, which inverts to $\hat{2}$–$\hat{3}$) may be used if the CF allows. (It is of course possible to avoid cadencing at the ends of periods completely, as Lassus' Ex. 13-9 shows.)

3. Because this is a continuous two-voice piece, each voice must occupy the normal range of about a tenth. In Example App. 5-1 the two statements of the CF in the lower voice stake out a more or less authentic Phrygian territory. Likewise those in the upper voice. The added counterpoint should not exceed these ranges. In Example Appendix 5-2, the CF statements in the upper voice outline an authentic Phrygian range, while those in the lower voice outline the plagal. In both examples suggested ranges are shown at the beginning of each line. Occasional crossing may be allowed by your teacher.

4. The intervals of inversion (transposition levels) must be carefully chosen. You must decide which voice to move, how far to transpose it, and to what extent the transposition maintains modal intervals. When you invert at the octave, the vertical intervals in the original combination should not exceed an octave; if they do, you should add an extra octave to the interval of inversion, inverting at the fifteenth, as in Example Appendix 5-1. In Example Appendix 5-2, the combination in mm. 15–22 is inverted at the octave, the upper voice brought down a fifth, and the upper voice (B²) is brought up a fourth. In both cases, the CF only appears on *E* and *B*, maintaining its semitone positions. When you invert at the twelfth, you may have to introduce notes not closely related to the mode. (For instance, Ex. Appendix 5-2 begins with a skip from *A* to *D*, not very Phrygian.)

Each of these decisions affects the others in a complex network.

If you use the type of elision in which the goal note of the cadence in the contrapuntal voice becomes the first note of the subsequent CF, then that cadence *determines* the level of transposition of the CF. In Example App. 5-1 the duo begins with a *B* octave, so the proper cadence facilitates the inversion at the octave. Example App. 5-2 begins with a vertical fifth, which, when inverted at the twelfth, becomes an octave, which are already there in the goal notes of the proper cadence at m. 8, making a smooth joint. In Example App. 5-2, the first two CF statements begin on *E*, but the evaded cadence in m. 15 introduces the *B* that is the first CF note in the third period.

Thought Experiment: If you use the other kind of elision, you have more freedom. Look at mm. 23–24 in Example App. 5-1; can you imagine a way to bring in the CF in the upper voice on some note other than *E*? You can do it by tinkering a bit with the start of *B²*. Try the same thing with Example App. 5-2 at mm. 22–23. You now have a new first note of the CF, and you must move the contrapuntal voice accordingly—what is the effect of this change on the range of the voices? What is the effect on the next cadence? What is the effect on the semitone positions of the CF?

If you are doing invertible counterpoint at the twelfth, and the CF is below in the first period of a pair, you must put the evaded cadence (5̂–4̂) at the end of the first period. If you were to treat the final CF notes as 2̂–1̂ you would have a 7–6 suspension above, which doesn't invert at the twelfth. Contrariwise, if the CF is above in the first period, you can use the normal 2–3 suspension below, which will invert nicely to an 11–10 suspension, leading to the evaded cadence.

Thus choice of range, cadence type, cadence note, interval of inversion, and type of elision all contribute to the overall architecture of little duos like these. These interrelationships are fiendishly confusing, but if you can master them in the simple context of the duo, you will have no trouble when they resurface in 3- and 4-part music.

Example A5-1 Invertible counterpoint at the fifteenth and nineteenth on "Da Jesus an dem Kreuze stund."

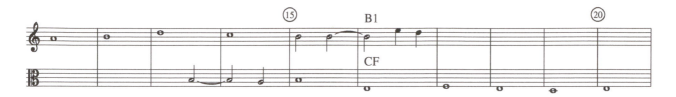

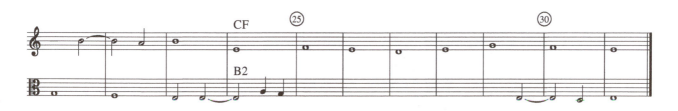

Example A5-2 Invertible counterpoint at the twelfth and octave on the same CF.

Bibliography

Treatises Cited

Angleria, Camillo. *La Regola del Contraponto*. Milan: Giorgio Rolla, 1622; facs. repr. Bologna: Arnaldo Forni Editore, 1983.

Artusi, Giovanni Maria. *L'arte del contraponto*. Venice: Giacomo Vincenti, 1598; facs. repr. Hildesheim: Georg Olms, 1969.

Banchieri, Adriano. *Cartella Musicale*. Venice: Giacomo Vincenti, 1614; facs. repr. Bologna: Forni, 1968.

Burmeister, Joachim. *Musical Poetics*. 1606. Translated, with Introduction and Notes, by Benito V. Rivera. Edited by Claude V. Palisca (New Haven and London: Yale University Press, 1993).

Cerone, Pedro. *Il Melopeo*. Naples: Gargano y Nucci, 1613; facs. repr. Bologna: Forni, 1969.

Cerreto, Scipione. *Della Prattica Musica*. Naples: Gio. Iacomo Carlino, 1601; facs. repr. Bologna: Forni, 1969.

Diruta, Girolamo. *Il transilvano, seconda parte*. Venice: Giacomo Vincenti, 1609; facs. repr. of 1622 edition Bologna: Forni, 1969. Translated by Murray C. Bradshaw and Edward J. Soehnlein (Musicological Studies v. 38/2): Institute of Mediaeval Music, 1984.

Montanos, Francisco de. *Francisco de Montanos'* Arte de musica theorica y pratica: *A Translation and Commentary*. Translated by Dan Murdock Urquhart. PhD diss. University of Rochester, Eastman School of Music, 1969.

Morley, Thomas. *A Plaine and Easie Introduction to Practicall Musicke*. London: Peter Short, 1597; facs. repr. New York: Da Capo Press, 1969.

Ornithoparchus, Andreas. Andreas Ornithoparchus his Micrologus, or Introduction: containing the art of singing Digested into foure bookes. Not onely profitable, but also necessary for all that are studious of musicke. Also the dimension and perfect use of the monochord, according to Guido Aretinus. By Iohn Douland lutenist, lute-player, and Bachelor of Musicke in both the Universities. 1609. Repr. New York: Dover, 1973.

Ortiz, Diego. *Tratado de glosas*. Rome, 1553; edited by Max Schneider. Kassel: Bärenreiter, 1961.

Pontio, Pietro. *Ragionamento di Musica*. Parma, Erasmo Viotto, 1587; facs. repr. Kassel: Bärenreiter, 1959.

Rodio, Rocco. *Regole di musica*. Naples: Giacomo Carlino e Costantino Vitale; facs. repr. Bologna: Arnaldo Forni Editore, 1981.

Sancta Maria, Thomas. *Libro llamado Arte de Tañer Fantasia*. Valladolid: Francisco Fernandez de Cordova, 1565; facs. repr. Geneva: Minkoff, 1973.

Tigrini, Orazio. *Il Compendio della Musica*. Venice: Ricciardo Amadino, 1588; facs. repr. New York: Broude Bros., 1966.

Vicentino, Nicola. *L'antica musica ridotta alla moderna prattica*. Rome: Antonio Barre, 1555; facs. repr. Kassel: Bärenreiter, 1959.

Zarlino, Gioseffo. *Le istitutioni harmoniche*. Venice, 1558; facs. repr. New York: Broude Bros., 1965. Part IV translated by Guy A. Marco and Claude Palisca as *The Art of Counterpoint*, New Haven: Yale University Press, 1968.

Modern Editions of Repertoire

An Anthology of Keyboard Compositions: Munich, Bavarian State Library MS MUS 1581. Corpus of Early Keyboard Music vol. 40/1 and 2. Edited by Clare G. Rayner. AIM, 1976.

Banchieri, Adriano. *Festino.* Venice: Amadino, 1608. Transcribed by Buonaventura Somma in *Capolavori Polifonici* vol. 1. Rome: de Santis, 1939.

Byrd, William. *The Collected Works of William Byrd,* vol. XVII. Edited by Edmund H. Fellowes. London: Stainer & Bell, 1948.

Cabezón, Antonio de. *Obras de Musica para tecla, arpa, y vihuela…* Madrid, 1578. Edited by Felipe Pedrell, revised by H. Angles. *Monumentos de la Musica Espanola*, vol. 27. Barcelona: Instituto Espanol de Musicologia, 1966.

Clemens non Papa. *Opera Omnia (CMM 4),* vol. I/3 Edited by K. Ph. Bernet Kempers. Rome: AIM, 1954.

La Couronne et fleur des chansons a troys. Edited by Lawrence F. Bernstein. New York, Broude Bros., 1984.

Crequillon, Thomas. *Opera Omnia (CMM 63),* vol. 3. Edited by Barton Hudson. AIM, 1974.

Elizabethan Consort Music, vol. 1. Transcribed and edited by Paul Doe. *Musica Brittanica* vol. XLIV. London: Stainer and Bell, 1979.

Festa, Costanzo. *Counterpoints on a Cantus Firmus.* Edited by Richard J. Agee. *Recent Researches in the Music of the Renaissance,* v. 107. Madison; WI: A-R Editions, 1997.

Gero, Ihan. *Il primo libro de' madrigali italiani et canzoni francese a due voci.* Edited by Lawrence F. Bernstein and James Haar. New York: Broude Bros., 1980.

Guerrero, Francisco. *Opera Omnia,* vol. 4. Edited by José Llorens Cisteró. Barcelona: Consejo Superior de Investigaciones Cíentíficas, 1982.

Jacquet of Mantua. *Opera Omnia (CMM 54)* v. 6. Edited by Philip T. Jackson and George Nugent. AIM: Hänssler-Verlag, 1986.

Josquin Des Pres. *Werken.* Edited by A. Smijers. *Vereeniging voor Nederlandsche Muziekgeschiedenis.* Leipzig: Kistner & Siegel, 1937.

Lasso, Orlando di. *Magnum Opus Musicum.* Transcribed by Carl Proske, Edited by Franz Xaver Haberl. Leipzig: Breitkopf & Härtel, 1894–1926; repr. New York, Broude Bros., 1973.

———, *Messen 10-17; Messen des Druckes Paris 1577. Sämtliche Werke Neue Reihe,* v. 4. Edited by Siegfried Hermelink. Kassel: Bärenreiter, 1964.

———. *The Complete Motets,* v. 11. Edited by Peter Bergquist. *Recent Researches in the Music of the Renaissance* v. 103. Madison; WI: A-R Editions, 1995.

Marenzio, Luca. *Motectorum Pro Festis Totius Anni* (1585). *Opera Omnia,* vol. 2. Edited by Ronald Jackson. AIM, 1976.

———. *Sämtlich Werke. Madrigale für fünf Stimmen, Buch I-III.* Edited by Alfred Einstein. *Publikationen älterer Musik* IV.1. Hildesheim: Georg Olms; Wiesbaden: Breitkopf & Härtel, 1967.

Merulo, Claudio. *Messe d'intavolatura d'organo (1968).* Edited by Robert Judd. *Corpus of Early Keyboard Music* v. 47, V. AIM, Hänssler-Verlag, 1991.

Morley, Thomas. *The first booke of canzonets: to two voyces.* London: T. Este, 1595; facs. repr. New York: Performers' Facsimiles, 1988.

———. *First Book of Madrigals* (1594). Edited by Edmund H. Fellowes. *The English Madriaglists,* vol. 2. London: Stainer & Bell, 1913; revised by Thurston Dart, 1962.

———. *Of Thomas Morley the first booke of canzonets to two voyces.* Published London: printed by Thomas Snodham, for Matthew Lownes and Iohn Browne, MDCXIX. Early English Books Online (http://eebo.chadwyck.com).

Othmayr, Caspar. *Das Erbe Deutscher Musik,* v. 26. Edited by Hans Albrecht. Frankfurt: C.F. Peters, 1956.

Palestrina, Giovanni Pierluigi da. *Opere Complete* v. 1, v. 27, etc. Edited by Raffaele Casimiri. Rome: Edizione Fratelli Scalera, 1939.

———. *Offertoria totius anni secundum Sanctae Romanae Ecclesiae consuetudinem.* Rome, 1593. Edited by Raffaele Casimiri. Rome, 1939.

Praetorius, Michael. *Gesamtausgabe de Musikalischen Werke. (1610).* Edited by Friedrich Blume. Wolfenbüttel: Möseler Verlag, 1928–40.

Recent Researches in the Music of the Renaissance, vv. 16–17: *Sixteenth-Century Bicinia: a Complete Edition of Munich, Bayerische Staatsbibliothek, Mus. Ms. 260.* Edited by Bruce Bellingham and Edward G. Evans, Jr. Madison: A-R Editions, 1974.

Rhau, Georg. *Musikdrucke,* v. 9: *Tricinia … 1542.* Edited by Thomas Noblitt. Kassel: Bärenreiter, 1989.

The Ricercars of the Bourdeney Codex. Edited by Anthony Newcomb. *Recent Researches in the Music of the Renaissance,* vol. 89. madison: A-R Editions, 1991.

Sermisy, Claudin de. *Opera Omnia (CMM 52),* vv. 3–4: *Chansons.* Edited by Gaston Allaire and Isabelle Cazeaux. AIM, 1974.

Sixteenth-Century Bicinia. Edited by Bruce Bellingham and Edward G. Evans, Jr. *Recent Researches in the Music of the Renaissance,* vols. 16–17. Madison; WI: A-R Editions, 1974.

Susato, Tielman. *Chansons Published by Tielman Susato.* Edited by Kristine K. Forney. *Sixteenth-Century Chanson,* v. 30: New York: Garland Publishing, 1994.

Victoria, Tomas Luis de. *Cantica B.M.V. vulgo Magnificat et Canticum Simeonis. Opera Omnia*, v. 3. Edited by Philippo Pedrell. Leipzig: Breitkopf & Härtel, 1904; repr. Ridgewood: Gregg Press, Inc., 1965.

———. *Opera Omnia* vol. 2. Edited by H. Anglès. *Monumentos de la Musica Espanols*, vol. 26. Barcelona: Instituto Espanol de Musicologia, 1965.

Villancicos de diversos autores ... Venice: Hieronymus Scotum, 1556; facs. repr. as *El Cancionero de Uppsala*. Instituto Hispano-Arabe de Cultura. Madrid: Emiliano Escolar, 1983.

Willaert, Adrian. *Opera Omnia (CMM 3)*, vol. 1. Edited by Hermann Zenck. Rome: AIM, 1950.

———. *French Chansons for Three Voices (ca. 1550)*. Edited by Courtney S. Adams. Madison: A-R Editions Inc., 1982.

Other Items of Interest

Agee, Richard J. "Costanzo Festa's *Gradus ad Parnassum*." *Early Music History* 15 (1996):1–58

Carapezza, Paolo Emilio. Introduction to *Scuola Polifonica Siciliano: Musiche Strumentali Didattiche (Musiche Rinascimentale Siciliane II)*. Rome: de Santis, 1971.

Collins, Denis. "Zarlino and Berardi as Teachers of Canon." *Theoria* 7 (1993): 103–123.

Jackson, Philip T. Introduction to v. 6 of *Opera Omnia* by Jacquet of Mantua. AIM: Hänssler-Verlag, 1986.

Newcomb, Anthony. Introduction to *The Ricercars of the Bourdeney Codex. Recent Researches in the Music of the Renaissance*, vol. 89. Madison: A-R Editions, 1991.

Rhau, Georg. *Musikdrucke*, v. 6: *Bicinia gallica, latina, germanica Tomus I, II, 1545*. Edited by Bruce Bellingham. Kassel: Bärenreiter, 1980.

Schubert, Peter. "Musical Commonplaces in the Renaissance." *Education Most Sovereign: The Teaching and Learning of Music in the Renaissance*. Edited by Susan Forscher Weiss, Cynthia J. Cyrus, and Russell E. Murray, Jr. (Forthcoming).

———. "Hidden Forms in Palestrina's First Book of Four-Voice Motets," *Journal of the American Musicological Society*.

———. "Recombinant Melody: Ten Things to Love about Willaert's Music." *Current Musicology* 75 (Spring 2003).

———. "Counterpoint Pedagogy in the Renaissance." *The Cambridge History of Western Music Theory*. Edited by Thomas Christensen. Cambridge: Cambridge University Press, 2002, pp. 503–533.

———. "A Lesson from Lassus: Form in the Duos of 1577," *Music Theory Spectrum* 17/1 (Spring, 1995): 1–26.

———. "Authentic Analysis," *Journal of Musicology* XII/1(1994): 3–18.

———. "Mode and Counterpoint," *Music Theory and the Exploration of the Past*, edited by Christopher Hatch and David W. Bernstein. (Chicago: University of Chicago Press, 1993), pp. 103–136.

———. "The Fourteen-Mode System of Illuminato Aiguino," *Journal of Music Theory* 35.2 (Fall, 1991): 175–210.

Index